FLYING TO BE FREE

The long awaited story of a man's passion for flying and how it changed his and other peoples' lives around the world is finally in print.

"When will you write this moving narrative?" has been for years the familiar question as a result of Mr. Schneider's far-reaching lecture tours and his many appearances on television and radio. Now that he has found the time to do so, we trust that the publication of *Flying to Be Free* will satisfy also this continuing demand. Autographed copies are available—see order form in back of book.

Schneider . . . and a companion, on a flying mission across Europe and Africa, "died almost 20 times."—*Evening Tribune,* San Diego, California.

In ten years of continent-hopping, he has visited almost 100 countries.—*Capital Journal,* Salem, Oregon.

OTHER BOOKS BY HANS J. SCHNEIDER

Masters of Legalized Confusion and Their Puppets (1968)
Timely and Profitable Help for Troubled Americans (1976, 1977)

(Both books can be obtained from
WORLD WIDE PUBLISHING CORPORATION.
See order form in back of book.)

* * *

NEWSPAPER COMMENTS ON HANS J. SCHNEIDER AND HIS BOOKS

There was Gibraltar. The small plane barely slid past the cliffs against which powerful northerly winds pressed it. Coming in for a landing on the small coastal strip–when three feet over the ground, red rockets were shot before the nose. Strict landing prohibition! The plane pulled up and banked on course over the ocean. With the last drop of gas they managed to get to Tangier; Africa was reached.–*Westfalen Zeitung* (German newspaper), West Germany.

Schneider . . . worked as an apprentice ship broker and became one of the first Germans licensed to fly planes [after World War II]. He then adopted a gypsy's life, travelling the world . . . –*Enterprise Record,* Chico, California.

Because of gas shortage in southern France they were forced down amid the Strategic Air Command of the Americans–on the old charts it was still shown as a civil aerodrome. Received with machine guns, an escort of five jets bade them farewell during their departure.–*Brackweder Zeitung* (German newspaper), West Germany.

(More comments and reviews regarding Hans J. Schneider and his books on the back of the dedicatory page and book.)

FLYING TO BE FREE

by

Hans J. Schneider

Illustrated by Roy S. Wathne
Cover designed by Michael Lee

Over 100 Photos and Illustrations

Published by

WORLD WIDE PUBLISHING CORPORATION

WORLD WIDE PUBLISHING CORPORATION
P. O. Box 105
Ashland, Oregon 97520

Library of Congress Cataloging in Publication Data

Schneider, Hans J 1935–
Flying to be free.

1. Schneider, Hans J., 1935– 2. Converts.
3. Air pilots–Biography. I. Title.
TL540.S34A33 629.13'092'4 [B] 77-26614
ISBN 0-930294-13-0

Printed in the United States of America

This book is dedicated to my most-beloved wife,
Inger Marie,
who, when airborne,
is unfortunately all too much like Klaus.

Far better is it to dare mighty things,
to win glorious triumphs,
even though checkered by failure,
than to take rank with those poor spirits
who neither enjoy much nor suffer much,
because they live in the gray twilight
that knows not victory nor defeat.

—THEODORE ROOSEVELT

Those who want us to conform have ulterior motives, for they desire that we strengthen their form in which they themselves proudly dwell at ease and with false confidence—destitute of all challenge by the unknown, which gives man that invigorating zest for life without which there can be no worthwhile and meaningful existence.

—HANS J. SCHNEIDER

Hans J. Schneider and his friend chartered an Aeronca Chief for a daring flight around western Europe to Africa with savings and receipts from conducting sightseeing tours over Brussels World's Fair. The plane had only 65 hp. Experienced pilots and engineers warned: "Such a flight will cost you your life."—*Zeitung für den Senneraum* (German newspaper), West Germany.

Schneider's . . . talks reflect the history of his upbringing and his travels to nearly 100 countries, as well as the "back-to-the-land" life style that his family now enjoys.—*The Daily Tidings,* Ashland, Oregon.

. . . he and a friend took a sight-seeing trip to Africa in a rickety, 65-horsepower plane . . . Since then, the young pilot . . . has preached in person and on radio to "hundreds of thousands of people all over the world." . . . The Schneiders, who now have five children . . . often travel together in the family plane, "Fire Eagle," as Schneider continues his speaking tours.—*The San Diego Union,* San Diego, California.

Subsequent world travels provided Schneider with much of the practical experience from which he draws in counseling his readers.—*The Mail Tribune,* Medford, Oregon.

After getting into West Germany . . . he became a licensed private pilot.—*The Arizona Daily Star,* Tucson, Arizona.

In 1955, when Germans were allowed to fly again, young Schneider obtained one of the first pilot's licenses and frequently made flying business trips.—*The Oregon Statesman,* Salem, Oregon.

He became a licensed private pilot and, on one dangerous flight from Europe to North Africa, was brought face to face with the reality and imminence of death.—*Bowman County Pioneer,* Bowman, North Dakota.

. . . Schneider studied extensively . . . held several jobs, became a licensed private pilot and later traveled through nearly 100 countries under survival conditions on pennies a day. . . .–*The Daily Tidings,* Ashland, Oregon.

Born in 1935 in Breslau, now East Germany, Hans Schneider began his life as a member of Germany's social elite. The son of a multimillionaire textile magnate, Schneider lived a life full of the most modern conveniences–until the latter part of World War II, when his family found themselves penniless.–*Daily News,* Red Bluff, California.

"Are you sick of it all? The rat race, pressures of modern-day living?" Schneider's book may provide some answers.–*Herald and News,* Klamath Falls, Oregon.

Hans J. Schneider not only made for the destination of his world trip with his private aircraft, he also used the airliners of the large companies. Thereby they offered him the opportunity to see his next destination from the cockpit in the air . . . At times the globetrotter was permitted to fly such a plane personally. –*Unabhängige Tageszeitung für den Grossraum Bielefeld* (German newspaper), West Germany.

Schneider and his 14-year-old son Roy flew into Salem Friday afternoon capping a nine-month cross-country crusade. . . . Father and son logged about 300 flights in his four-place aircraft. During those nine months they covered the United States from top to bottom and spoke in over 200 meetings. . . . The elder Schneider speaks with the accent of his German homeland. He spent five years under the communistic regime in Eastern Europe and learned to fly in post-war Germany.–*Capital Journal,* Salem, Oregon.

Hans Schneider and son Roy, 14, return from a nine-month, 25,000-mile lecturing tour criss-crossing America by private plane. Logging over 204 flying hours and 200 flights, they spoke for hundreds of meetings as well as on television and radio. His wife, Inger, and their four younger children meet him at the airport. (Statesman photo)

ABOUT THE AUTHOR

Born on April 25, 1935 in Breslau, Germany, Hans J. Schneider, author, lecturer, pilot and world traveller, began his life as a member of Germany's social elite. The son of a multimillionaire textile magnate, he lived among ultramodern conveniences—until the latter part of World War II, when his family became penniless.

While suffering five years under another ruthless and cruel dictatorship, this time Communism, his recurring dream from earliest childhood days, *flying*, continued to haunt him. When still a young boy and full of untamed enthusiasm, he, like Daedalus of old, constructed a pair of wings under the most primitive circumstances.

After coming to West Germany, heaven and earth were moved to satisfy his longing. As a first step to become mobile, he obtained all four classes of driver's licenses. Living on pennies a day while busy going to school, including the High-Sea Academy and Foreign Trade Seminar in Bremen, and working as an apprentice ship broker for a monthly wage of $7.14, he somehow drummed up enough time and money to go to the *"Fliegerschule"* (flying school) and obtained the *"Luftfahrerschein für Privat-Flugzeugführer"* (Private Pilot License). Trained by famous air aces, he thus became one of the first pilots licensed in Germany after World War II and soon held airman certificates of several nations.

The stage was set. Many unusual years of barnstorming in Europe, the United States and other parts of the world followed.

During that time Hans continued to study intensively various religions of mankind and philosophy. He also worked for a number of companies in different nations.

While still in his early 20's, the author undertook a formidable flying venture with a photographer friend around Europe and into Africa. Their escapades, numerous brushes with death, and the way these were instrumental to launch Hans on effective, influential missions circling the globe, are described in this book.

Multilingual and nicknamed by his friends "a man of seven lives," he has travelled and lectured since in nearly 100 countries around the world, including Afghanistan, Australia, Bolivia, Bora-Bora, Bahrain, Burma, Cambodia, Ceylon, Chile, Curaçao, El Salvador, Fiji Islands, Haiti, Iceland, India, Indonesia, Jamaica, Kuwait, Malaysia, Nepal, New Caledonia, New Guinea, New Zealand, Papua, Saudi Arabia, Surinam, Tahiti, Taiwan, Thailand and Uruguay. You will read of the touching encounters in his new life and higher calling.

Now married, with five children, Hans looks back upon the trips and marvels that he lived through them. He flies these days in his own plane on extensive speaking tours, but the circumstances are much different from those written about in *Flying to Be Free.*

A self-made all-arounder and also a consultant, economist, evangelist, and publisher, Mr. Schneider's principal other interests include good music, reading, research, field study, classicism in some aspects and romanticism in others. A dynamic idealist, he doesn't smoke or drink, but loves individual outdoor and water sports, especially swimming and sailing. At a beautiful lake in Germany, his family owned a weekend house and yacht for many years which Hans used frequently.

The author has visited nearly all national parks, monuments and forests in the United States where he now resides. Mr. Schneider enjoys hikes in wilderness areas and expeditions to remote places of great scenic beauty, much wildlife, archaeological interests and different cultures.

He has found that the happiest and most interesting people he meets in his international travels usually show commendable characteristics, such as open-mindedness, a great affection for nature, genuine sense of humor, amiability, thriftiness, honesty, warm-heartedness, and spiritual vigor. They are generally serious-minded but happy in virtuous and higher things of life.

Hans Schneider, who is listed in *Contemporary Authors,* has been writing for many years. His first two books received almost instant fame upon publication. The initial edition of an amazing 40,000 copies of *Masters of Legalized Confusion and Their Puppets* is almost gone. The first publication of *Timely and Profitable Help for Troubled Americans* was sold out in a matter of months and is now in its second, enlarged edition. Because of Schneider's many television and radio appearances during his national and world-wide lecture tours, his third book, *Flying to Be Free,* one of the most heart-warming chapters in the exciting life of the author, promises to enjoy great public acclaim as well.

CONTENTS

ABOUT THE BOOK

FLYING TO BE FREE is an authentic account of how boyhood dreams became an aviator's nightmare.

Truly, the most fascinating aviation endeavor of its kind in this century . . . a sensational, factual narrative detailing spine-chilling exploits of two daring skytrotters who made Europe vibrate and set young and old aflame with enthusiasm for unlimited adventure. Rarely did anything so galvanize the subconscious yearning of a generation and serve as a harbinger for decades to come.

Years ago, Hans J. Schneider, champion of flying, roamed the sky alone. The wind and clouds, the sun and stars were his only companions as he tasted the exhilaration of doing that which is different and difficult. Pitted against the untamed elements in search of a meaningful existence, excitement and challenge, he risked his life many times. This spirit of exploration brought forth a virtually matchless aviation tragicomedy: The story of two daredevils you will never forget . . . the day when a deafening roar of an engine charged the atmosphere with suspense as one of history's most incomparable and breathtaking air dramas began.

Veteran pilots, flight engineers and other pros all solemnly warned, "It can't be done–you will not return!" Little did they know that Hans had never known fear until . . . . There he was, young, determined, high-spirited and with a bold dream that couldn't be stopped–which frequently brought him and Klaus face to face with death.

You will be thrilled as you read how these captivating experiences with a small motor and a pair of wings in post-World War II Europe changed Schneider's ambitions and sent him around the world touching the hearts and lives of millions of people. Danger, humor and excitement all combine to make this book one you will always remember.

☆ ★ ☆

"Hans J. Schneider made his childhood dreams come true. The adventures which Schneider brought home from all over the world are overwhelming. He took more time than Jules Verne. For seven years he travelled on all continents–retraced the trails of the Incas in Peru, was a guest of the ex-king in Bali, and in Iraq was thrown into prison without reason. In short: He encountered country and people in almost 100 nations."–*Westfalen-Blatt,* Bielefeld, West Germany.

☆ ★ ☆

FLYING TO BE FREE is Hans Schneider's third book. He has been a pilot for about 25 years.

PREFACE

FLYING!—the dream of mankind for ages. Weightless soaring over a seemingly peaceful world of mountains, plains and rivers has long fired the imagination of young and old alike. To mount up on wings of the wind, to drift along freely with the clouds or far above in the realm of a golden sun with a countryside below bathed in the cold, foggy shadow of a rainy day—what an inspiring thought!

Oh, that I had wings like a dove! Then I would fly away, and be at rest—the longing of man's heart for millenniums—since history began. The ultimate escape from a vale of tears . . . ?

Come with me and discover what such hopeful aspirations and lofty dreams are all about. Before you lies the exciting, colorful account of an absolutely fantastic, yet true, 18-day life and death aerial drama spanning two continents. Even without added ballyhoo, the episodes related within this narrative are unbelievable.

Let's turn back the pages of aviation history to a time when flying was what it should be—daring, exciting and full of the unknown. Then *taking to the air* was simple and exhilarating. One did not have to worry about the myriad of instrument requirements, noisy communication procedures and exhausting regulations so prevalent today.

It was good that way, for it produced capable pilots. Not relying on so many complicated devices and other outside help, they were on their own, finely attuned to the fast-fluctuating, temperamental weather and other flying hazards. An occasional breakdown of navigation equipment did not distress those aviators as it does today. They were in harmony with the elements and possessed a keen sixth sense so much dulled in our time. Even under the worst flying conditions, these pros usually found a way out. Their piloting and plotting were remarkably accurate and did not provide them with the highly intoxicating "I am lost!" syndrome so often encountered now, especially after mechanical failure.

With all the modern gadgets an aviator finds himself surrounded by at present, flying has lost much of its excitement, explorational spirit and originality. Occupied with the instrumentation and talking to flight service stations, airport towers and control centers, he has been deprived of the sense of flight, the time for enjoyment and the ability to adapt to the elements around him. Technical intricacies have robbed all the splendor connected with a genuine flying experience, degrading him to a button-pushing, strikingly bizarre robot.

Gone are the days, under ever-present and increasing government stipulations, when a person could find freedom and unbounded joy in

Batteries of instruments, radio equipment and other gadgets form an entangled maze in the cockpit of a modern airliner.

flight. The aviator has become just like a bird in a musty, dreary cage whose wings have been clipped after having been snatched from a colorful and constantly changing world of rivers, mountains and sunsets. The massive industries and impedimental "red tape" monoliths, representing bureaucratic uniformness and consequently unyielding, rigid attitudes and rules, are the profiteers. Though part, but not all of it, of course, has been necessitated by the increase in air traffic, too much interference by regulatory agencies (also adding intolerable expense) has never strengthened any good cause.

But at this time, let me introduce you to the *world of flying* I knew then in contrast to what it is today.

Every small and great achievement begins in someone's thoughts and heart. I still remember when I was very young and confined to a school bench in the unbearable environment and monotony of a stifling classroom. Being a visionary, the apathetic languor, the weary treadmill, the much learning and cramming of nonstrategic and superfluous material into one's brain had no appeal to me. My verve was not jaded by the cold and colorless walls of that school. As in the life of Thomas A. Edison, my mind explored beyond what was offered. Thank God, there was a window in that building. But my eyes swept over a dreary landscape below a rainy sky. It was simply too much. I needed wings to escape that drab, dull and spiritless world.

I was dreaming about coral reefs, an atoll with a crystal-clear blue-green lagoon and palms gently waving in a balmy breeze somewhere down in the South Pacific. Why had I been detained in this stodgy, stereotyped milieu? Not for me! In fact, I already flew when a toddler!—but at that time merely with my imagination. In many ways, it was more beautiful then! One upward look into the unclouded blue sky of a bright summer day and my idealism kept filtering out disturbing and unpleasant realities so often associated with any worthwhile and beatific endeavor.

I think Providence intended it, for if man knew the detailed, complicated and seemingly never-ending tasks associated with most great and noble accomplishments, he, in the face of such overwhelming obstacles might have been discouraged in the beginning and never set out to attain these goals, which achievements have enriched mankind immeasurably through the centuries.

Exactly such was the case when we were *winging out for fulfillment.* Had we known the formidable difficulties, the dangers and breathtaking challenges which lay ahead, we would have never started on this endeavor. The world then, would be without this book and the impact my changed life had on it afterward.

In the past I declined many requests to narrate this flying adventure because of the extent and magnitude of the story. To these many willing, potential listeners I have given the tentative promise one day to write the romance. Well, here it is!

Let me now take you back to earlier days when 65 horsepower over Europe and Africa brought challenging highlights to our lives and *those born to fly were flying to be free!*

PROLOGUE

Suddenly we were caught by deadly, inexorable downdrafts south of the Rock of Gibraltar. With relentless force and madness, they threatened to smash us against the commanding, century-old fortress of global seapower. Desperately I hung onto the controls, wrestling as the plane wildly reeled in the air, tossed to and fro by these winds screaming with fury, filled with foreboding and whipping to tatters the storm flags then flying and fluttering above our very lives. Maneuverability had become nil—I wrung from the controls all they would yield.

In those agonizing moments, time seemed to turn into eternity. Again and again we were almost smashed into this monolithic giant, while terror stricken, we apprehensively circled this outpost at the western edge of the Mediterranean on our approach to the runway.

Barely escaping certain destruction, we came in on "final." With the end of our flight at hand, the landing strip, like a timely haven, stretched out below, directly ahead of us. Coming in with nearly empty tanks, and no other airfield within our safe range, we uttered a quick sigh of relief.

Almost simultaneously, and just about two or three feet over the extricating runway, we were jolted by the startling sight of red signal flares rocketing into the sky. We could not fail to understand this unmistakable warning. An aviator's nightmare was coming on apace as, snatched from the only safe refuge, I was forced to abort the landing. Reluctantly reapplying power, I passed over.

Incredible! What had gone wrong? Had our Seville flight plan been refused after all? It was a mystery which remains unsolved.

"AFRICA!"—was going to be our next stop as the closest alternate airport was located there. We were only able to come to a decision following minutes of utter confusion in our cockpit, and headed for Tangier, Morocco.

Soon, while nearing the middle of the Strait of Gibraltar, the gas gauges registered "Empty!" It was a time of total crisis.

We found ourselves in a seemingly inexpiable situation far from home, with nearly 200 fathoms of shark-infested waters forming a death trap below. Certain doom before us, our fate seemed sealed. Hopeless and forlorn, we were teetering on the brink of penultimate disaster . . . !

How did it start? Before finishing this bone-chilling isolated account later in sequence, let me first introduce you to the beginning of one of the most unique, fascinating flying adventures you have ever read.

PART I

GETTING READY

Here begins the true narrative of deadly suspense about a man who was determined to find fulfillment in his passionate love for flying even though it might mean death.

1

Setting the Stage

"The base Air Police Sabotage Alert Team got an unexpected opportunity to test their effectiveness on April 21 when an unidentified aircraft landed here . . . . before its pilot could cut his engine, the APSAT had completely surrounded the craft and its occupants. The Air Police team was heavily armed with the necessary weapons when they swooped down on the unexpected, unsuspecting pilot and co-pilot.

"The French Liaison Officer, Commandant Major Jean Claude Faure, who had also been called to the scene, arrived with base-assigned French Gendarmes and an immediate search of the plane was instigated. Klaus Rügge, of Hamburg, Germany and Hans Schneider, of Bielefeld, Germany . . . were escorted to the base Provost Marshal's office for interrogation," blazed the *Laon Sentinel* of the Laon Air Base on May 1, 1958.

It all began on April 3, 1958, 13 years after the Second World War. I shouted, "One, two, three–contact!" as my hand flipped the magneto switch.

Monsieur Ricart promptly flung the prop. A few backfires of the engine and then a surge of power. The metal walls of the old hangar building vibrated. "Be careful, your venture is dangerous," yelled my French instructor, trying to penetrate the noise. He was only one of the experienced pilots who had issued strong warnings against this trip.

I nodded and shoved in the throttle as he jumped back. The plane rolled toward the active runway of the Grimbergen Airport at Brussels, Belgium. I glanced back. There was Monsieur Ricart waving good-bye like an old friend.

Perhaps all these Cassandras are right, I thought. I am not too familiar with the plane. It has only 65 horsepower, a low service ceiling and short range. And with aeronautical charts about 10 years old as well as no navigational equipment–no radio, nothing besides a little compass, I was really taking severe risks!

By now I had taxied to the end of the runway. For a final check-out I pulled the plane onto the run-up area. "1700 rpm. Magnetos–right O.K., left O.K. Carburetor heat on–no ice." Everything like clockwork . . . until now!

Klaus, my partner in this flying venture, would arrive soon in Ghent where I was to meet him. We planned to start our journey there and make Paris our first stop, if . . .

I looked up. Dark clouds rolled across the sky casting foreboding shadows upon the land. Again doubts entered my mind. The wind seemed to be increasing, too. Was this a warning? How would the weather behave on our paths of flight?

Twelve miles to the south, the decisive and final combat of the French military genius, the Battle of Waterloo, was fought on June 18, 1815. There Napoleon Bonaparte saw his hopes and dreams smashed forever in a stunning defeat. Even 6,000 bayonets of his "Old Guard" could not reverse the tide of a crushing onslaught. With the odds against us–like then–were we going to meet our Waterloo, too?

What had brought me to this fateful moment? My enthusiasm for flying . . .

It went back a long time. To this day I remember how I would look longingly up to the sky when just a toddler and watch airplanes passing overhead. I dreamed about being way up there one of these days, especially after I read about the flying ventures of Otto Lilienthal and the Wright brothers.

Then came the terrorizing World War II. Next, an invasion of my homeland by the Russian army in 1945. My father, a multimillionaire-industrialist, was turned into a pauper overnight as he was robbed of everything. Forced to work as a manager in one of his former factories, his monthly wage equalled the value of one pound of butter. For five years we had to stay under those conditions.[1]

Even when coming eventually to West Germany, it was not feasible at first to fly because of restrictions imposed by the Allies. But finally, finally . . .

The year was 1956. Eleven years after the Second World War had ended, once again Germany was allowed to issue private pilot licenses to motor plane fliers.

---

[1] *Timely and Profitable Help for Troubled Americans* also published by World Wide Publishing Corporation contains a full account of those years behind the Iron Curtain. See order form in back of book.

Gliders could be flown before that, but I simply did not have the time to put in one thousand hours in model building which the schools then required before I could even get close to a real plane—no matter how appealing glider flying was to me. I yearned to glide soundlessly through the sky like a bird beholding the beautiful countryside below. Now the persistent longing of my childhood days, still lingering with me, was to receive a dramatic fulfillment as boyhood dreams turned into aviation nightmares.

A bird's-eye view of the harbor at Bremen, where I made my first solo flight and pilot license.

The road toward it was arduous, but my great idealism kept spurring me on. I worked at that time as an apprentice in a large ship broker corporation in Bremen, Germany, for a monthly wage equivalent to $7.14. This company also acted as an agent for several steamship firms, and about once or twice every week the department I worked in would have what we called an "expedition." During those periods we usually worked for two days far into the night—even into the wee hours of the morning—in order to prepare all the many documents (bills of lading, manifests, etc.) required. Often an expedition would stretch over the weekend. For the many hours of overtime in each expedition we were paid the spectacular total sum corresponding to $1.67.

I also received a small allowance (approximately $36 per month) from my father at that time to enable me to rent a room and buy some food. By subsisting on mostly dry bread and water, and living ascetically in a room in which I kept the heat turned off during the winter (an act that lowered my room rent considerably), I managed to save enough money to make my private pilot license. When I showed the impressive certificate to my parents, their amazement was great.

In that manner I became one of the first German motor plane pilots after the war, trained by an experienced and weathered Danish flying daredevil[2] and some of the old German air aces of past World War fame.

Taxiing to the active runway on Bremen's airport in a Danish KZ 3, a two-seater, in which type I took most of my instructions and soloed.

In January of 1956, one of those old bomber pilots took me into the air for the first time for what he apparently considered the initiation ceremony. At times I wondered if flying really was for me, as we kept rolling, diving, and climbing around. I had difficulty with my equilibrium, wondering where the sky and ground were last. It was a new experience filled with challenge and adventure.

---

[2]Konstman, the Dane, a master of feats displaying unusual skill and daring, taught me many of his unique stunts that later were probably instrumental in saving my life many times. He could land, for instance, in a small clearing amid a wild forest by performing the following acrobatic maneuver: with minimum speed, barely sufficient to keep the plane in the air, he approached the open space just high enough to clear the trees in the path. Then, as soon as he passed the last ones, he cut off all power and the immediately stalling plane would drop until, scarcely above the ground, he recovered it by quick reapplication of power and landed within a few feet. I was glad to have him as one of my main trainers.

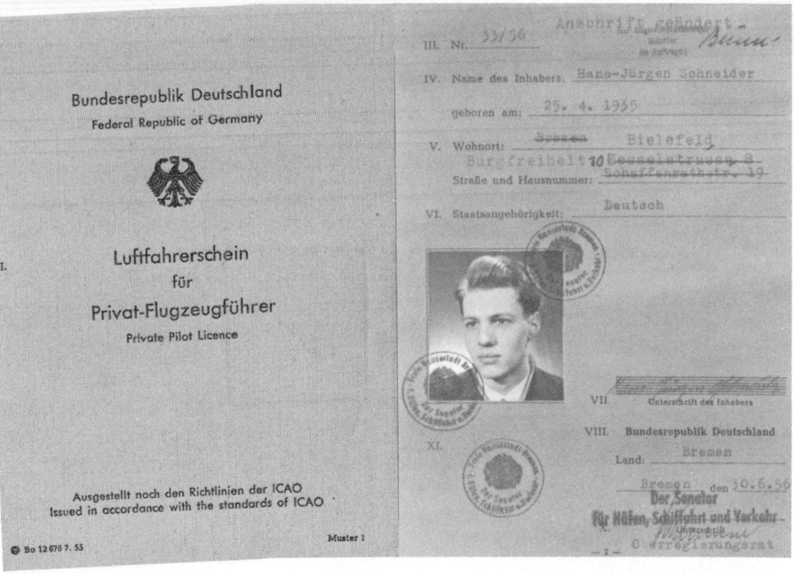

I. Bundesrepublik Deutschland
Federal Republic of Germany

II. Luftfahrerschein
für
Privat-Flugzeugführer
Private Pilot Licence

Ausgestellt nach den Richtlinien der ICAO
Issued in accordance with the standards of ICAO

Bo 12 676 7. 55
Muster I

III. Nr. 33/56 Anschrift geändert
IV. Name des Inhabers: Hans-Jürgen Schneider
geboren am: 25. 4. 1935
V. Wohnort: ~~Bremen~~ Bielefeld
Burgfreiheit 10 ~~Besselstrasse 8~~
Straße und Hausnummer: ~~Schaffenrathstr. 19~~
VI. Staatsangehörigkeit: Deutsch
VII. Unterschrift des Inhabers
VIII. Bundesrepublik Deutschland
Land: Bremen
Bremen den 30.6.56
Der Senator
für Häfen, Schiffahrt und Verkehr
Oberregierungsrat
— 2 —

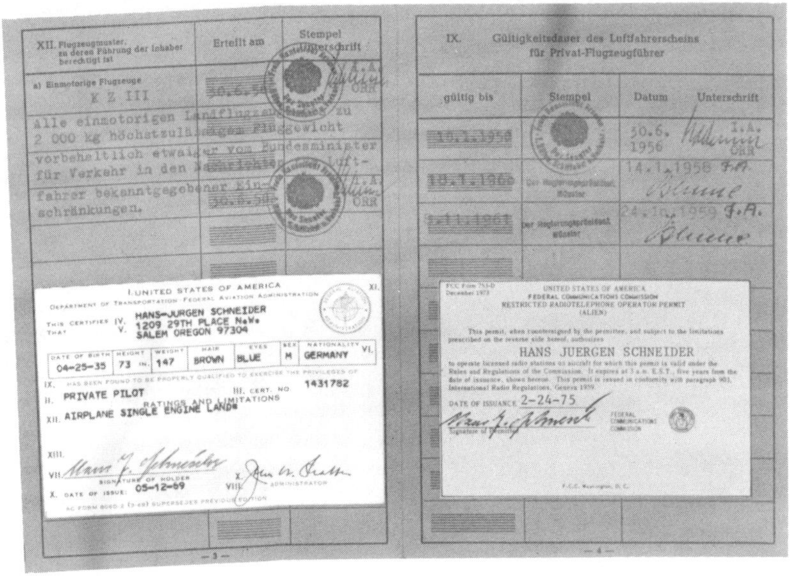

XII. Flugzeugmuster, zu deren Führung der Inhaber berechtigt ist | Erteilt am | Stempel Unterschrift
a) Einmotorige Flugzeuge
K Z III | 30.6.56
Alle einmotorigen Landflugzeuge bis zu 2 000 kg höchstzulässigem Fluggewicht vorbehaltlich etwaiger vom Bundesminister für Verkehr in den Nachrichten für Luftfahrer bekanntgegebener Einschränkungen. | 30.6.56

UNITED STATES OF AMERICA
DEPARTMENT OF TRANSPORTATION · FEDERAL AVIATION ADMINISTRATION
THIS CERTIFIES THAT IV. HANS-JURGEN SCHNEIDER
V. 1209 29TH PLACE N.W.
SALEM OREGON 97304
DATE OF BIRTH 04-25-35 | HEIGHT 73 IN. | WEIGHT 147 | HAIR BROWN | EYES BLUE | SEX M | NATIONALITY GERMANY
IX. HAS BEEN FOUND TO BE PROPERLY QUALIFIED TO EXERCISE THE PRIVILEGES OF
II. PRIVATE PILOT III. CERT. NO 1431782
RATINGS AND LIMITATIONS
XII. AIRPLANE SINGLE ENGINE LAND
VII. SIGNATURE OF HOLDER
X. DATE OF ISSUE: 05-12-69
VIII. ADMINISTRATOR
— 3 —

IX. Gültigkeitsdauer des Luftfahrerscheins für Privat-Flugzeugführer
gültig bis | Stempel | Datum | Unterschrift
10.1.1958 | | 30.6. 1956 | I.A. ORR
10.1.1960 | | 14.1.1958 | I.A.
1.11.1961 | | 24.10.1959 | I.A.

UNITED STATES OF AMERICA
FEDERAL COMMUNICATIONS COMMISSION
RESTRICTED RADIOTELEPHONE OPERATOR PERMIT
(ALIEN)
HANS JUERGEN SCHNEIDER
DATE OF ISSUANCE 2-24-75
— 4 —

I obtained my German Private Pilot License on June 30, 1956. Note the size and simplicity of my U. S. Pilot Certificate *(lower left)* in comparison (both reduced 50%). My U. S. Restricted Radiotelephone Operator permit is at the lower right.

My next great milestone was the one every pilot remembers for the rest of his life. It was in March of the same year . . . One of those beautiful spring days when the birds were singing, the trees shooting forth buds and the air and environment seemed to be charged with the excitement of sending forth new life–a perfect time for my first solo flight. What a thrill to take that little bird into the air all by myself apparently leaving all the cares of this world far behind–just like being born into a new realm of life–a life far superior to what had been.

Little did I know at that time all the dangers and bone-chilling escapades which were lurking in the future and into which this new life was to carry me. I conquered a new dimension and, like a young eagle who had just learned to fly, I was anxious to use those wings. Fear was practically unknown and emotions ran high in that time of first excitement.

Then on May 5, with only 26 hours of logged time, I made my final test flight. Shortly afterward, I buzzed my landlady. Mrs. Ahnelt and her children were dying to see me fly and I could not keep them waiting forever. They stood in the yard, waving excitedly, as I drew my circles overhead. Every pass was so brief that I decided to put out full flaps. This enabled me to make them slower and more enjoyable.

Upon my return to the airport, deep trouble waited. The president of the flying club, who was also the head instructor, fired some pointed questions at me. Soon I found out that some killjoy had called in, complaining about me flying too low and slow over his neighborhood.

"I'll see to it that your license will be withheld from you for one month," said Mr. Schulze, who took a dim view of anyone buzzing friends and relatives. My certificate had not been issued yet since I just made the check ride. I could hardly wait to get it.

"What you were doing causes many plane accidents. I hope you will learn from this and always remember to be careful. I am trying to make a good, cautious pilot out of you. I'm sorry, but it is the best thing to do!"

"Who was it that told you?" I asked.

"That doesn't matter," he replied and never revealed the secret.

One of the longest months in my life followed. I desired to take friends with me and enjoy the freedoms of a licensed private pilot. My instructor knew this well enough to realize that his harsh measure would teach me the lesson. In retrospect, I am glad for what he did. It may have been instrumental in saving my life by preventing me from doing reckless things at a later time. Since that day I have always been careful when making "visits from above."

My other instructor, Konstman, the Dane, besides being one of my best friends, was also in charge of the aircraft rental in Bremen. He acted as the chief representative for Sönderborg Flying Service. This company leased the KZ planes to Bremen's flying club, the only ones available to us because of the Allied restrictions on German aircraft construction.

Konstman always saw to it that I had instant access to the few planes when I needed them.

Immediately after obtaining my pilot certificate, I began to conduct sightseeing flights. Many of them were made during the lunch hours designated by our employers, so we could enjoy ourselves in the air rather than in a smoke-filled restaurant. There was barely enough time for me to dash out to the field with new clients in my V.W. bug, squeeze in one or two trips, and then rush back to the office. It would have been impossible for us to wait for an aircraft.

In the evenings, after finishing the ship broker work for the day, I flew more people around. A combination of idealism, fiery enthusiasm, and industriousness kept me going, even though it was hard on the stomach and nerves.

At times it aroused the jealousy of other flying fans and members of the club. Many of them hung around the airport, engaged in wishful thinking. Occasionally they would take a four- to five-minute trip circling the field. Not getting the same service, it was hard for them to understand why my extensive flying was worthy of more attention than their hops.

"Where in the world do you get all your clients?" asked one of them. They didn't realize that I worked hard for it by spending many hours on the phone. I called the large firms our company dealt with and had their people pass the word.

I felt no inclination to keep hugging the same old field after obtaining my license. To wing out and see other places–that's why I learned to fly. Continuously I took people on flights, and many of them were cross-country. In that way I became the main charterer at the club, adding considerably to the financial status of it and the Sönderborg Flying Service, whose personnel enjoyed and supported my love for aviation. All this in turn strengthened its cause, and even the short-sighted members of the club benefited. Soon I was also ferrying planes to and from Denmark for Sönderborg Flying Service.

Once Konstman and two other veteran pilots invited me on a business flight to England. I remember this particular journey distinctly! All three of them consented that I fly the plane to gather more time in my logbook. What a challenge to aviate under the scrutiny of these old pros. My inner call and instinct to be airborne made me feel at home among them, even though my experience was practically nil.

On our return from England to Calais, France, we had fog problems. All kept a watchful eye to see how I would fare with the flight across the misty channel. At times they advised me to fly more to the left or to the right, but I followed my inbred sense of flight and held the heading I felt was correct with the compass as a steady companion. When the French coast finally appeared below us through the fog, we were directly over Calais. Everybody on board was amazed about the remarkable precision of this newcomer. I visibly gained in their esteem as I had taken another step in the field of aviation.

It is true, I had earned a lot of respect from my instructors and fellow pilots from the start—ever since soloing quicker than any of the other students. Then, with only a few more hours in the air, I made my final test flight. Again, this was a record unachieved by any of the other trainees.

Not so bad for a start, I kept hitching my wagon to a higher star. More territory was destined to be conquered.

BARNSTORMING DAYS

I had a number of humerous episodes in my barnstorming days. Once three ladies in their 70's were my sightseeing customers. I was rather surprised that they would be willing to fly in a small plane piloted by such a young chap. But they were a happy-go-lucky bunch and it was a real pleasure to take them. While airborne, the weather turned sour. When coming in for a landing, I battled strong gusts and poor visibility as snow piled up on my windshield. I was wondering how we would make it in, but on board were three old ladies, singing and enjoying life to the fullest.

Around midmorning on Mother's Day, May 12, 1957, I took off in a KZ 7 with special plans and a heavy load. Two of my three passengers were of noble peerage and Manfred von Gerkan was one of them.

My parents lived in Bielefeld and I worked in Bremen. Our vacation house on Dümmer Lake, situated right between the two cities, was our regular meeting place most weekends. I was going to conduct this visit from the air. It was about time for everybody at the resort to learn officially that, besides driving motorcycles, cars and sailing, I could also fly. This might result in more customers for sightseeing trips, which it did.

Approximately 35 minutes after our departure, the silvery-white waters appeared before us. We were now close to our destination. Soon my parents would find out if I really knew how to be an aviator. With the weekend house at hand, I cut the motor power and came diving toward it. I then reapplied full throttle. With a sudden roar we came whistling low over the cottage. Everyone was in a mad scramble, trying to rush through the door at the same time. With an abrupt wing over right above them, I turned the plane and came hurtling back.

Not yet recovered from their first shock, my parents and the local inhabitants were in for the next. By now many people had gathered to see this wild stuntflyer perform his tricks. I initiated a slip, and moments later opened the right door as everyone watched in stunned silence. I could almost hear them say: "What will be next? Is Hans going to jump out of the plane? It couldn't be! He has to fly it. Anyhow, he is too low for the parachute to open."

They didn't have to wonder long. Next to the place where people had gathered, we noticed a pasture—a good place to land our drop shipment. Heading that way, I counted, "One, two, three," followed by, "let go," when over it. Instantly Manfred tossed my sack of dirty clothes through the open doorway. It plunged toward a canal.

"Oh, no! They're headed right for the water! My clothes will be in the soak cycle before my mother gets to them." One foot from the channel, the bag struck the ground with vehement force. Bystanders later told me that it sounded as if a rock or meteor had hit.

What we just did was not strictly legal. Aviation laws forbid the act of throwing objects from a plane. Also, we were a little lower than we should have been according to regulations limiting the altitude over settled areas. But since flying had just started out again in Germany, people were not fussy about these technicalities. Everybody was glad to see a plane and, even more, to see it perform some interesting feats.

Our mission was not yet complete. Again I cut the motor power and came gliding over my parents' place. This time, I threw a pretty bouquet of lilacs out of the window, tenderly wrapped in transparent paper with the note: "Mother's Day airmail greetings for Mrs. Marga Schneider." Caught by a strong air current, the flowers vanished in the distance.

"Did you see where they went?" I asked the passengers.

"Yes, I saw them blown to the next little village on the lake. I believe they'll land about a mile or so from here," one of them replied.

"I sure hope my mother gets the nosegay," I said, flying around the entire lake. "What a difference to make this circle by plane in a few minutes! With the sailboat it takes hours!"

I always enjoyed the invigorating feeling of sailing our boat *(above)* on the Dümmer Lake in Northern Germany in the face of an approaching storm.

Exactly 98 minutes after leaving Bremen, we were back. Manfred and I jumped into my V.W. bug and drove to the lake for an in-person visit. There we received a hero's welcome and delighted in it.

Blackbird was among the first to greet us. We called him that because hook-nosed, cross-eyed, hoarse-voiced and of a tall, haggard stature, he reminded us of this feathered creature. Still very much excited, he declared in his usual but now much more pronounced stutter, "The, the, the, clo- clo- clo- clothes -es, al- al- . . ."

"Almost got soaked," I completed.

One day after my "Mother's Day" escapade, farmer Schodde, Jr., the main landholder and big shot at Dümmer Lake, drove his truck up to Bremen and requested a jaunt in the sky. He chose to sit in the co-pilot's seat, wanting to steer the plane once airborne. Instead, "Junior" was so scared that he clung to the iron braces in the cockpit as if he were just about ready to fall out. He looked like a monkey hanging from tree branches. The funny billed, earflapped cap he wore made him look still more comical. Once we hit the first airhole, Schodde immediately panicked. With a trembling voice, he requested an instant landing, not realizing in his predicament that we had to return to the airport first. His world was the ground and the soil his bread and butter. This lofty state of affairs was strange to him and he was not yet ready to say good-bye to his earthly fortunes.

As we came in "on final," a distinct odor caused by a disgorging ceremony drifted across the cockpit. However, no trace of naughtiness was in sight. Upon intent questioning, the passenger who sat behind me confessed his wrongdoing and sheepishly pointed to the pocket on the back of my seat. Examining it, I nearly flipped when I saw the results of airsickness all nicely stashed away in an orderly fashion.

"Why didn't you use the funny hat of our farmer friend?" I asked, and could readily tell that Schodde, Jr., being proud of his headgear, didn't appreciate that joke.

We had to take out the whole seat and practically dismantle it in a clean-up operation.

Even less pleasant was a trip when an unexpected explosion occurred behind me. Fragments of vomit covered the windshield as well as my hair and brand-new jacket. I had to wipe the windows to be able to land. It was good that we were just at the end of the flight.

After stopping the plane, I turned around to face the culprit and demanded courteously but firmly, "What have I done that you must treat me like this?" Then it dawned on me that the countenance I looked at was dark red as if ready to burst.

"I'm sorry. I tried to hold it back until the pressure got too great. Then I had to let go. I am awfully sorry," stuttered a feeble voice.

My displeasure turned into compassion. "The next time, it would be wise to use the container provided for this purpose in the backrest compartment. This way you can find release before the problem gets 'explosive,' " I kindly replied.

Immediately after obtaining my pilot certificate, I faced the glorious opportunity of giving a ride to one of the main bosses of the company I worked for. In the past his lofty behavior had bugged me and now was the time to test his bravery.

It was a lovely day. No reasons for turbulence were in sight, so I had to create some. Gently we took off and continued the smooth flight just long enough to gain sufficient altitude and calm my tense passenger. Then, all of a sudden, I performed a wing over, letting the plane plummet on his side. To him, it seemed as though the plane were disintegrating and he was doomed. Sweating profusely, he confessed that these wingdingers were not overly appreciated.

I had performed my little tenderhearted trick and was satisfied. I made up for it by giving him a nice ride the rest of the half-hour we were airborne.

Not quite as gently, I treated a fellow of rather hilarious nature. One day he performed a deed for which I meant to get even. While sailing with me on Dümmer Lake, he clowned around before some girls in the boat, apparently trying to impress them. In addition to putting on all that commotion, he jumped to the wrong side of the boat as I was tacking. The ship leaned way over because of his added weight and was ready to capsize. Not wanting to get wet, he leaped to the opposite side, giving the boat the final jolt which tipped it into the lake. While all of us slowly went under, he managed .o jump into the middle of the expensive mainsail with a loud shout, leaving a large gaping tear through which he bobbed up again in short order. Heinz apparently thought that he was funny. Besides causing us a lot of expense by getting everything wet and damaging things, he could easily have been killed had he not found the hole again. It would have been possible for him to get tangled in the sail below the water and drown.

Now Heinz was sitting beside me in the plane. As soon as we were airborne, I gave him all the fun he wanted. In every sense of the word, he received a roller coaster ride through the sky. Wing overs, lacy eights, chandelles, diving flights with sudden pull-ups and vice versa gave him plenty of excitement. All through the maneuvers, he kept yelling and hollering at the top of his voice. I felt he just meant to be silly as usual. After this flight, I didn't see him for several years. When I finally met him again, this formerly lanky person had turned into a cigar-smoking 250 pounder and looked like an overgrown baby with a lollipop—a strange sight indeed.

Not all my flights were of this rough nature. One weekend Konstman, two other Danish friends and I flew down to Bielefeld to visit my parents. Dr. Gerhard Gabler, a dentist, lived in the same house. A very intelligent man, he was a walking encyclopedia. It seemed that no matter what someone asked him, he had the appropriate reply. For instance, he was able to answer every question of TV quizzes immediately. I briefed my companions about him in advance. As soon as I introduced them, he asked, "Where are you all from?"

One of my Danish friends came from a very small, virtually unknown island. Being sure that Dr. Gabler had never heard about the place, he asked him with a big smile of triumph, "Do you know where it is?"

"Of course!" was the reply. "I vacationed there long ago."

The next day, before our return to Bremen, I took this dentist and my father on a plane ride. When I landed on the bumpy grass strip, Dr. Gabler exclaimed, "Alfred, did you feel that smooth landing? You could have shaved yourself while touching down (straight razor blades were still common in those days). I couldn't even feel when the wheels made contact with the ground!"

I was happy about the compliments of that knowledgeable man.

I used this Danish four-seater, a KZ 7, on many sightseeing flights I conducted in Germany as well as for trips to Denmark, Netherlands, Belgium, France and England. To my left is Konstman, the Dane, and to my right are two young customers for a plane ride.

OUR WINGED 65-HP FRIEND—THE AERONCA CHIEF

About three years later, while living in Belgium for a while, a keen plan was being conceived which sent spine-tingling thrills through my body even at that early stage. It was spring of 1958 and already I had amassed the "tremendous" amount of 131 flying hours–not very much for the launching of such a spectacular flying odyssey as I now cold-bloodedly planned.

After all, with only twenty-three summers to my count, I was still young and filled with vim and vigor, ready to challenge the world with the 65 horsepower of the control-wheel-equipped Aeronca Chief I was to rent from "Le Club National D'Aviation à Bruxelles" in Brussels, Belgium. The low hourly rental fee of $7.60 was about all I could afford at that time. My father did not share my flying enthusiasm and therefore I could not count on any help from him. I knew there was not going to be any problem in keeping the daily flight-hour minimum the Club had imposed–not with the gigantic trip I had envisioned.

However I had never flown a craft with a control wheel before. Just having been acquainted with the left-handed (as in the English Auster Autocrat) and mostly right-handed sticks, this wheel "bit" was new to me, and required my full attention to get the hang of it.

First, I was a little apprehensive about going without becoming more accustomed to that different approach, but a good 41 minutes, encompassing five flights, with my trainer were sufficient for him to okay me in that new bird. Another 13 minutes of solo, and I was confirmed. After all, I had piloted quite a number of different types of planes previously including the Tiger Moth (a biplane with an open cockpit), Piper, Bücker 181, and Klemm–nine altogether–with most of my time in the Danish KZ 3 and KZ 7.

Earlier, I had obtained a "validation" certificate issued for a limited time by the Administration de l' Aéronautique of the Ministere Des Communications in the Royaume de Belgique on the basis of my current German pilot license, so that I was able to fly planes with Belgian registry. It was vital, for they could be chartered there for less money than in Germany.

Mr. Ricart had initiated me to the Aeronca Champion in January of that year during three "touch and goes" totalling 18 minutes. In contrast to the Chief, it was equipped with a control stick and tandem seats and had somewhat different flying characteristics. With this plane I had made numerous sightseeing flights for interested parties.

My instructor was a friendly, sympathetic person, but the trouble was that he, like most of his countrymen, spoke only French. My knowledge of that beautiful sounding language was very limited. I knew practically no words whatsoever related to flying. This communication barrier did not help much and prolonged matters somewhat, as we had to resort mostly to sign language. When I was familiarized with the Chief, therefore, I had already amassed 11 hours and 47 minutes in two Champions and was glad again to have Monsieur Ricart on my side. We had become used to each other, and a close-knit friendship developed between us. On one occasion he even transferred some of his customers for sightseeing rides to me, for he knew how much I enjoyed flying.

Then during the afternoon of the third of April, I moved the plane from Brussels to Ghent so it would be ready to carry Klaus and me off into adventure land the next morning. I made this a combination flight by taking a Belgian sightseer and flying fan along.

On April 4, 1958, we now launched one of the most breathtaking and dangerous aviation ventures probably anyone ever undertook in modern aviation history with such a tiny, underpowered plane. Never have I heard of anyone even coming close to equal such a fantastic and reckless flight endeavor—not in all my travels through almost one hundred countries of the world, meeting airplane captains and bush pilots galore, some of them with over 40,000 flying hours to their credit.

There were admonitions from engineers that my plan was crazy. Experienced pilots also intensely warned me not to take that trip. They knew that the inadequate, underpowered plane might be unable to withstand such high winds as accumulate along the Pyrenees between France and Spain and still gain ground. They figured that I would be driven far out into the ocean by those forceful gusts and might not have enough power and speed to counteract them.

They also knew that the range was too small despite an additional reserve tank behind the seats, and that it was absolutely unbelievable to fly without a radio or other navigational instruments besides the little magnetic compass it had. All of them literally assured me it would mean a certain end of my life if I were to go ahead with that project. Unanimously they all said, " . . . it can't be done—you won't return!" Little did they know that I had never known fear until . . .

But there I was, young, determined, high-spirited and with a dream that couldn't be stopped—that brought me many times face to face with death. Even 100 horses could not have pulled me away from my idea. Soon I was to feel bitter remorse many times for not having followed their advice—but I am getting ahead of my story.

MEET MY COMPANION—THE PAWN IN THE GAME

Let me introduce the poor victim I had chosen to accompany me on this undertaking. It was on a boat trip to Vigo, Spain, when I met Klaus, who was quite a character. He almost didn't make the connection, as the train he was travelling in changed cars and his coach was one which was disconnected.

Unnoticed by him on account of his carousing around, he sooner or later found himself in a lonely car on a dead track. This, however, could not detain Klaus from a fun-filled journey. Enterprising as he was, he threw himself into a taxi and arrived at the ship at the last moment when the boat's crew was getting ready to haul in the tows and gangplank.

He was quite a person to watch, and I knew soon that he would be the one to pick if an out-of-the-ordinary deal would be contemplated.

Whenever something ecstatic, unusual and incredible was going on, Klaus was there and often the motivating factor behind it. I therefore wrote to him about the forthcoming adventure and he sent me his "okay." I had expected it, for Klaus could not say "no" to such an intriguing proposal.

In the meantime, I obtained special plane insurance since the African section of our flight was not included on the regular policy held by "Le Club National D'Aviation à Bruxelles." They insisted that we be covered for the entire trip. "Compagnie Belge D'Assurances Aviation" was willing to take us as a risk for a fat fee, and our African leg of the journey was assured.

Klaus soon arrived at my residence in Kortrijk (Courtrai), Belgium, filled with expectations and mischief. I could hardly wait to show him the proud ship which soon was to wing us all over Europe and into Africa.

But when Klaus first saw the plane, he didn't like it at all. He looked at it as an object of a prank and insisted that it resembled one of those toy planes which children snap off with a little rubber band.

I didn't like that joke, and he felt almost insulted that I had invited him to accompany me in such a rickety conveyance, thinking that I would have presented him with a big, executive aircraft according to fashionable multimillionaire style. Having previously met my father and learned that he was a former multimillionaire industrialist who was just making a good financial recovery in West Germany after his evacuation from the eastern territories where he had lost everything, Klaus thought that I, his son, would come up with something better and more fancy than this flimsy craft. Doubling up with laughter, he said, "No, Schneider, you have a nerve to invite me on a world tour in a flimsy tail dragger! Is this a joke or do you mean it?"

Proud of the ship I had so laboriously searched for, I was utterly taken by surprise about those disrespectful words so lightly spoken and gasped for breath. *"Was ist los Du Dummkopf?"* I finally uttered.

But before I could say anything else, he continued, "If you had told me what type of an antiquated, ridiculous plane you were going to use, I would never have come all the way over here by train to join such a crazy venture."

And as if to underline what he said, he walked toward the bird, poking his finger into the delicate fabric airframe cover and then proceeded to rattle the wings and tail of the craft. "Do you see how the skin like that of an old lady stretches and shrivels and how the wings and tail bend and flap around?" he snapped. "With such a lame duck you want to take me on a world tour?"

Knowing little about planes, he did not realize that he had moved the ailerons, elevator and rudder of the plane and that indeed without those moving parts a plane could not fly. What he called *"flatternde und klappernde Teile"* were very much needed for our forthcoming venture.

"Go back home to Hamburg and tell your mother to feed you more Wiener Schnitzel, Bockwurst und Hamburgers until you become

AGENCE : **Monsieur A. DUCHATELET à SCHAERBEEK**

Exemplaire à nous retourner signé

COMPAGNIE BELGE D'ASSURANCES AVIATION

AVIABEL

S. A. D'ASSURANCES CONTRE TOUS RISQUES D'AVIATION

SIÈGE SOCIAL : 90, RUE ROYALE - BRUXELLES

CAPITAL SOCIAL : 40.000.000 de Francs

AVIABEL S.A. 18 JUIN 1958 BRUXELLES

REG. COM. BRUX. : 81.655
C. C. P. : 134.78

Adresse Télégraphique AVIABEL BRUXELLES
TÉLÉPHONES : 17.21.62
18.36.33

AERONCA(Chief OO-L.E.M.

AVENANT No I2/447I à la Police No II0.709

souscrite par le CLUB NATIONAL D'AVIATION à Bruxelles

Il est convenu et agréé d'un commun accord entre les parties ce qui suit:

I-Le preneur d'Assurance déclare que l'avion Aeronca-Chief OO-L.E.M. piloté par Monsieur Hans-Juergen SCHNEIDER entreprend à partir du 4 avril I958 un voyage en Afrique du Nord pour une durée d'un mois. La Compagnie en prend note et consent à étendre les garanties de la police à ce voyage qui sont les limites géographiques prévues à la police.

2-Il est également entendu que la valeur de l'appareil assuré est portée à Fr.B. I50.000.- à partir du 4 avril I958.
La prime annuelle est désormais fixée comme suit:

R.C.T.N.T. (Inchangé):	Fr.B.	2.000.-
R.C.T.T. (Inchangé):	Fr.B.	2.000.-
CASSE valeur Fr.B. I50.000.-	"	I5.075.-
		I9.075.-
Réduction pluralité I5%-	-	2.860.-
Total Fr.B.		I6.2I5.-

3-Le supplément de prime à percevoir se décompose comme suit:

a) Surprime pour voyage en Afrique du Nord:	Fr.B.	I.62I.-
b) Prorata de prime du 4-4-58 au 23-6-58	: Fr.B.	9I2.-
Total:	Fr.B.	2.533.-

4- Il est perçu à l'émission du présent avenant et contre quittance séparée pour la période du 4 avril I958 au 23 juin I958 la somme de Fr.B. 2.533.- + 274.- d'impôts et frais.

Fait en double à Bruxelles, le 23 mai I958.

LE PRENEUR D'ASSURANCE. COMPAGNIE BELGE D'ASSURANCES AVIATION.

CLUB NATIONAL D'AVIATION
Le President Ph. QUERSIN

A. de WALQUE
Directeur

This insurance policy shows the additional premium I was forced to pay for the African portion of the trip, because of its high risk factor.

more courageous to match me *'Du Angsthase!'* (you scared rabbit)" I challenged.

This apparently had a sobering effect on Klaus, for he suddenly realized how "foolish" he had been. Slowly he began to develop more of a respect for our lovely little bird and finally he decided to come along.

It had taken quite some persuasion to bring him down to the more realistic level of our pocketbooks. As far as he was concerned, most of his money had to go into new business opportunities, and this trip had to be done on a shoestring—although he wanted luxuries (such as gourmet meals), but at rock-bottom, bargain prices.

Klaus was also a fellow of many high aspirations, such as getting rich in a hurry, foreign investments, running many enterprises—a real go-getter and manager type. He was all for an exciting life and had strange "talents" which were almost immediately to become our downfall. Little did he know what dreadful excitements were soon to turn him into a nervous wreck and knock off one-third of his 150 pounds!

He assured me, for instance, that he was well versed in terrestrial navigation and would ably perform the function of chief navigator while I was to use all my wits to keep that little overloaded plane in the air. He made it rather plain that he had learned all there was to learn about piloting on his sailing trips on various lakes.

"Aber klar, das ist doch kein Problem (But certainly, this is no problem). I never have gotten lost with my sailing boat," he bubbled.

"What lakes have you sailed on?" I inquired. After listening to his eye-opening revelations, I realized that he had merely been on a little *pond* here and there.

Not sharing his overt confidence along that line, therefore, I gave him a quick minicourse in pilotage and Klaus was a fast student with a willing heart. His unlimited thirst for adventure went so far that he pressed toward a quick and almost immediate departure.

Weather information was secondary, for he was an "old pro" in that matter, so he thought—an idea he was to face soon with nervous regret. I consented, knowing that he had only a certain amount of time before he needed to return to his business enterprises in Hamburg, Germany. Klaus might draw back if excitement were not kept at a high pitch and if I delayed.

The next dilemma we found ourselves faced with was the somber fact that, according to the plane's manual, the combined weight of us and the filled tanks nearly exhausted its capacity. Certainly we had not picked a cross-country craft but just a little hedgehopper.

Klaus, a lanky professional photographer, had brought a heavy little suitcase of fancy photo equipment, such as expensive telephoto cameras and what have you.

I had no interest in his gadgets or picture-taking. To me it was merely an added nuisance and expense. Because of the new trouble I was running into with him now, I said laconically, "What do you need all that junk for—aren't we overloaded enough as is?"

"Wenn ich meine Kameras und die dazugehörigen Ausrüstungen nicht mitnehmen kann, dann werde ich selber auch nicht mitfliegen—es ist entweder alles oder nichts (If I can't bring along my cameras and their necessary accessories, then I won't come—it is either all or nothing)," he answered, full of determination.

To my dismay, he insisted that his photo laboratory had to go, too, even though we were counting every ounce by now. It was either that, or he wouldn't go at all. He was quick to assure me one of the main reasons he decided to come along was that he could take a lot of exotic pictures on this trip, most of them from the air.

"I would rather leave any of the other stuff behind as long as my cameras with their equipment can go," Klaus assured me magnanimously, as I began to realize that in a sudden burst of benevolence he had included my pack of belongings *amongst* "the other stuff"!

I saw he was not kidding and again reluctantly consented. Since we could not go on such an extended journey with at least some of the necessities of life, we painstakingly went through all our stuff again and came up with one bag of most essential items.

While sorting out more, Klaus once again amazed me, when asserting that many of my personal effects were not needed while most of his were absolute necessities.

By now the plane was really loaded. It didn't matter to Klaus as long as his exceedingly heavy photographic equipment could be included. This was the way we started on the first leg of our journey in the beginning of April, 1958.

PART II

HEEBIE-JEEBIES

IN THE COCKPIT

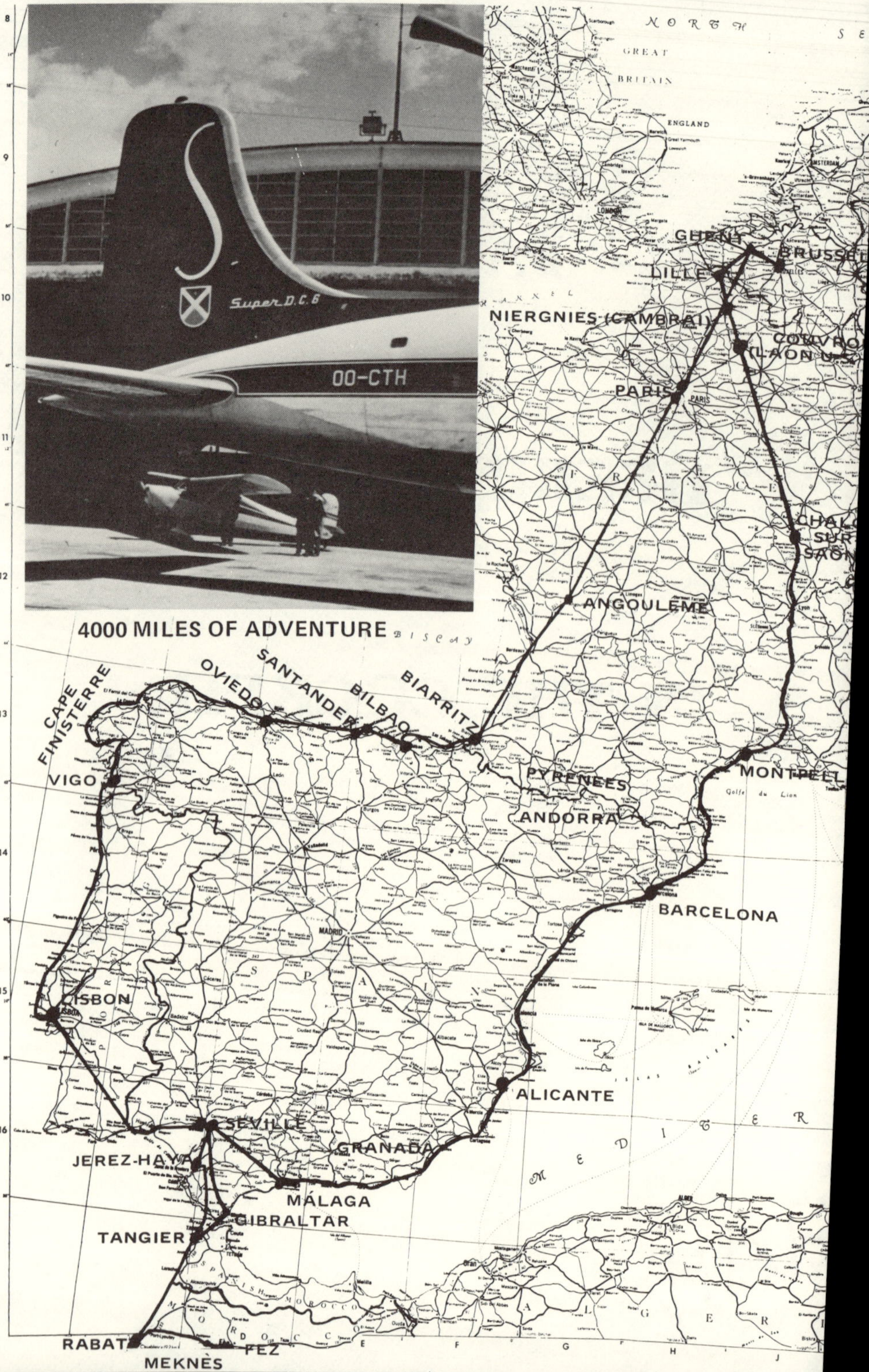

4000 MILES OF ADVENTURE

2

Panic Over Paris

(Ghent, Belgium to Paris, France)

Now hold on and fasten your seatbelt.

"One–two–three–CONTACT!" I hollered enthusiastically, whereupon Klaus expectingly jumped into action, pulling through the prop. A few seconds later a deafening roar of the engine charged the atmosphere with excitement. Our troubles began immediately and on this very first flight we almost never made it. Our lives nearly faded away that early, thanks to Klaus's great haste and navigational "talent."

After taking off in Ghent–and amazingly enough, we *were* able to take off using most of the runway available–we immediately enjoyed being airborne. Soon this joy received the first jolt as about in the middle of the flight the motor started to cough and sputter. Not being very familiar with that aircraft, we both wondered what we had gotten into, and Klaus muttered a quick doubt whether our plane was any better than those toy planes he had referred to earlier. *"Ich habe Dir doch gesagt, dass diese Klappermühle nichts taugt* (I told you this clackermill was no good)," he was quick to remind me.

However, I could tell he became more soft spoken, because suddenly he realized that his life depended on the goodwill of this little bird and I, as chief pilot, had a good leverage on him and could perform a few quick little flying tricks to frighten him yet more if undue words of insult were being spoken about my much-treasured flying machine.

At any rate, an airport appeared below our wings and, circling the field, I pulled the carburetor heat and made a few other adjustments.

This apparently did the job, for the motor recovered and once again purred along nicely, pulling us right into our next adventure.

"Make absolutely sure that everything is O.K. with the motor and otherwise," commanded a voice to my right. Klaus wanted to be certain that everything was all right before leaving that harbor of safety.

Immediately I resumed course toward Paris, not realizing that what had just happened was a bad omen and, in fact, connected with certain disastrous conditions which were to give us the heebie-jeebies not much later. We had barely recovered from this incident when we were in for the next, infinitely worse, one. It nearly ended fatally.

Only when we started to notice a remarkable deterioration of visibility and weather conditions as a whole did we realize it was the great moisture content, already present in the air, which had caused a near motor failure through carburetor icing. So far my friend had performed his function as chief navigator quite well, but he had not yet proven himself in acid tests under adverse conditions. We did not have to wait long for these conditions to arise, for they lurked just around the corner.

I chuckled as I noticed that Klaus, with increasing frequency and jittery hands, drew one navigational reference circle after the other on the map. These circles were drawn around points providing easy terrestrial navigation, such as ninety-degree bends of railroad tracks, intersections of such with major roads or rivers, a crossing of our flight path with them, or the appearance of a town, airport, high tower or lake.

Soon he had those marks only four and one-half to two miles apart! In the meantime, the visibility started to turn sour on us. Finally, greatly humbled and wildly fumbling about, Klaus had to admit that he was lost and did not have the slightest idea, whatsoever, where we were. As a further encouragement, he stammered that this had been his lot for quite some time—ever since we were still about forty to fifty miles away from Paris.

"I didn't want to tell you that I goofed because I was sure that I still could find my way on this crazy map—how could I know that this _ _ _ _ fog would get worse by the minute," he groaned.

"What do you like best—the plane, the fog or being lost?" I jested.

"I'll take the plane any day!" he bellowed.

"Do you remember the derogatory words you spoke when first seeing *our* brave little bird?" I reminded him.

"Don't talk about this now," he reprimanded.

"Well, then you'd better repent and make peace with our little winged friend, because if he quits on us now it's going to be *furchtbar* (terrible)!" I urged at last.

Had he earlier conceded his state of affairs, I could have looked for an alternate airport on the map and, computing my new course, been able to fly and land there before conditions turned into an inferno. At this late stage of the game, with Paris right ahead of us, we were running quite low in gas, forbidding a turn around to look for another field, not even knowing where we were.

With my eyes glued to the compass, I decided to fly straight on, doing the best I could under such circumstances by following our computed course and hoping for the best.

"Klaus, have you ever been in trouble?"

"What do you mean—we are in trouble *right now,"* he snapped.

"Then what can we do?" I inquired.

"Only one way to go—keep your eyes on the compass!" he hollered through the drone of our fogbound aircraft. "That's about all you can do—it's our only hope now," he affirmed in a voice becoming somewhat softer.

"How about your other troubles in life?" I persisted.

"Will you leave me alone—I have no time or inclination to think of other troubles right now!" This time his voice was furious.

"Just meant to tell you that if you ever do have problems in life which you cannot handle, like now, remember to keep your eyes on the compass."

"Have you lost your marbles, are you crazy—do you think I walk around with a compass in my hands?" he inquired with amazement.

"I am talking about a different kind of compass, Klaus—you will soon know what I mean," I said as if by prophetic utterance. How could I know the full meaning of what I had just spoken at this fateful moment? And how could I have known at the time that we would only survive each confrontation with death to be ready for the next?

In the meantime I was forced to keep on lowering my flying altitude so I could maintain a minimum of visibility to enable me to stay barely clear of high structures and other dangers, including flying objects.

The last thing I remember appearing in the haze off to my right, before arriving over Paris, was a rather high tower with "rotating light with flashing code beacons." According to the air regulations, an aircraft when over congested areas such as cities or towns has to observe a minimum safe altitude of 1,000 feet above the highest obstacle within a horizontal radius of 2,000 feet of the plane.

As the altimeter slowly unwound, we approached Paris at an altitude from only 240 to 180 feet above ground level—a definite violation of this regulation. Instantly I wondered if somewhere out of the mist the Eiffel Tower would arise.

"Keep a lookout for that foreboding iron skeleton which could rake us out of the clouds in an instant. Even though experiments are performed on the upper platforms, I hate to utilize these facilities this way. Neither do I plan to join their dinner party by trying a table-top landing in their skyline restaurant!" I hastily cautioned Klaus.

"There is a weather station up there. Why not give them a close pass to see if they have any idea when the fog is going to lift, since you don't have a radio on board?" Klaus suggested, startling me with a sudden flux of humor.

The Eiffel Tower on a clear night. Searching for an airport, we were almost raked from the sky by this 984-foot iron and steel monster during a panic-stricken, fog-trapped flight 180 feet over Paris.

After this, an icy silence spread throughout the cockpit as both of us suddenly realized that by now we were flying *so low* that even these platforms, wrapped in a dense layer of fog, towered way above us.

This seven-thousand-ton colossus on the Champ de Mars in Paris, which was for many years the highest structure and engineering marvel in the world, rises to a height of 984 feet.

Considering this, I should have flown at an altitude of at least 1,984 feet above ground level, but with an altitude of only 180 feet, I found myself flying exactly 1,804 feet too low. As I was just below a dense layer of fog, fighting occasional skirmishes with lower patches, I would have been completely unable to see had I flown any higher.

Then, all of a sudden, we found ourselves right over the "art capital of the world," 185 square miles in size, and one of the most crowded cities on earth. I also realized that several hills between 300 to 500 feet above river level were adding to our danger. They were Mont Sainte-Geneviève and Montparnasse in the south, Mont Valérien in the west and Belleville and Montmartre crowned with the Sacré Coeur (Church of the Sacred Heart) in the north. On top of that, Paris is one of the world's greatest centers for air transportation, with Le Bourget and Orly as the two chief commercial airports of the city. Besides running into a hill or building, we could easily be rammed by commercial aircraft, especially if close enough to some of those airports.

After minutes of panic, we arrived over, what I guessed to be, the Seine River, following its course as our last lifeline. Many of its 30 bridges passed below. At this point our compass went haywire, as we spent the next 30 minutes in a desperate struggle between life and death hugged to the deep, tranquil river which winds through Paris in a general east-west direction. It was the only area in that great metropolis I could fly over with at least some hope of survival. Death-defyingly and with forlorn hopes, I clung to the controls, tearing the airship around each succeeding curve–of which there were all too many. At this time, my flying altitude was the lowest ever, and at each new turn I could see the walls of buildings come crashing toward me as I kept wondering if I would make the never-ending horseshoe bends. I forced all the aileron and rudder control the plane could muster to get it around that next river loop, our wings barely avoiding the buildings hurtling by us. Our flying position was changing continuously between a predominantly southwest to northeast position and the compass float was wildly gyrating, passing the north mark many times.

I managed to spare a few seconds to share my observations with my greatly "talented" companion, who looked then as white as snow.

"Paleface, do you see the compass–I am wondering where we are headed with such continuous course changes. The compass is showing one moment near north and the next near south."

Full of the "willies," he immediately snapped back, "Shut up, I see that myself!" He had noticed every bit of it, as his taut nerves revealed and, thinking that his certain end had arrived, he did not want to be reminded any more of our desperate situation.

We had not the slightest idea of our geographical position as we trailed the sinuous stream for about 30 minutes. There was no time for me to study the map, and my friend was too jittery to help or even look straight–his strange "talents" suddenly went by the wayside. Even at that low altitude, visibility was so poor I could scarcely keep flying. We had doubts if the weather would hold up that much or get worse, necessitating a nearly impossible try at an emergency landing in that forbidding area. Both of us had given up hope, as our tanks were emptying rapidly after we had flown like that for about 37 to 55 miles along the Seine River without an airport in sight.

Then, suddenly I sighted something which seemed to me like a "fata morgana" (mirage). This "something" looked like a grass landing field stretched along the side of the waterway. Without delay, I passed on my observations to fidgety Klaus, who thought that because of the tension and stress I had gone crazy. The news sounded too good to him to believe, and after all we had been through, it was incredible that in those moments of imminent doom help came in sight.

Crazy or not, I circled around the field to discover the windsock. "Watch this one!" I shouted at Klaus. With a short approach, wanting to get in before the motor quit or the field hazed in, I made a giant slip landing. Coming down like a rock, I slipped the plane nearly right into the ground, making sure that it would not be a go-around. We touched down at the Marine Nationale Airport in Meulan les Mureaux, 32 airline miles west-northwest of downtown Paris. Our first jaunt had just ended.

Klaus, with trembling knees, slumped out of the plane and, still pale, promptly announced with a gasping voice, "No, Schneider, that was the last trip I ever made with you! I will take the next train and go home." All my persuasions to continue the trip with me whenever the weather cleared up were of no avail. He repeated his statement over and over, still shaking so badly that I began to wonder if he would come out of it.

But then it was my turn to pull a joke. "All along you professed to seek an exciting life and it has just started to become interesting. After receiving the first crack at it, are you wanting to quit?" I could quickly see that he did not receive the joke very well, for all his humor had suddenly left.

Meanwhile, the Marine Airport personnel arrived at our plane, unable to hide their amazement, for our arrival was just as if we had suddenly been spit out of the sky. After uttering a compliment about my wonderful slip landing, they asked, "Why didn't you notify us via radio?"

When they found out that there was no radio on board, they were in for their next surprise. French aviators are known to be daredevils of the sky, but what they then heard and saw, staggered their imagination. Actually, this was not a civil airport and we weren't allowed to land there, but it was of little concern to us after what we had just been through—nothing could have been worse than that.

A slowly recovering Klaus and I spent two days in Paris, with its remarkable fauna mostly consisting of dachshunds, poodles, cats and sparrows, and this apparently had a calming influence on him. The next day we ferried the plane to the Toussus Le Noble aerodrome just southwest of Paris, as we were not allowed to keep it at the Marine field, and my log book entry indicates that this again was done in haze.

Refueling at Paris' Toussus Le Noble Airport for further ventures ahead. I am talking to one of the attendants behind the gas truck. Notice the neat uniform of the driver and our entire baggage consisting of two items. The small leather briefcase was devoted exclusively to Klaus' photo "laboratory."

Klaus and I had agreed that we would share the entire travelling expenses and, since he was a gourmet and I an ascetic, he decided that he would pay for food and hotel accommodations and I would pay the plane expenses. It was apparent that the airplane would not enjoy anything fancier than gas and oil, but this was different in his case, so he assured in this manner that his good meals and lodging were nicely taken care of. This, of course, induced me at times to eat more of things very nectareous to the palate. After all, I was the pilot and had to be kept in good health to perform well in such adverse circumstances we were flying under, and the plane expense was not negligible either. He looked at that differently, apparently wanting to keep me in a weaker condition so I would not be up to so many reckless flight endeavors which, in turn, would be better for his nerves and his well-stuffed innards. A bumpy flight does indeed make things a little uncomfortable for a lover of much good food, and occasionally he might even have to let go of it in a not-so-pleasant way, which we referred to as "eating backward." Or could it be merely a pocketbook consideration, for at times he was audacious enough to ask me what in the wide world I had all consumed, because the bill ran so high.

He was also a lover of many nice girls, a peculiarity not uncommon with me, either, and at every turn I saw him with another one of the "weaker vessels" on his arm. The good food, wine and champagne in Paris, in combination with the fast French girls, apparently suited this Don Juan well, and after our two days' stay in that city a well-pleased Klaus decided after all to continue the journey with me.

Unknown to Klaus, though, was the fact that the unavailability of current and proper aeronautical charts would endanger our flying yet further. This past flight, for instance, was covered by an old, outdated 1:500,000 ICAO (International Civil Aviation Organization) map compiled, drawn and reproduced by the War Office in London in 1950 with aeronautical information as of January, 1950—more than eight years out of date. Worse yet, portions of our journey were covered by French "Pnue Michelin" automobile road maps. They showed many details in color, and included airports. Used on occasion by daring French aviators who were more familiar with the countryside than we, those charts were inadequate for flying because of the absence of much vital aeronautical and airport information. All of Spain, Portugal and North Africa were represented by grossly outdated and, for our purposes, very insufficient 1:1,000,000 World Aeronautical Charts (Carte Aéronautique De Monde), which again were about six to ten years old. At times the airports had been printed into the wrong places on the maps. In some cases the old aerodromes were abandoned and replaced by new fields or none.

CROSSING THE FRONT TO MEET "NAPOLEON"

(Paris to Angoulême)

Finally the weather had cleared up and early in the afternoon we were able to continue our trip. We could not leave the Paris area until I had backtracked for about five miles and, by much circling, enabled Klaus to make quite a number of aerial slides of Versailles. Then the green light was given for our onward journey.

In a 3¼-hour south-southwesterly flight, we covered about half of France. This time our travel over the flat, but charming, French countryside was challenged by a bad cold front which stretched across the middle of our flight path, lowering the visibility almost to zero. The resulting fog became so dense that at times we were about ready to turn around. Sud-

Below our wings are the famed gardens and the magnificent palace at Versailles that once housed the French kings and nobility. Louis XIV started its construction in 1661 and hired the best architects, sculptors and landscape gardeners. The present palace with hundreds of rooms is now a national museum. It was here that the Treaty of Versailles was signed after World War I, "the war to end all wars."

denly rain started and our visibility improved greatly as we passed the front. Looking back, we rejoiced to see the dark, rolling clouds behind us. Soon we made a smooth landing at the refreshing grass strip called "Angoulême Bel-Air."

A very enjoyable feature of travel by small planes is the proverbial worldwide camaraderie among pilots. Most aviators feel a common bond, even more so than representatives of many other professions. They all have had similar experiences, fought the elements in lonely cockpits, been lost in the weather, thrilled to the setting of the sun while gliding over a sea of clouds or enjoyed the reinvigorating tranquility of a romantic night flight under the clear moon and stars. They all alike have learned what it means to be at peace with the elements, to absorb all of nature's splendor in a relaxed mood and then to be delivered suddenly to the brutal force of turbulent storms with thunder and lightning crashing all around them which threaten to tear apart their little cabins in the sky. Pilots of the world, therefore, are like a big family and share many things in common. This applies especially to areas which are not quite as commercialized as the United States, for instance, and to those people who carry a sentimental value in their hearts for flying as one of their favorite endeavors. To them it has not just become another commercial arm.

The highest peak in the Americas, Mt. Aconcagua (22,834 feet), only 65 miles from Santiago, Chile, towered to my right as I crossed the Cordillera de los Andes in the cockpit of a Comet *(above)*. This monarch is part of the Andes, the longest mountain chain in the world which stretches 4,500 miles from Cape Horn to Panama and is about 500 miles across the widest part. Only the Himalaya (house of snow) of northern India and Tibet is higher.

This traditional friendship at times even carries into mercantile echelons. I remember a flight from Buenos Aires to Santiago when I was invited by the captain of a Comet airliner to the cockpit for the entire duration of the flight. The view from the windows of that cabin was spectacular. The 22,834-foot-high Mt. Aconcagua, highest mountain in the Western Hemisphere, just off to our right, the snow-covered Andes Mountains to the north and south, the lowland and ocean ahead, and Santiago coming up below us all blended into one of those magnificent scenes a person can never forget. As soon as we had passed the high Cordilleras, the captain reversed the jets and we started descending like a meteor in a full-fledged dive into the depths. Santiago was zooming toward us like a racing car and soon we were 30,000 feet lower as we landed.

On another flight, from what was then known as Sokarnapura (Hollandia) in West Irian, the pilot of that airliner also invited me to the cockpit when he learned that I was a fellow airman. After a while, he arose from his seat and motioned me to sit down and, for the first time in my life, I flew an airliner. Under the observation of the co-pilot, I headed toward the Island of Biak and was only released by the pilot a short time before we came in for the landing.

Let's return to Angoulême, France, which, like so many stopovers on this trip, brought back treasured memories.

At this particular airfield, we ran across a whole group of flying fans—eight of them—and all members of the "Aéro-Club d'Angoulême." Upon our arrival they immediately gathered around, and soon whisked us away on motor bikes. We shortly found ourselves sitting at a dining table loaded down with goodies, again surrounded by our new friends. Among them, of all people, was "Napoleon." I assigned to him the name of this former French demagogue because of the way he looked, acted and had his tirades in full swing. To him, the Algerians did not exist, and Algeria was not a colony of France but part of the motherland itself. There was no alternative; another Napoleon, who, according to him, was the only decent ruler France ever had, was badly needed to remedy his nation's fate. With his persuasive speech, he dominated the entire time of fellowship. He was a man of strong convictions, one not easily forgotten. He and the others clung to us like burs and it was a sad time when we had to say good-bye the next day, for we had to move on.

The French have long been known for their contributions to aviation. Posing for a picture are the enthusiastic members of the Aéro-Club d'Angoulême who instantly became our friends. "Napoleon" *(third from right)* stands next to me.

OVER THE PEARL ON THE OCEAN
(Angoulême to Biarritz)

A busy seventh of April began for us with a 2½ hour flight to Biarritz, France, which is very close to the Spanish boundary line and the Pyrenees Mountains–an area, old veteran pilots had warned us about, because of the excessive winds which usually lambaste this territory. This was our last flight for the time being over flat country. At about midway, Bordeaux passed below us. There were some beautiful lakes enroute, and it

The glistening waters of the Bay of Biscay *(above)* partly encircle the cliff-top castles, hotels and shoreline pools built on and into the rugged coastal promontory at Biarritz, France, a famous resort. A more complete view of the city, its beaches and the white surf are shown below.

interested us to see the sharp outlines in the form of color contrasts and a white crest which the Gave de Pau River created for a long stretch after entering the ocean just north of Biarritz.

Biarritz is a famous beach resort on the coast of the Bay of Biscay. Adjacent to the city, its rugged promontory studded with pools and buildings offered quite a sight from the air. "Unbelievable, unreal," Klaus cried, amazed at the spectacle.

We circled a lot before we landed, which gave us a wonderful opportunity to get acquainted quickly with this pearl on the ocean and enabled my friend to take slides to his heart's delight. Had we not taken his photo equipment along, I would not today possess over 100 beautiful color slides of this voyage. Apparently we hit a good day, for so far it was not very windy north of the Pyrenees. When coming in for a landing, however, the gusts really hit us. After a two-hour stay and compliance with some minor custom procedures, we were airborne once again.

Not very far south from here, in Pamplona, Spain, bulls were going to be turned loose in the streets during the fiesta of San Fermin in July and then engaged by young amateur matadors.

3

Frenzied "Dancing" in the Air

(Biarritz, France to Bilbao, Spain)

We passed to the north of the Pyrenees without any problems. The dreaded portion of the journey was behind, and seemingly we had become masters of the air and also experienced navigators. Little did we know at this time what lay ahead and that we had received only a small taste of flying hazards so far.

Meanwhile, we enjoyed seeing beautiful San Sebastián, which we flew over. This world-famous, seasonal resort, situated on the Bay of Biscay, is one of the most fashionable in Spain. At one time it was the summer residence of the Spanish royal family; then the government started using this city as its official seat during the hottest 70 days of the year.

Reaching Bilbao, no windsock, tetrahedron or landing "Tee" could be found, but only a wide landing strip to make up for it. Again there were few custom procedures, and we had arrived at a land whose civilization dates back to the Stone Age.

The ancient Phoenicians had settlements there more than 3000 years ago. After that, Spain was a colony of the Carthaginians in Africa and became then one of the most treasured provinces of the Roman Empire. Later, under the Moors, it was the center of the splendid Moslem civilization for several centuries until 1200.

Three hundred years later, Spain was the most powerful country, with its empire including most of the Americas and other possessions around the world. At one time, the once-mighty and dreaded Spanish Armada reigned as undisputed ruler of the seas. Today it is a land of gaiety, color, and song, with many reminders of its past glories, including more than 1,400 beautiful castles and palaces built by Spanish and Moorish noblemen. These edifices rise amid blooming gardens. Massive El Escorial, constructed in the 1500's near Madrid, contains 300 rooms, 86 staircases, 88 fountains and 16 interior courts, encompassing nearly 400,000 square feet. There are great contrasts between its past wealth and the present poverty as a whole.

Most of the Spanish farmers still harvest their grain the old-fashioned way. They cut it with scythes and sickles and bundle it by hand. The straw is discarded with pitchforks after the grain has been removed through the trampling of horses or oxen. This remainder then is tossed into the air with wooden shovels so that the breeze can separate the lighter chaff from the grain.

Notwithstanding, there are about 3,000 textile mills and close to 1,500 hydroelectric stations in the country. It ranks third among wine-producing nations. Most of Spain's mercury, supplying about half of the world's demand, comes from mines near Almadén which have been worked for more than 2,000 years.

A high, nearly treeless plateau covers three-fourths of the mainland. The circumnavigation of its 1,698-mile-long coastline, studded for the most part with many steep cliffs jutting into the sea, lay just ahead of us. A relatively level, smooth French coast along the Bay of Biscay offered us a good degree of safety in the case of an emergency landing and it also provided more calm wind conditions. On the Spanish coast, however, there was to be a drastic change, with many unsuspected dangers lurking in the distance.

GIANT SLIP INTO A SPANISH FIESTA
(Bilbao to Santander)

For the third time on the same day we took to the air. Our destination proved to be a frustrating experience at first, but then held some wonderful surprises in store. After a short flight, we were over Santander but could not find the airport. It was not very astounding, as we began using the outdated 1:1,000,000 World Aeronautical Charts that guided us most of the way.

While keeping up our search, I noticed a place which looked like a former dumping ground with a rather narrow, crooked dirt strip through it; however, there was a hangar and a windsock. Our map indicated a joint civil and military airfield at Santander. I could not fathom how it could possibly serve any planes of the latter category. There were no aircraft visible. The place looked deserted–maybe an abandoned field, I thought. But since we were unable to find another landing area, we decided to go into that one.

Once again I used the "giant slip" approach, which, in the absence of flaps, made a good substitute. Much to my amazement, I was able to bring the plane onto this short "banana" field smoothly. When we finished our ground roll and stopped before the hangar, two or three people had gathered, who informed us that we had arrived at the wrong facilities. At once they wanted to send us to the right place, as there seemed to be regulatory problems in Spain when nonofficial airports were used. We expressed our unwillingness to go on a fourth flight for the day as we were getting tired, and succeeded with this approach.

Another congratulation was bestowed upon us for a good landing on this rough strip, with an aside to Klaus that he flew with a skillful pilot, which really boosted his morale.

"Did you hear what they said?" Klaus boasted.

"What?"

"They said that you really know how to handle the plane."

"Well, do you want me to prove otherwise," I rejoined.

"No . . . never, no need to . . . we have enough on our hands the way it is," Klaus quickly flashed. It was a much-needed encouragement for him to know that as far as the pilot was concerned, he had placed himself in capable hands on such a haphazard journey, particularly for what lay ahead.

We were introduced to the owner of what turned out to be a small airplane factory on the field. They hand-constructed the "Jodel 112," a beautiful two-seater. When informed about the rock-bottom price of the craft, because of the very low Spanish wages, we immediately considered importing them into Germany. It would have been quite a profitable venture, since Germany almost completely lacked aircraft industry at that time, so shortly after the war. Because of the shortage of planes, a ready market was waiting. Klaus, of course, got rather excited about this potentially very profitable prospect.

"Let's go home and make some money," he urged.

"Oh no, I won't let you get out of this odyssey that cheaply. First you have some more pounds to lose. Think of all the goodies still before us."

"Sure, I knew that was going to be your answer. You are a hopeless *Wolkenkutscher* (coachman of the sky). I just can't share your idealism, your aerial dreams to that extent. These continuous dramas in the sky, the whipping by the wind and all the rest has me completely worn out already."

"Wait a minute, just cool it. You are needed as part of the *dramatis personae.* Now, baby, don't cry–you will make a million by and by." With this I left him and turned my attention back to the planes.

The rough "banana" strip at Santander, Spain, with a Jodel 112 in the foreground.

While still getting acquainted and checking over the Jodels, a taxi arrived and we were asked to enter, accompanied by the factory owner, whom I will call Fernando, as I do not remember his name. For two hours the driver chauffered us in that cab on a big sightseeing tour all over the beautiful City of Santander. The explanations were given mostly in Spanish sprinkled with a little English and German here and there. We wondered why Fernando was doing all his travelling this way. "In Spain cars are about four times as expensive as in Germany, for instance, because of the 400 per cent duty on automobiles," he said. Then we could understand.

Soon we arrived at Fernando's modern, cozy home. He introduced us to his wife, a typical Spanish señora, and they whisked us off to the fanciest restaurant in town. Here we were treated to the most luscious dinner of our entire trip. The menu included so many servings of various delicacies that Klaus and I began to wonder whether there was going to be an end of eating. The atmosphere in the restaurant was magnificent. The culinary odors kept our digestive juices flowing and the lively Spanish music brought joy to our hearts. The interior partitions consisted of antique wooden wine barrels.

"I am sure glad that we didn't return home yet," confessed gluttonous Klaus chameleon-like. "This is really something else. I feel right at home. What a treat—just according to my taste and lifestyle," he continued eagerly as he dove his fork into the sumptuous meal before him.

I still remember how we drank wine from delightful little pitchers with long, narrow spouts by pouring it from a distance into our open mouths. Since, according to custom, the end of the spout had to be held about seven inches away, it took a little know-how through practice on our part not to pour the wine all over our faces. The Spaniards, being very adept at this, had a hilarious time seeing us being drenched under an ever-so-sweet stream. They were eager to help us perfect our technique for a twofold purpose: first, they wanted us to take part in the native ceremony they were proud of, and second, it would prolong their glee in watching us unsuccessfully attempt to avoid additional showers. Still somewhat tremulous from our risky flying, our hands and feet did not cooperate well as we stood there, endeavoring cross-eyedly to aim the liquid properly.

At the end of the extravagant meal, a waiter appeared with a tray filled with flaming crystal bowls. They were full of the most delicious tropical fruits floating in ignited rum. This succulent dessert was placed before us with the sugary tongues of fire dancing across its surface. Ever so slowly we consumed this last serving.

By now Klaus was really at his best. *"Lange lebe Spanien und die spanischen Fräulein* (Long live Spain and the Spanish señoritas)," he exclaimed. "This is the place to live. I think I will make my residence in this country–it's the place I have always been looking for!"

"First wait and see if we survive this journey," I interrupted, fearing that he might get completely out of hand. "The Spanish men are heroes. They fight bulls singlehandedly and they also fight for girls. You'd better toughen up some more first by gathering more time in the air–think of all the wonderful adventures still ahead! Then you may be able to keep pace with the local protagonistas. Just remember, dagger fights still abound. It's going to be rough one way or the other. No easy going around here. At least up there you'll be in safe range of the sword. I know you are fond of the señoritas–it may save your life."

Still this was not the end of the day. Next we were hauled off to a lavish nightclub with a raised dancing area in the center. I have never been a good dancer and, other than an occasional waltz, have not thought much of it. There is too much turning, twisting and smoking involved. I don't count it a healthy exercise, and it usually leaves me with a slight headache or a little dizziness. In the pandemonium of crowded dance floors, surrounding couples deeply engrossed in each other under the spell of a flamenco often land an agony-inflicting smash on one's unsuspecting foot. It is particularly painful when one is nailed to the floor by the spike of a fiery señorita. Those circumstances seemed to me to require the agility of a funambulist. When waltzing, I can simply stay on one spot and turn, and in this way the girl usually has to make three or four steps to one of mine. I don't have to sweat so much and if I do something wrong it is not so noticeable.

That evening I decided to play a more passive part, as I felt I had done my share of "toe dancing" and "jitterbugging" in the air, but soon was asked to dance by a charming señorita. My friend met with the same fate and, very much to our surprise, we turned out to be accomplished at this art. Those girls apparently were professionals and Fernando probably had asked them to befriend us. They knew how to synchronize with our clumsy steps so there was no treading on feet or stumbling; but, to the contrary, it seemed so easy to dance that both Klaus and I marvelled.

"I've never been able to dance that well in all my life," an excited Klaus funneled into my ear while he passed me as he came jitterbugging along.

"Watch the daggers," I warned, as he trailed off with gusto.

Indeed we never were able to dance that well before or after. Soon I was to find out that the eurhythmic portion of this night brought about near-fatal consequences for the remainder of our journey.

It was getting late and we were very tired. We had had a long day and three flights were already quite a load. Fernando, apparently noticing our increased yawning, inquired next whether we desired to spend the night with those girls in our arms—and at his expense, at that. This was a clear signal for us to break off the party.

"So was gibt es doch garnicht—das können wir unmöglich annehmen! (This sounds unbelievable—it is impossible for us to accept this)," exclaimed Klaus and I.

Fernando had spent an enormous amount of money entertaining us in many ways, and there had to be an end. To go so far as to take this last offer that night would have been presumptuous. Even philanderer Klaus agreed. He felt that after all the things Fernando had done for us, it was extraordinary that he would come up with such an overture and still be concerned even about our night's comfort. It was amazing for a fellow like Klaus to decline such an offer; but, being so bone tired, he had to admit that he could not have enjoyed and vigorously lasted through this added episode. Maybe, if Klaus had been approached with an offer of that kind at a more opportune time, he would have been more inclined to accept. Under the present circumstances it was just too much, potency- and courtesy-wise. Certainly we would not have wanted this man to pay additional money so we could have further fun and pleasure.

Klaus's decency in this regard, therefore, was apparently of ulterior motives and circumstantial dependence. Or could it be that this *"Cockaigne"* (imaginary land of luxury) had a sobering effect on Klaus and began to make a sensible fellow out of this Casanova? It seems like all he ever wanted, he was suddenly getting—plenty of excitement, adventure and romances or *"affaires d'amour,"* as the French would say. Was it more than he could bear, or did life's *ultimate* values dawn on him amid such opulence? It would not be the first time when a Croesus had a turning point at the very time when he found what he thought he most desired—a life steeped in luxury and splendor. Historical records are replete with such accounts, including the lives of Siddhartha Gautama (Buddha) and Moses.

Many of the young people in America today have turned from a course of affluence and ease and are searching for a deeper fulfillment. Unfortunately, quite a few of them are looking in the wrong direction. So many great opportunities and worthwhile rewards are offered, that it is very saddening to see young folks drifting by the wayside through the use of dope, liquor, rock-and-roll, jazz, illicit sex and other perversities. Would it not be wonderful if more people were seeking challenges similar to the ones we found in this flying odyssey?

Could it have been that, high up in the air numerous times and with no apparent hope of survival, Klaus quietly began to re-evaluate his life, stretching out at the same time tender threads or feelers toward his Maker, the Creator of all life, the only One Who knows the beginning from the end and the purpose of our existence? Only God Who made us knows what the heart needs, for, having put that craving desire for peace and happiness into it, only He can satisfy it. People all over the world and of all careers have experienced tremendous climaxes in life through reorientation when in the middle of superaffluence and in their prime.

On the other hand, there were many mighty men who, to the vexation of their souls, never came to this point. Napoleon Bonaparte is reported to have confessed: "There is not a man who would lay down his life for me." His great renown dwindled into miserable failure. Voltaire wrote: "I wish I had never been born." Byron lived a life of pleasure if anyone did. He wrote: "The worm, the canker and the grief are mine alone." The pleasures of sin do not satisfy, even while they last; so soon they will be gone forever. Oh! the grief of the life frittered away in the empty pursuit of pleasure. Gould, the American millionaire, had plenty of that. When dying, he is reported to have said: "I suppose I am the most miserable devil on earth." Thus, they all agree and confirm Solomon's verdict: "All is vanity and vexation of spirit." (Ecclesiastes 2:17b).

In my case, this trip brought about a definite turning point. Indeed ours was not a fortuitous journey.

Our friend Fernando accommodated us and insisted we stay for at least two days. The next morning, he took me on several flights in his Jodel D-112 plane. Two were sightseeing flights, which included a landing at the official airport we would have to stop at, before leaving the Santander area. This way he made sure that we could find it. The third one was acrobatic; his craft performed beautifully and held up well.

We felt that we could not leave without showing our gratitude to Fernando in at least some small way. Klaus ordered flowers. When they arrived at Fernando's home, we could hardly believe our eyes, for two big basins loaded with about 150 beautiful pink and red roses had come.

Klaus, filled with surprise, commented, "In other European countries the same money would have bought just a modest bouquet. Such a thing is possible only in Spain, where everything is more voluptuous."

I was glad that Klaus's spirit had been lifted, for otherwise, I am sure, he would not have endured what lay immediately ahead.

Lovely Santander, a summer resort on the northern coast of Spain.

ALL HELL BREAKS LOOSE

(Santander to Vigo via Santander Miliano and Oviedo)

We left Santander la Albericia after a short stopover at Santander Miliano to keep everything perfectly legal. Then we continued on to the Lugo de Llanera Airfield next to Oviedo.

Wherever we landed in Spain, we noticed that people eyed us, as though we had just come from Mars. It was exceptional for them to see a small, private plane, especially one from so far away, touring their country.

Different was the treatment we received from the airport commandant at Lugo de Llanera. There had been some erasing on the registration certificate's plane picture which we had never noticed because it was so negligible, and we were sure that the "Club National D'Aviation à Bruxelles" did not give us improper papers. He raised a big fuss over this technicality, and we could readily perceive that he had an envious spirit. Occasionally you meet those bureaucrats who cannot stand to see anyone else do things which they themselves have missed in their boring, everyday rut.

Much of Spain looks more rugged than this from the air. The small, scanty fields do not offer a good place for an emergency landing. Many high plateaus give it the driest climate of Europe. The average altitude of Spain is second only to that of Switzerland.

At Oviedo, on account of cross-wind conditions, I had to come in by banking and applying opposite rudder. A few squalls hit us violently just at that time, dumping our wing edge onto the runway. Other than a few scratches, no harm was done. This place did not have much to offer—we had been at better, friendlier areas before. Why stay here? We moved on to our next destination, Vigo, Spain, as it was yet fairly early in the day. What was ahead just about finished everything.

We had started a flight which turned into a "Corybantic" marathon rock-and-roll with death, almost leaving us with the chorea or St. Vitus's dance for the rest of our lives. Never, in all my aviation experience, have I been in such an aerial cancan. The flight started out fairly well, more like a fandango, as we were angling back toward the Spanish north coast, meeting the ocean at Luarca. Next, a saraband became a Lindy and, soon after, turned into a frantic jitterbug as the plane shimmied along, with me performing the tap dance on the pedals.

We preferred to return to the coastline and follow it for several reasons. For one, the heavily loaded, underpowered plane had a low "service ceiling," and in this way we could stay clear of the excessively mountainous inner territory. Next, we figured that a flight along the coast, especially the stretch before us, would offer a much more interesting flight—which indeed it did. The further we proceeded toward the west, the more the winds gathered momentum, making the plane revolve with the turbulent formlessness of a frenzied dance, like a tarantella, while the whirl of the elements played hokey-pokey with our senses. On and on the gale blew, turned into squally, screeching twisters by the rugged, craggy coastline.

As soon as we passed Punta de la Estaca and Cabo de los Aguillones all "hell" broke loose, laying the shaking, reeling plane under the spell of tarantism. As we struggled for our lives between the sky and forbidding cliffs of a wild shoreline, the foaming ocean waited below with seemingly endless and outstretched arms, ready to receive us into a watery and icy grave. With all of its untamed, tempestuous fury, the raging storm all around screamed in high shrieks and momentarily tossed the plane up like a feather, plummeting us thousands of feet only moments later like an elevator which had suddenly snapped its suspension ropes. Rolling, tossing, turning and aimlessly moving about in every conceivable direction so that even the fullest counteracting application of the controls was of no avail, whatsoever, the plane acted like a lame duck. With no power at all, we were flung up and down–just about plunged into the high waves of the sea.

Every time our ship dropped precipitously at accelerations exceeding that of free fall, rushing us headlong toward the bottom of the vindictive body of water, our altimeter and vertical speed indicator went wild. Over and over we were lifted out of our seats and jarred against our safety belts as the plane dove forebodingly into the depths toward the fiercely foaming waves immediately below, clashing resoundingly with madness against the protruding headlands opening wide the ocean's jaws of death all along that forbidding coastline. To make matters worse, the plane's rate of climb during my intermittent attempts to recover altitude was practically nil.

It looked as though all the forces of torment had conspired to bring the world around us into a wild crescendo and present us with this needless, unnerving and fidgeting jamboree in the air which almost left us with "the creeps" for the rest of our lives. Certainly "Old Nick" could have looked for someone else to dance his jig with. All we could afford with our weak mini-bird was a Charleston or the conga or something along that line at the most. "How much longer can we last?" "How will we escape certain death?" These were the thoughts which tortured our minds for so long in this unbelievable, impossible flying situation. Surely our end must be near, perhaps around the next precipice. Endlessly the flight dragged on with no hope in sight, and the storm continued to blow "to beat the band." For hours we had been fighting to the last of our strength and with desperate grit.

There it was–Cabo Finisterre, the world-renowned cape, feared by sea captains and crews alike for its terrifying weather conditions and highly dangerous coastal area. "There is still hope if we can just make it around that one," we thought. Tottery and shaky, we held on. With failing energy we scraped around that bluff, and around yet another one called Punta de Louro. We arrived over the Ría de Muros y de Noya, forming the mouth of the Río Tambre, and followed its bank with many sighs of relief. Klaus and I shared the same feeling a boat's skipper would have when he first sees the beacon of an approaching lighthouse near a friendly harbor after he had been lost for many weeks, fighting heavy seas raging below dark, billowing clouds.

After following this river for a while, we turned east and, arriving over Santiago de Compostela, decided for some reason to fly on for another 50 miles to Vigo.

It would have been a pleasant change to stop at this important national monument, university city and pilgrimage center of world fame. The city, retaining its ancient character to that day, rivalled Rome and Jerusalem in the Middle Ages. St. James the Apostle and his two disciples are said to have been buried in the Twelfth Century Roman-style cathedral which has an architectural overlay of baroque carving and is one of the most magnificent in Spain. We could have enjoyed strolling quietly through Santiago's old streets with adjoining arcaded houses and little charming plazas to cool our greatly abused tempers.

It is possible, though, that we were unable to locate the Santiago de Compostela Airport or found it unsuitable. Flying this last stretch on an inland route over Padron, Caldas de Reyes and just west of Pontevedra, we found that the wind had abated considerably. Having been in Vigo before by ship, we did not anticipate any problem with finding the airport.

Finally, finally, after a 3-hour volational struggle, with little gas and no strength remaining, we hauled into the Vigo Airfield under very gusty conditions. Wobbly, we left the plane with swaying and staggering movements, feeling lightheaded and giddy. The ground below us, even though still careening, felt good. Our highland fling was over and another experience, this time with the treacherous winds displaying their fury over mountainous Spain, lay behind us.

Klaus found it more difficult this time to suggest a quick train trip home, because Germany was so far away. Maybe, though, he had become somewhat more inured or perhaps, not having had much previous flying experience, he thought that it had to be that way.

Vigo, located at the small stretch of the western Spanish seaboard, by no means an overrun tourist resort, provided a much-needed two-day stopover. Somewhat protected, it is situated at the southern edge of a big bay, spanned by several islands. Opposite from Vigo and out in the bay is a beautiful islet approximately one-half mile long, emblazoned with an old, pompous castle. On a boat trip to Vigo, as mentioned earlier, my father almost bought this island for DM 300,000, equalling a little over $70,000 at that time. It was a bargain.

We still had friends in this town, and of course we could not leave until I had taken one of Klaus's Spanish girl friends on a sightseeing flight. Also, I was very happy once again to meet my old friend, Antonio Sieiro, who owned a fancy men's apparel store called "Pañetria Rumbo." There a

Klaus with one of his beauties in Vigo, Spain.

person could buy the most beautiful, best-fitting tailored suits ever, for an unbelievably small amount. As a whole, prices were very low in Spain in those years, but that has changed, too, with increased tourist trade and a general cost-of-living raise. The devaluation of the dollar, of course, has had its effect on American travellers.

Also interesting was the visit with another Spanish friend who was just in the process of making wine. All the harvested grapes were dumped into a big, open wooden barrel, whereupon our friend took off his shoes and, without washing his feet, jumped in barefooted and then the grape dance started. He pressed his grape crop, as customary, by treading the grapes with his bare feet with a rhythm all his own. When I inquired whether this served at the same time to wash his feet, I was given a big grin. After this experience, I wondered if I would be able to appreciate the Spanish wines with the same savor as before. Even after our friend assured me that all the impurities would ferment out of the juice and only the pure, refined product left, I was not so sure. This unique type of winemaking left a rather permanent impression in my mind, and still today I can see our joyful Ortego jumping around in that open wine barrel like a bunch of bush negroes who were putting on the sun dance with gusto.

It was about at this time that an old sickness (osteomyelitis) in my right foot acted up again. For years in the past it had caused me torturous pain, leaving me sleepless night after night, until the foot would break open following months of suffering. During those periods I had to be extremely careful. Actually, I should have been in bed and off my foot altogether, but this was not possible then. With this most unwelcome new guest around, nearly everything seemed to be against me. Apparently that fast dancing with those Santander beauties had not done me much good, and I was to pay for it with bitter remorse. How could I possibly travel, hike around and pilot the aircraft without sleep at night and tremendous pain in my all-important foot? Every time I depressed the rudder pedal in the plane I would be struck by sharp pains as if hit by needles clear into the marrow of my bone.

Because of the suffering with my foot for many years I began to question the purpose of existence. What was man's mission in this world? Why was he confined to a vale of tears and sorrow in a robe of mortal flesh? What was the ultimate reason? A life under two dictatorships, a complete economic crash and the near-fatal sickness when only 9 years old . . . it all brought me to a confrontation with those questions!

Early in life, therefore, tender arms were raised toward a Great Creator—the One Who must hold all the answers to my questions.

It was now, during this dangerous trip, that my dependence on this "Eternal One" grew immeasurably. Somehow, when tossed to and fro in the sky, when being lost in the fog and facing death many times, I couldn't help but feel that I was in the hollow of His hands. Deep down in my heart I knew that my time and life depended on Him.

Many more dangerous encounters had to be endured, however, before I found myself *"on final"* in this long-lasting search for the *"ultimate!"*

The two days in Vigo went by fast, and soon we were airborne again.

4

Our Plane Suffers Damage

(Vigo, Spain to Lisbon, Portugal)

This almost 3-hour-long flight led us along most of the Iberian Peninsula's West Coast, with nearly all of it in Portugal. It was a sunny day and the weather rather tranquil as we headed strictly south. With the coastline to our left leading us all the way, we passed many rivers such as the Rio Minho, Rio Lima and Rio Mondego. We saw numerous cities en route, including the important seaport Pôrto (Oporto), the second largest city of Portugal, with its beautiful Rio Douro lined with many picturesque homes and boats. Coming from the highland region, it drains northern Portugal. The famous wines and the country itself derive their names from the region of Pôrto, which was the first regained by the Christians from the Moorish rulers around 1000.

When later passing Cabo Carvoeiro protruding far into the ocean below us and the Island Ilha Berlenga about eight miles offshore to our right, we knew that our destination was not very far ahead. Soon we passed Cabo da Roca, made very noticeable by an approximately 1,500-foot-high mountain on an otherwise level coastline. Cabo Raso came next, and then we turned west.

Another 20 miles, and the splendid City of Lisbon lay below us, bordered to the south by the wide bay formed by the mouth of the river Tagus (Tejo in Portuguese), one of the three biggest rivers of Portugal. This metropolis was almost completely destroyed in 1755 by an earthquake which killed about 10,000 people. Since the ocean teems with sardines and tuna nearby, we could also observe many of the country's 16,600 fishing vessels. The fish industry is second only to grape growing in Portugal.

Our view from the cockpit, with the great city, the huge bay and the Atlantic just at our fingertips, was simply fantastic.

"This alone is worth the whole trip," Klaus assented. "What a sight—only flying can do that for you."

"There you go—that's being a good boy," I joined in. "Compare this with the view you get from the window of a car, if you can. Cities, with all their turmoil and confusion, sure look nicer from the distance—don't they?" That's the way in life—many things look better when viewed from a distance. Therefore, it is important for one to dwell on a higher plane.

Following ample circling, we came in for a landing at the main intercontinental airport after receiving a green light from the tower. Immediately after our touchdown, we witnessed a tremendous number of incoming airliners. It was quite a sight to see so many large planes stacked in the holding pattern on account of the delay we had caused with our slow-flying-and-taxiing bird. As soon as we had crept off the runway, they were cleared one by one for approach and landing, and came in without interruption. A busy international airport had been temporarily thrown out of gear by the arrival of that unusual little intruder and was endeavoring quickly to resume a more normal schedule. I wondered whether I had made some enemies among the many captains of the air who were bringing in their giant ships from long, tiring flights.

Anyway, this flight was a "dandy" compared to what we had been through and, above all, what was to come. Some of the most unbelievable hazards were yet ahead. They were to occasion us at a later time to pause and look back in amazement and wonder why we made this crazy, reckless trip, seemingly playing with fate, but still believing that everything had to go all right. Shudderingly, we would marvel that we came through it alive.

We had arrived at the "República Portuguesa," as the Portuguese call their country, the westernmost in Europe and only a little larger than the State of Maine. It is a land of Madeira wines, citrus fruits, sardines and cork. The latter item is taken from the cork oak and supplies more than half the world's demand. This is also a nation of Bartolomeu Dias, Vasco da Gama, Pedro Álvares Cabral, and other daring Portuguese sailors who, through their brave ventures, made their country at one time the world's third largest colonial empire. Its permanent alliance with England of 1386 is considered the oldest political alliance in Europe.

The former Finance Minister Antonio de Oliveira Salazar, premier since 1932, ably led the state toward greater economic prosperity, especially compared to Spain. Even when crossing from Spain into Portugal by car, a person could at that time notice an immediate improvement in road conditions.

The Portuguese people are also skilled in the making of pottery, lace, and beautifully decorated tiles in many colors. With pride in their place in history, they have a deep love for their country.

Their language is softer than Spanish and not as emphatic, although very similar.

With sea food being served at almost every meal, the Portuguese have many famous cooks preparing such chowders and dishes.

One more glance back at our plane revealed an interesting sight. There stood our little yellow bird with blue stripes parked below the tail of a "Super DC 6." The Belgian black-yellow-red flag was proudly displayed on the fin along with the airclub insignia "CNA" and the registration mark "OO-LEM." The contrast of the tiny craft with that giant airliner which had swung its tail right over our ship was overwhelming, and the thought of such a minute conveyance carrying us over much of Europe was likewise staggering. After bidding our plane an affectionate farewell for a while, we unfortunately entrusted it to the care and safekeeping of the airport and hangar personnel in particular, while we were getting acquainted with the capital of Portugal.

We spent two very interesting days in Lisbon and the immediate surroundings, including the country's famous seaside resort Estoril, with its beautiful beaches and pleasant climate. Nearby Palacio de Sintra, a Moorish castle, offered an absorbing attraction at a place which Lord Byron called a "little Eden."

I enjoyed climbing the many narrow, but quaint, stair-step, "tunnel-vista" streets found in Lisbon, which is, like Rome, built on seven hills. Some of the houses found along those narrow streets are almost 1000 years old.

Had we known what was happening in the meantime to our winged friend, little "OO-LEM," at the Lisboa-Portela de Sacavem Airport, we could not have relaxed for a moment in this faraway exotic metropolis. It was hard to do without this lifeline of our trip!

The broad, colorful Avenida da Liberdade with its monuments, fountains, lanterns, large facades covered with mural-like posters, street cars and many-hued busses and automobiles, located in one of the fashionable parts of Lisbon, made quite an impression. There were also many unique cobblestone streets, parks and gardens with tall, sculptured shrubs. We marvelled at the exotic local flora in the botanical garden Rua da Escola Politécnica and at one of the best greenhouses of Europe at Parque Eduardo VII. The harbor, the native fish market with their costumed lady vendors *(varinas)*, and another Moorish castle of the Tenth Century crowning Lisbon were among the other engrossing sights.

We stayed at a tall hotel with roof garden and blooming, small potted orange trees aromatizing the air. From there we had a panoramic view

Left: An ocean of red roofs and white houses. This is a view from one of the many narrow, but quaint, stair-step, "tunnel-vista" streets found in Lisbon.

Below: Cobblestone streets, statues and government palaces in picturesque Lisbon.

over the hilly city with its many white- and red-roofed buildings, the large boat-studded bay, and a low mountain range in the distance.

Klaus promptly met a beautiful American girl with a red flower in her hair who was enjoying life by touring the globe. He couldn't help but fall deeply in love with her. Most of his time in Lisbon was spent catering to his newly won love with elaborate meals and all the other trimmings.

"You have to tighten your belt now, Hans. This affair is costing me plenty and there won't be much left for us to live on."

As usual, I became the fifth wheel on the car whenever he went off on another jaunt with his latest diva. This lasted until we were back in the plane. Then, as pilot in command, I suddenly became all-important once again.

In the meantime, he was revealing to her his foremost secret—that she was the one and only true love for life and lucky heir to his fortunes. Little did she know that those great secrets had been breathed to many baffled, now-forgotten young ladies long before.

Quick marriage proposals were made, but the girl was determined to see the world first. In his endless crave for adoration of that charming beauty, he overspent himself in an effort to procure the most delicate tidbits for the dining table.

One evening, while overindulging at such a meal on rich, hard-to-digest items, like lobsters, crabs, desserts, and followed by plenty of wine on top of that, poor Klaus took sick and, performing the hootchy-kootchy, started to vomit in an arm-thick stream. His facial color reminded me of the time when we were lost over Paris, and he seemed thinner than ever.

Our nerve-racking way of travelling, much sightseeing, changing climate and foods, yielding to the desires and whims of that pretty girl by trying to obtain her favors, and then getting sick, was starting to have a profound effect on him. The love affair came to a sudden halt as he dared not face the young lady in such a condition. As soon as he felt better, he was ready to move on, with no wife and considerably less money to his name.

When we returned to the airport to pick up our plane, we were in for the next shock. After pulling it out of the hangar, we noticed to our dismay that one of the wing tips was badly bent, especially the vital corner of the leading edge. What were we to do now? No one, of course, had done it and not a soul had any knowledge of how it might have happened. Must we stay in Lisbon for time without end until it could be repaired? Already we were running behind schedule with still a big trip ahead of us! Would we have enough money left to return home after paying for the repair bill and our additional stay in Portugal? Those questions came to our minds.

As we pranced about nervously, wondering what we should do, and the situation began to get embarrassing to the hangar personnel, they sent us a so-called plane "expert." He fiddled around with the damaged area trying to see if it still had some strength and, to our great consternation,

Left: For centuries man has walked through these arched gates that reveal their Moorish influence. Now tourists visit these romantic castles near Lisbon, Portugal.

Below: Another beautiful landscaped estate with sculptured trees near Lisbon with the American "knockout" posing in the foreground.

bent it more in every conceivable direction. He finally assured us that we could continue to fly the plane this way until we got home. We had the distinct suspicion that they just tried to get rid of us before we made any claims against them. The situation did not look good to us, but under these special circumstances, we finally decided we would fly on. We never found out whether they had pushed the craft into the hangar door or into another ship while sheltering it, or what. The mystery of the damaged wing was never solved.

Our next stop was to be Seville, Spain. We went to the proper airport office to dispatch the required telegram for this upcoming international flight to our next destination. A Mr. Franko signed and stamped my pilot flight log and we were ready to leave this big city for new adventures ahead.

LISBON, PORTUGAL TO SEVILLE, SPAIN

Early that tensive afternoon we were once again rolling down a runway as the surge of the engine caused the prop to grab increasing amounts of air.

"I sure wonder how this plane is going to fly with that bent wing," a scared voice faltered through the buzz. "Do you think it will be a lopsided take-off?"

Endless seconds later the ship was airborne. Amazingly enough, the plane was still willing to fly, with bent wing and all. After leaving the Lisbóa-Portela De Sacavem Airport, we first passed over the seven-mile-wide Tejo Bay. Then came a peninsula with the City of Setúbal to our right and after that the big Rio Sado Bay. We continued our southeasterly course toward Ayamonte on the Portuguese-Spanish border line. The generally low region, with its great river valleys, extends far inland. In this southern part of the country, vineyards, oranges, lemons, tangerines, figs and almonds are plentiful. The roughness of the area below us, with many jagged little hills, gave us shudders when thinking of a potential emergency landing.

After about one and one-half hours of flight, we passed a fairly large mountain range to our right and soon we intercepted the Golfo De Cadiz at Ayamonte. Then heading eastward, we followed the coast to Huelva. From there, continuing on an eastward heading, we flew straight to Seville over a rather flat countryside with some of the large Spanish mountain ranges to our left.

After a rather lengthy flight, we landed in high grass on Sevilla Tablada, a military airfield. We were not allowed to stay there, and a brief hop, including a sightseeing jaunt over beautiful Seville, got us to the civil airport of Sevilla-San Pablo.

This was to be a most pleasant stopover before we were nearly trounced on each of our next three flights. Our last three were relatively smooth sailing, even though we had encountered some problems such as the bent wing and the landing on the military field. It was nothing, however, compared to what was before us. Some of our most bone-chilling adventures waited, ready to receive us into their arms one by one, flight after flight, time and again. A whole series of shocking escapades of unbelievable magnitude not, by any means, for mollycoddles, were going to jolt all wits out of Klaus and me and leave us temporarily namby-pamby.

As we climbed out of the plane, we were greeted by the most paradise-like odors and climate on our entire trip so far. A beautiful, clean airport, ringed with blooming orange trees, especially next to the small, cozy terminal. They, in fact, were blooming while at the same time also exhibiting ripe fruit. After asking permission, we sampled some and found them rather sour. Apparently we dealt with an ornamental variety.

"How can those beautiful-looking oranges be so sour?" a surprised Klaus commented.

"That's the way it is with some of those lovely girls like the one in Lisbon. Remember how she dumped you when the fun was all over and when your wallet was getting thinner? If I were you, I would forget about that outward charm and search for inner values instead. That's the way I feel about it, and even more so as the days go by. Have you never noticed that the prettier they come, the more shallow they usually are? It is because they rely solely on their attractive appearance. The many Adonises they attract help along to make them even more vain. They get all they want. Another magnetic smile and one more great deflation of the admirer's billfold. After all, if there is no cooperation, they can readily find another inamorato. One by one, like moths flying into a nightly flame where they die, these spooners are attracted by their radiant display and perish in style. Not all that glitters is gold!" was my last warning observation.

How could I know that soon I was going to fall into the very trap I had warned Klaus of!

The touchdown on the former grass field was apparently rough on our landing gear. After noticing some damage, we quickly performed the repair job on our wheel fairing. Next, the airport commandant stamped and signed our log books–the airplane log and the pilot flight log.

All flying in Europe, principally conducted according to ICAO regulations, was handled, however, a little differently and with more complications. Before and after every trip, a person had to report to the appropriate airport office in order to get his log books stamped and signed by some authority as proof. Furthermore, a flight plan had to be made personally before each journey at the office and then cancelled the same way upon arrival. Weather information was also part of the obligatory procedure. It was just more paper work and another pain in the neck. The only good part is that all those stamps, still in my log book, make it easier for me to retrace this venture accurately. Those many and diverse stamps with fancy signatures of the various nationalities add to the flavor of the book and enhance the memories. (See pages 144-147.)

Seville once was one of the capitals (besides Tangier, Morocco and Córdoba, Spain) of the formerly powerful Moorish Empire which came into existence through the merger of Arabs and Berbers and reached its zenith in the Middle Ages. Many of the Berbers, especially from the Rifs in Morocco, have fair hair and light skin. The common, but erroneous belief, apparently due to William Shakespeare's play *Othello,* that Moors belonging to the above-mentioned larger Berber group are negroes, is in contradiction to the fact that the Moors belong to the Mediterranean group of the caucasoid (white) race. Long ago those people were also called "Mauri" by the Romans and their area of habitat "Mauretania."

I mention this important matter because for over 500 years this city was under Moorish rule and still to this day shows a lot of Arabic architecture (Moorish culture is mostly Arabic). The Moors also constructed some of the most beautiful buildings of the world in Granada. Especially the southern cities like Córdoba, Granada and Seville show their influence. Iron balconies overlooking narrow streets adorn many stone homes which, in some cases, surround shady, romantic courtyards containing fountains.

In my humble opinion, Seville is one of the most beautiful, graceful and interesting cities I have ever seen in all my travels through about 100 countries around the world. Permit me, therefore, to elaborate on this remarkable provincial seat for a few more minutes. Already while flying over it and observing the beauty from the air, both my friend and I exclaimed, "My, what a place! It is tremendous–just unbelievable. We have to land here and look around. We cannot pass up a spot like that!"

This, by the way, is the advantage of flying. A person can recognize quickly the worthwhile places with such a vast, sweeping panoramic expanse below that he does not waste time with insignificant sites and boring details. He gets the nub the easy and pleasant way, and can at once decide where he wants to stop. It is different from the limited view out of a car window.

The vision from our lofty height encompassed gorgeous parks with lush, red soil, fantastic buildings reminiscent of *The Thousand and One Nights,* the remains of a great wall with 64 towers which at one time surrounded the city, courtyards with adjoining white balconied houses with florid iron gates and shaded, narrow streets and beautiful squares with unique fountains.

"That's the *only* way to see the world and to pick out the nice places quickly. What a fabulous dream world! Look what is coming in sight below us now," declared a still-excited Klaus.

All of a sudden we saw the famous over 300-foot high Giralda Tower –a Moslem minaret built in the 1300's–guarding the Court of Oranges, the splendid Hotel Alfonso XIII, all kinds of ornate churches, monuments

Main courtyard of the romantic Dueñas Palace where flowers, tiled roofs and walls as well as lacy iron grillwork abound. It belongs to the Duke of Alba.

and other works of art, including museums, the resplendent Maria Luisa Park, and the Palacio de las Dueñas.

To enhance all of this even more, canals and the winding Guadalquivir River provide the city with a valuable inland port amid a setting of orange groves and sunny vineyards. What a jewel of a metropolis!

It was the only place (besides our point of departure in Belgium) we visited twice on our entire tightly scheduled, fast-moving journey. There was an additional reason for this, however, for we learned on our first visit that in a few days the world-famous "Feria in Sevilla" would be held. A festival-fair we could not miss for anything. After all, we had a plane, and distance did not mean that much to us. Also, there were very many beautiful señoritas in that lovely city and the "Feria" was a most ideal place to meet and get acquainted with some of them.

We knew that our next visit was going to be completely occupied by that development. Therefore we decided to do all our other sightseeing right then, much of it by walking in this pleasant environment. Only very few cars drove on the roads. Instead of a bicycle path, the streets were adjoined by red dirt horse trails lined with trees, and most of the trekking was done on horseback. Proud and elegant people were gracefully using

The famous 12th century Giralda Tower in Seville stands guard over the Court of Oranges and the tomb of Columbus in the adjoining 15th century Gothic Cathedral.

this mode of transportation. Noticeably absent were the noisy confusion and the ill-smelling fumes so prevalent in most modern cities today.

In Spanish education, literature and art, Seville comes second only to Madrid. Bartolomé Murillo, whose best productions are in the local "fine arts museum," and Diego Velázquez were born there. They are among Spain's greatest painters. *The Barber of Seville* and *Carmen*, two famous operas, had it as their setting. Even Don Juan, whose colorful life supplied many composers and writers with much material, dwelled there.

"Maybe you can qualify as the next Romeo around here and donate new material for the ever-searching writers and poets," I insinuated.

"Why don't you suggest this to yourself. After all, you are not excelling either in the virtue of chastity—or are you?" replied a peeved Klaus.

Then, after giving it a few more moments of thought, he suddenly boasted, "O.K. Hans, the competition is on . . ."

Being unable to match him in that game with a sick foot and strong language impediments, I preferred to change the subject.

"Did you know that this place is also of great archaeological and artistic importance?" I asked.

Certainly, of interest was the 14th Century Salon Arabe, a Moorish palace in Seville, with its exceptionally lovely outer courts, pools, fountains, gardens, palace rooms and courts, all showing exquisite decorations. The cathedral in 15th Century Gothic style, with rich interior works of art, Seville's greatest building, which was constructed from 1402 until 1519, ranking as Europe's largest next to St. Peter's in Rome, stands on the site of a Moorish mosque. It is claimed that in 1898 the tomb of Columbus was brought here from Havana and placed in the south transept. Many of the fabulous buildings decorated by varicolored tesserae forming radiant mosaics, are situated in and surrounded by romantic parks with their lush southern flora and the fiery red soil which we could see so well from the plane.

We thoroughly enjoyed every minute of our tranquil stay in this lovely spot and hated to leave the next day for contradistinctive Africa.

5

"Empty Tanks" Between Two Continents

(Seville, Spain to Gibraltar and on to Tangier, Morocco, Africa)

It was noon on the 14th of April when forebodingly we left Seville. We intended to land at world-renowned Gibraltar for refuelling the plane and then to fly on into Africa. A flight plan was properly filed at the airport before our departure with destination "Gibraltar." Premonitorily the Spanish airport officials had us wait for a while to see whether it would be accepted by the English authorities there. During a tense but reasonable waiting period, we received ironically no negative reply which, according to the Spanish personnel, meant that our flight plan was indeed accepted. Unfortunately, we did not fill our tanks completely in order to cut down on our weight. It was a hot day and we would have to deal with the effects of increased density altitude on our aircraft performance. Also, mountain ranges had to be crossed en route.

The first part of the flight took us over the Guadalquivir River delta with its many tributaries, and then we entered the mountainous regions somewhat east of Jerez de la Frontera. After flying for about 30 minutes over this fairly rough terrain, we noticed that the country sloped down toward the Mediterranean Sea. Soon the Rock of Gibraltar or, as it is also commonly called, "The Key to the Mediterranean," lay clearly and distinctly before us.

At this point allow me to give you a few of the fascinating details about this strategic point. The recovery of Gibraltar, held by Britain since 1704, has been a major goal of Spanish foreign policy, especially since 1964. The colony's population, however, voted overwhelmingly to remain British in a referendum in September 1967. On these grounds, Britain also refused an United Nations proposal in December 1968 to end this colonial reign. It was they who made it a strong fortress built in, above, and around the rock, covering an area of roughly two square miles. The town itself was constructed mostly on the southern and western slopes of the peninsula. A 1½-mile-long flat, sandy isthmus, less than a mile wide, which also accommodates the airport, forms the connection to the Spanish mainland. Designated as a "neutral zone" to separate Spain from Gibraltar, it is strongly guarded. Steel nets shield the harbor from attacks by submarines. In addition to this, the base is protected by seaplanes and battleships. Heavy guns galore have been installed into the rock. The local armed forces are supplied with food, water tanks, ammunition and even a hospital and living quarters, all of it located in 10 miles of tunnels built into this limestone giant. About 28,400 people, mostly of Spanish and Italian descent, live in Gibraltar.

It was referred to by the Greeks as one of the two "Pillars of Hercules." Across "The Key to the Mediterranean," on the African coast, stood the other pillar. The word "Gibraltar" comes from the word "Gebel-at-Tarik" (Rock of Tarik), which was given to it by the Moorish invaders who took possession of it at times. Spain tried to regain Gibraltar in 1779 when England was engaged in the Revolutionary War in America. Joined by France in 1780, the greatly outnumbered British were able to withstand a more than three-year blockade around the stronghold in an effort to starve the garrison. During both world wars Gibraltar was a strategic Allied Mediterranean base.

If we had known what was to come, we could not have enjoyed this marvelous sight. One of the worst experiences of our trip followed.

RED SIGNAL FLARES OVER GIBRALTAR

A strong north wind was blowing, carrying us to our intended destination even faster. Gliding in a descending flight, we approached the Rock of Gibraltar from the north, passing it just to the west and then, in an approximate 280-degree turn to the left, we flew around it, being soon south and a little later east of it before coming in for a landing. As the airstrip stretches across the narrow land tongue, a plane would plunge into the water when either touching down too early, too late, or rolling too long.

Then, as soon as we approached the vicinity of this 1,408-foot-high monolith, furious winds, torn to shreds by it, began to hit us. Since the gale came from the north and we were passing Gibraltar to the south near Point Europa, we were caught by horrendous twisters and squalls which made our ship rock around like a nut shell on the ocean. Temporarily the winds pushed us down with great force, threatening to tear up our conveyance, and just about smashed us against the rock. As the aircraft emitted repeated cracking sounds while caught in the downdrafts to the south of it on account of the northerly winds, I was unable to gain hardly any altitude to make up for the plunging of the craft. The severe vertical gusts caused a sudden increase in the angle of attack which, in combination with the banking of the plane, resulted in large wing loads. These were resisted by the inertia of the airplane and it increased the load factor beyond safe limits. Not very far from a blackout and temporary loss of vision, we had already reached the point where we noticed the sensation of the blood draining from our heads and the tendency of our cheeks to sag, both signals of extreme danger. I was unwilling to slow the craft too much below the maneuvering speed because of the likelihood of imminent stalling. My log book has an entry indicating that the turbulence we found ourselves in at this time was even worse than what we had experienced at Cape Finisterre. You can imagine what it was like, though for a shorter period.

"I am surprised the plane is holding up—staying in one piece in this pandemonium," Klaus mumbled in utter amazement, apparently remembering the fun he had poked at it when he first saw what he considered a flimsy toy.

"How would you like it to be as unreliable as you had thought in the beginning?" I joined.

"We would be all dead by now," he stammered.

Surely, the air traffic controllers in the airport nerve center must have seen our dilemma, and one would have expected some commiserate actions on their part. Such, however, was not to be the case.

When in our final landing approach, we encountered more stable wind conditions only a few feet over the runway. While getting ready for the touchdown, we were horrified to see a red rocket and signal flares go up at the tower. What an enigma that was! For the first time on our trip we were treated in this fashion. The firing of these objects meant "disregard any former instructions and do not land at this time." In other words: "Absolutely no landing!"

I immediately pointed Klaus's attention to the signals.

"Just forget it! What kind of secrets do they think they still have at this centuries-old fortress anyhow? Never mind their ridiculous and silly show of strength! What damage or espionage work can a little plane like ours with two tourists on board possibly do? What else is there to observe

Our last countdown began at Gibraltar as red rockets and flares seemed to signal our demise over the shark-infested waters of the strait between Europe and Africa.

than we can see right now? Go ahead and land and forget their fireworks—make it another emergency landing!" he flashed.

"I would like to, but I fear that the authorities at Gibraltar most likely will keep the plane in custody for weeks or months and probably cause other complications. I am not going to risk confiscation or settle for additional troubles at this stage of the game."

"Land! Don't you see how little gas we have?" my companion said full of determination.

I was however reluctant to disobey the signalling, even though the situation was extremely odd. Also, we were just about out of gas.

"What's the closest airport?"

Klaus fumbled for the map. "Tangier, Morocco."

Again I had to do some fast thinking and decided heavy-heartedly to forestall the termination of the flight. "I am aborting the touchdown," I said hastily. Thereupon I reapplied power by shoving in the throttle, cut off the carburetor heat and headed south to Africa. The plane climbed as I pulled back the elevator controls providing the wings with greater lift.

"They must have some oddballs working in the tower. Either that or they aren't all there. We gave them notice of our arrival when we filed the flight plan. They never rejected it."

"I would like to know what caused them to fire the red signal flares. Wouldn't you, Klaus?" Indeed, while going through, the two of us did not have many kind words on our lips for that tower personnel.

Our fuel indicator was a wire sticking out of the gas cap on the cowling in front of us. It was bent to a 90-degree angle at the upper end so it would not fall into the tank. By floating on a cork at the lower tip, this wire would show how much gasoline was left, depending on how far it protruded out of the cap. We had already run our auxiliary tank empty, as the fancier gauge on that one registered even more inaccurately. I trusted the simple device on the front tank more. This way we could be fairly confident of the amount of fuel left for any potential emergency. That practice came in handy at the time, but the trouble was that the wire had dropped nearly all the way down. It meant we were just about out of gas.

SHARKS BELOW

A flight of agony and torture was ahead, with the closest alternate airport located in Africa. Before us lay the shark-infested conflux of the Mediterranean Sea and the Atlantic Ocean. Fear gripped our souls as apparently our last countdown had begun. With increasing frequency, our eyes swept over the gas indicator as we crossed Gibraltar Bay. After a seemingly long time, we passed Punta Acebuche to our right and then for about 13 minutes flew along the southernmost tip of Spain next to a rather large restricted area. Tarifa lay at the very end of it. There went our last chance for an emergency landing on dry ground. From then on we flew diagonally across the 1,000-foot-deep Strait of Gibraltar in an effort to conserve miles and gas by trying to reach "Tanger-Bou Half" on the straightest line possible. About half an hour of further terrorizing flight lay still before us–mostly over waters teeming with nearly 400 kinds of fish, including the Common Sandbar, or Brown shark, lurking like death below us. The Mediterranean flows out at the bottom of the Strait, and the chilly waters from the Atlantic Ocean rush into the Mediterranean at the surface, which would have made it an icy dip for us in case of the expected power failure.

In the meantime, our wire had hit bottom, indicating that we were, or at any moment would be, out of gas. We felt like we were sitting on powder kegs with the fuses already lit, waiting for the dreadful moment of having the engine quit at any time. We knew it could not last much longer, and the purr of that little motor in front of us sounded ever so good. "Please, please, brave engine, turn a little longer! Don't quit on us now, dumping us into the cold waters and ending it all!" was our hearts' cry in that hour. I adjusted the fuel setting for maximum cruising-range conditions in order to stretch the few remaining drops of gas. We almost wanted to get out to help push the plane, but this unfortunately was not possible.

At that moment, we were right in the middle of the 32-mile-long and 8- to 23-mile-wide Strait of Gibraltar, watched over for millenniums by the two "Pillars of Hercules" at its eastern end–one in Spain and the other in Africa. Hopefully assuming the unlikely eventuality that we had sufficient fuel to fly the added leg from Gibraltar to Tangier, we were then passing the "point of no return"–the spot beyond which, in this contingency, we wouldn't have enough gas to get back. From here on it would be safer to proceed than to turn around.

Our eyes were by then glued to the wire indicator to see if we perchance could notice an occasional bobbing of the same or maybe even a rising, in case the cork or the wire had gotten stuck. There was no such sign at all, and a sinking feeling overcame us as that last glimmer of hope vanished. The red signal flares had led us right into a deadly and acute "energy crisis" over the shark-infested waters between two continents.

Really, deep down we knew we were out of gas and would meet our Waterloo, but like any living being, in his last struggles for life, we refused to give up hope altogether. After all, we had been through so much; there must be a way out of this, too.

There it was–a stuttering of the engine, a shaking of the plane! Or were our senses playing havoc with us? It is well known among pilots that in most dangerous flying situations an apparent engine roughness is noticed. Perhaps the anticipating fear had just suggested that faltering of the regular hum of the motor. Still we were airborne, still we were heading toward Tangier, Africa. I had regained several thousand feet altitude, so at least we could have some gliding distance if the engine quit and time to figure out what to do in that case.

INTERCEPTION BY MILITARY AIRCRAFT AHEAD?

In addition to our many trials and distresses, we began to face at that time the distinct possibility of being intercepted by military planes. We were just about ready at any moment to penetrate the airspace of another foreign land without an international flight plan or any other advance arrival notice to that nation.[1]

But there we came, contrabanding along between Spain, English-held Gibraltar, and Morocco, Africa, with an American-made plane regis-

---

[1]The United States, for instance, is pretty well surrounded by the Pacific Coastal, Northern Domestic, Atlantic Coastal, Gulf of Mexico Coastal and Southern Border Air Defense Identification Zones (ADIZ). With the exception of these, all airspace of the United States is designated as Defense Area. The operation of civil aircraft and security control of air traffic within, into or out of the above-mentioned territories, including the Alaskan Distant Early Warning Identification Zone (DEWIZ), is governed by Federal Aviation Regulations. According to them, even pilots of planes with a true airspeed of less than 180 knots have to file a Defense Visual Flight Rules (DVFR) flight plan prior to operating VFR within or penetrating an ADIZ in the following cases:

1. Before entering a Coastal ADIZ south of 25° north latitude and east of 85° west longitude. (This includes the Florida Keys south of Tavernier, Long Island, Florida.)

tered in Belgium and manned by Germans, completely disregarding all specified requirements. At the brink of crossing over into Moroccan territory, we were unable to talk to them by radio. In the absence of any communication equipment whatsoever, it was impossible for us to explain our dilemma, such as what had happened, why we were arriving without proper procedures after having been refused on the other side, and that we were rapidly running out of gas. What if they should repel the "enemy," and herd us back, making us run the gamut? Certainly we did not have enough fuel left to return to Gibraltar and land there amid red rockets and signal flares. Coming close to that country's territorial waters, all we hoped was that they wouldn't crowd us off, repulse or rebuff our last chance for survival, or even shoot us down.

What an insurmountable number of odds had accumulated against us. It was hard to say which of our predicaments so far was the worst: the panic over Paris, jigging around Cape Finisterre, or this one. Never had we encountered such a combination of disastrous circumstances in a single flight. It all began when the wind blew with furious gusts which angrily tore the small waves of the Strait's waters into spindrift below our fighting, faltering Aeronca south of the Rock. What a carking and exigeant journey for two haggard die-hards with an almost constant cockpit fracas. Arduously charging and dashing forward, the flimsy plane had pulled us through our Gibraltar experience and, still hanging on, was bravely heading toward an inevitably last recourse with the unexpected cheechakos. Vibrating on the wave of those current events, we knew that our unplanned, unwonted high-altitude daredeviltry had to terminate soon. Our longing desire for a vagabond life already had been abundantly and overly rewarded.

The northern tip of Africa was coming closer. Soon we would reach the shoreline of safety and rescue if–only if–the motor would just run a little longer. Finally, finally, there it was! The coast of Africa to our left and soon Tangier, like a white jewel bathed in scorching sunlight in near-noon heat, lay below us. Known as the "Crossroads of the World," it looked like a giant amphitheater from the sea. Hills lined with rows of white houses curved around a lovely bay. At that time Tangier, with its famous beach resorts, low prices, and ever-perfect climate, attracted many American artists among its international inhabitants. Lying at the western opening to the Mediterranean Sea, it is the second largest seaport of

2. On flights between Mexico and the United States.

Furthermore, the pilot must report the time, position and altitude of passing an identifiable reporting point and estimate the moment of arrival over the next appropriate one along the route before flying into an Air Defense Identification Zone. If there is no such conspicuous landmark, the pilot is required to give an approximate time, position and altitude for ingressing an ADIZ to a proper aeronautical facility at least 15 minutes before entering. The Air Defense Command has advised that even an air-filed flight plan makes the aircraft subject to interception for positive identification. This can be avoided if one is filed prior to takeoff.

Morocco and was until 1956 an international zone controlled by leading world powers.

The ticklish time of illegally crossing over into foreign airspace had passed. Anxiously we scanned all around to see if some fighters were zooming toward us, ready to drill their noses into our delicate, little fabric-covered bird. This inherent danger loomed on the horizon ever since we entered. Our perturbation gradually subsided, as there were no signs of imminent confrontation. The utterly absorbing flight neared an alleviating end as the plane logged the last stretch.

Now we could reduce the power and possibly make it the last nine miles to the airport by mostly gliding. Why couldn't the airfield be on *our* side of town? Did it have to be so far away on the other end, in a south-westerly direction, prolonging our flight? With the worst behind, though, we could take heart, and already things started to look brighter indeed.

"But what if we don't find the airport, or if it has been abandoned, as was the case at so many other times on our flight? Since we made it this far, wouldn't that be terrible?" Klaus hinted.

We quickly tried to discard such a nasty thought.

A few more minutes and the field was in sight. What a feeling of euphoria overcame us! How wonderful life suddenly was! We felt like embracing the entire world. Without wasting any more time, I came in for a landing on a tight pattern and within a few more minutes we had genuine earth below our feet. We had made it with the last drop of gas—maybe we even had run partly on fumes.

Truly, life can be very exciting without the ruinous, crazy habits so many people indulge in, such as smoking, doping, drinking and carousing around. If you are looking for challenge, plenty of wholesome and enriching ventures can be found in the world today. There is no need to destroy your life, consuming products of industrial and other selfish interests. Let the ones who make and profit from that stuff take it. They then would probably quit this production. But as long as they find feeble, debilitated subjects willing to abuse their health and bodies with their criminal merchandise, they will continue to take advantage of that situation. Life is full of beauty and pleasant surprises if you have eyes to look and search for them.

Once again our merciful Creator had been very good to us, perhaps for a reason. There might yet be a job for us to do. In times like these, all but the dullest and most hard-hearted persons cannot help but utter a few words of thanks to the omnipotent and omnipresent Power of the universe. Little did I know then that compassionately and tenderly God was calling me for a different, greater mission in life.

A 2½-hour gruelling flight had ended. It was a nice airport, giving us a good initial impression of Africa. However, the personnel at the airfield simply didn't know and couldn't share our deep feelings. To them we had intruded just at their noon hour when they preferred to nap. It was 2:30

P. M., but still they were resting. Apparently the siesta runs there for four hours or more. We were stuck with the payment of an additional fee because our arrival inconvenienced them at the wrong time.

"I guess that's Africa for you. I am already missing Spain," grumbled a disenchanted Klaus.

I almost joined in. It was hard for the two of us to settle down to a more quiet way of life, particularly in the middle of an action-packed journey.

"Another country, with different customs, and we might as well get used to it," I returned. After all, Klaus and I did not travel to find conditions the same as at home. If this were our desire, it would have been better to stay where we came from. We were eager to taste different lifestyles.

The way they refuelled our plane was something else. There came one of those Arabian fellows, rolling a metal barrel through the sand. At first I thought it was for him to stand on, but no, it was full of gas and intended to be our filling station. Next, a dirty funnel was picked out of the sand and the refuelling ceremony started, but not before I wiped off the funnel and made sure that things were at least as clean as possible. One of our handkerchiefs or was it an old felt hat from the Arabian—my memory leaves me at this point—served as a much-needed filter for likely dirt particles, including the ever-present African sand.

"Have you ever seen anything like it? Don't we have enough problems keeping our ship afloat?" a quick-triggered Klaus chuckled.

"I agree, I am not at all that keen either on fighting the African sand in our gas supply. How can the poor little bird possibly last through all of that persecution? But what can we do? We wanted to go to Africa and here we are!" I finally added.

We were on a new and large continent in the interesting country of Morocco—a land where "The Desert Fox," German Field Marshal Erwin Rommel, left many tracks. In the days to come, I was to hear a lot of high praise about this brilliant general, who fought with clever tactics commanding the "Afrika Korps." When the Allies landed large military units from 500 troop and supply ships under the escort of about 350 warships on the shores of Algeria and Morocco on November 7, 1942, it caught the German high command by complete surprise, further aggravating the situation for the Axis powers after they had already been halted at El Alamein. Ultimately the Allied forces had suffered a grim total of about 70,000 casualties in the North African campaign and the Axis powers lost about five times as many killed, wounded and captured.

ASLEEP AT THE CONTROLS

(Tangier to Rabat Ville)

After a brief stopover at the Tangier Airport, we were on our way once again, but not before we had thoroughly drained the glass carburetor

An exotic castle garden in Africa *(above)* and a unique wheel used to lift water *(left)*. The old fortress and indigenous flora are in the background.

float bowl. We needed to be absolutely certain to get rid of any and all water, sand or other dirt which might easily have been dumped into our tanks from that strange fuelling facility. Without any emergency supplies or even water on board, we definitely didn't want to go down somewhere in the wilderness of Africa. This was the least desirable of all places to get stuck. We did not know what awaited us yet on that flight and how close we came to a crash.

Before us lay 135 miles of straight, shallow and rather boring coastline. Besides an occasional river running into the sea, the only other remarkable sights from the plane were scattered settlements of clean, beautiful-looking European sections with modern buildings, broad streets, nice parks and, next to them, dirty native slums of unbelievable, extreme poverty, crammed with rows of huts made of canvas, corrugated iron and other rusty metal sheets, and whatever was available.

"What in the world are those places? They look like city dumps or collections of giant pack rats! You don't suppose that people, real human beings, can live in trash heaps like that—do you?" I asked Klaus, full of bewilderment.

Likewise flabbergasted, he replied, "Just remember, we are now in Africa. Everything is possible here. Who knows what else we will run across on this continent!"

Soon we were to find that this was a prophetic utterance indeed.

The poorest of the poor live in those tarpaper and "what-have-you" shacks. Numerous times, and in the absence of any modern development, we would see only one of those squalid hamlets, seemingly lost all by itself on that long, fertile coastal plain along the Atlantic.

It was a very hot day. The tank behind us was leaking gas, filling the cabin with anesthetizing fumes, and my foot hurt. For many nights I had not been able to sleep on account of sharp pain in my leg, and was extremely tired. The combination of my physical weakness, the boring countryside below, the monotonous droning of the engine, the relatively uneventful flight—at least so far—and the narcotizing cockpit situation lulling my senses (the heat and fumes) was almost to be our end! We came mighty close that day to finding our final resting place on the far-off shores of Africa.

With sudden jolts I was jarred back into alertness. While flying along, the shoreline of Africa to our left, a bright and deep blue sky above, and the wide, endless ocean below us, I had fallen asleep. Klaus was hanging onto my arm, violently shaking me. For the first time on our journey, he had an object of our seemingly permanent flying troubles at his finger tips and was making good use of it by promptly jerking me mercilessly from my refreshing and much-needed rest.

"Wake up, wake up!" Klaus yelled. He continued mercilessly, "If you want to die, that's one thing. I am not ready to go yet. First I'd like to see more of Africa. After that, I need to return to Seville for you know what."

I could tell that the last statements were a false show of bravado, for the strain of the trip had left its mark on him.

I awoke to the danger with a start and no interest or time to listen to his silly parlance.

Snapping back to the real world of flying, I immediately noticed that we already were in a full-fledged dive toward the territory below us. Easing back on the elevator controls, I ever so slowly recovered the aircraft from its downward plunge. As, sharply descending, we had developed a rather high speed for this bird, I did not dare to overcontrol at this stage, lest I cause damage to the plane. At this excessive velocity, the lifting capacity of the wing was so great that a sudden movement of the controls could have increased the load factor beyond safe limits.

Klaus, likewise not any longer at his best, being worn out and tired much of the time as well, usually took frequent naps in the craft. Considering this, we counted it a miracle that he was not asleep at that time. A rather sudden contact between the plane and the ground or water might have been the only thing which then would have awakened Klaus and me from deep sleep–or should I say moved us from this state into the land of no return–death!

I could readily see that he did not like this type of flying very well. He anxiously inquired if I were really awake and still astir.

He pleaded, "Do something to keep from going back to sleep!"

Being as tired as I was, and having no idea what this "something" could be, I probably would have fallen asleep again shortly. Almost instantly, though, he offered me a cigarette, which I refused, not being a smoker.

"What do you think is worse, to crash the plane and kill us both or to smoke a cigarette?" he hollered.

Obviously, not having much of a choice, I smoked that cigarette and managed to stay awake until we arrived at our destination. That cigarette, too, was dangerous on account of all the gas fumes in our cockpit, and it could have blown us to bits. The opening of the air vents lessened that danger somewhat.

Before arriving in Rabat, we passed the large United States military airbase Port Lyautey to our left. The size of the runways, the large planes, and the elaborate constructions and buildings offered quite an intriguing contrast to the indigent native shanty villages we had seen. When, in Operation Torch, the Allies sent to the shores of Africa one of the greatest armadas in military history, fierce fighting broke out between French colonial troops under command by Vichy officers and the Allies at Port Lyautey. The United States needed the airfield there. Resistance at that place held out longer than at Fedala and Safi, which fell in less than 10 hours to Major General George Patton's forces.

We expected to land at Rabat in another half hour. Soon we passed the joint civil and military airfield Rabat-Salé to our left and just northeast of Rabat. A few minutes later the Moroccan capital lay below us. As usual, we spent some time sightseeing the town first from above. There were many small, white, flat-roofed houses. Also we saw mosques, lovely gardens, gateways cut through the ancient city walls, the immense 12th-Century Tower of Hassan and the European section with its broad streets and modern buildings. The city was founded by the Moorish Chief, Abd-el-Mumin, in the 1100's. When the French established a protectorate over much of Morocco in 1912, they made Rabat their headquarters.

A little later, we landed against the sun and in high grass on the Rabat-Ville Airfield. We were then only about 50 miles northeast of Casablanca.

This night we stayed in the deluxe Hotel Balima with a beautiful view from our window. The stately boulevard before the hotel was quite a sight in itself—divided by a center section with lovely palm trees and lanterns. The long-needed rest—even though I was again unable to sleep on account of the pain in my foot—did us good.

In the morning Klaus was ready to go on a detailed sightseeing jaunt all over town.

"This place looks interesting. Before we leave I have to look into things here. I'd like to find out what makes this city tick. Everything looks quite different. It's an intriguing site to explore," he most intelligently concluded, while I was wondering what things he was trying to look into.

"I'm sorry, Klaus, but not now. We'll return here. But first, let's make a little side trip to the interior," I replied, interrupting his venturesome plans.

At this time, it would probably be appropriate to say a little more about Morocco, so that you will be able to understand better some of the things we experienced during our three-day stay in that country.

Morocco, a small, mountainous nation in northwest Africa, is a little larger than the total area of Oregon and Washington. Two great dynasties, the Almoravides and the Almohades, united Morocco from 1064 to 1269 and at times they ruled North Africa and southern and eastern Spain. The country has had four capitals simultaneously: Fez, Marrakech, Meknès, and Rabat, with the king living in each of them at various times. Morocco became independent in 1956, after it was ruled by France and Spain by a French resident-general at Rabat and a Spanish "caliph" at Tetuán from 1912 on. Nearly all Moroccans are Arabs, Berbers, or Moors (of mixed Arab and Berber descent). They are the descendants of the people who built the mighty Moorish Empire from the 700's to the 1400's that included Spain, Portugal, and most of northern Africa.

The United States and Morocco have the longest unbroken treaty relationship in United States history. Much of the country has stayed unchanged during the centuries, with the exception of a few modern cities.

It has a 620-mile coastline. Mount Toubkal, rising 13,661 feet, is the highest peak in the dry, rocky Atlas Mountain range, where the wild boars make their home. There are also gazelles, Moroccan foxes, and hyenas in the country. Towering palms, huge cacti, cork forests, orange and thorny argan trees, and enormous roses make up some of the flora. Arabic, French and Spanish are spoken widely. City people live mainly in little, centuries-old adobe (sun-baked clay) homes without windows to keep them cool. Mostly along winding alleys, these old buildings huddle together and form sections of the town which are called "medina." At times the streets are so narrow that you can stand in the center and touch both walls with outstretched arms. Two small Spanish overseas provinces are still in Morocco. They are Melilla on the northeastern coast and Ceuta on the northernmost tip.

Some of the other items, unforgettable about this part of Africa, were the beautiful old castles, the fine mosaic works at many places, the wide avenues with sidewalks, palms and other ornamental trees and flowers separated in a center section. The colorful native markets, veiled women, hooded characters, the narrow, coffee-brown faces of the men, the beautiful subtropical flora as a whole, including the unique trumpet-flower trees—all combined into a rare, outstanding, exotic flavor we would always remember.

A desperate fisherman with high expectations and no results. We could readily tell that this tiny waterhole had no fish. But he tried nevertheless, apparently hoping Allah would come to his rescue. The coffee-brown face shows interesting features. This picture aptly depicts typical clothes and the slow tempo of Moroccan living amid the country's poverty.

RAMADAN
(Rabat to Fez [Fes] Via Meknès)

This was the only occasion that we took to the road for long-distance travel. Flying temporarily had become a burden and a bugbear. We were ready for something different, and this country, with its unusual customs, was a good place to do it. So we decided to go the next day the native way—that is, on a bus to Meknès and on to Fez. After leaving the coastal plain, the road wound over a mountain and down through a river valley. Then again we climbed steadily until we reached the walled city of Meknès at an altitude of 1,890 feet. Founded in the 1100's, it is a main trading center in the northern part of the country and also has a fine Moroccan art museum. It became one of the nation's four capitals when Sultan Ismail built a large palace here in the 1670's. After a short stopover, with Klaus, as always, busy shooting pictures, we continued.

With a relatively long ride and many stops along the way finally behind us, we arrived at Fez. The approximately 145 miles of street travel from Rabat lay in the past, and we sincerely wondered whether flying was not better after all. This bus trip seemed like eternity when compared to travelling by plane—even though the craft was small and slow, generally making about one mile per minute. This, of course, depended upon the wind conditions. On our flight from Tangier to Rabat, for instance, we made 58 miles per hour, covering approximately 135 miles in 140 minutes. At least we didn't have to worry about the many curves and grades. With the bus, a similar distance was nearly an all-day journey, tiring as well as noisy.

We were in Fez, the religious center of Morocco and another one of its former capitals. Kairoween University, founded in 859 and one of the world's oldest, is located here, also the famous Moslem shrine, the Mosque of Mulai Idrisse. The city lies in the Fez River valley and was founded by the Moorish ruler Idris II as his capital in 808.

It was a logical place for me to buy a fez, a tall, red brimless cap with a colored tassel of wool or silk, because it was first made and worn here. At times called a "tarboosh," it is in wide use in Egypt, Turkey and North Africa.

The stay at this very interesting, strange city was dominated by a self-imposed guide, whom we called the "Little One" because of his small stature. We don't know where he came from, but there he was, forever trying to get us to buy some of the native crafts, copper plates, hand-made rugs or fabulous leather goods. He received compensation at the places we bought from and made no bones about immediately collecting his rake-off from the vendors. We didn't need him, as we knew our way around sufficiently to take care of ourselves, but this did not make any difference to him. He clung to us like a bur. His English vocabulary, slightly more extensive than that of some boys we were soon to drag behind us as unde-

On the way to Fez, Morocco. The crude means of transportation, the car and the Westerner among the natives *(above)* are one of the few signs of the 20th Century. Morocco is a dry land whose inhabitants often quench their thirst at an old mosaic-walled water place like the one below.

sired tourist guides, was strictly limited to his commercial "talent." Obviously he had been at it for a long time and was obsessed by a limitless thirst for earning commissions. He must have thought our pocketbooks were without bottom.

I finally bought that fez, a leathern letter folder with beautiful green, red and 22-carat gold-covered flat modelings. Also, a sham leather lady's purse was forced on me. It was to be a present for my mother who, in turn, passed it on to my wife at a later date. I had wondered about the featherlight weight of the handbag, and soon we found out that the inner layer was ordinary pasteboard, covered by razor-thin leather which wore through during the second use.

That night, while trying to rest in one of the native hotels, a rattling noise was heard at our door and woke us up. I think it was the first time I had fallen asleep for many nights. As the knocking noise and rattling did not abate, Klaus got up and opened the door. Instantly he sighingly uttered, "Hans, the 'Little One' is here again!" There, in the middle of the night, stood the "Little One," loaded down with commercial products and trying to conduct some more business with us. He didn't care if he had to wake us up, nor what time it was. He apparently thought that our only mission was to buy continuously. Naturally, that was about the last time we wanted to see him and, with hands motioning wildly and words sounding rough and harsh, we sped him on his way in no uncertain terms. This time there was no language barrier as we came through crystal clear and plain. Indeed, and much to our relief, it was the last time we ever saw him. He had vanished for good, and heaven knows where the little man came from or where he went.

We hit Morocco at an unfortunate time. Ramadan, the Moslem's holy month of fasting, being the ninth month in their year, was upon the land. From dawn to sunset Moslems may not eat nor drink. They were lying around everywhere. When we walked all over the countryside, through high grass, or wherever, they appeared out of nowhere and settled down again.

On one occasion we visited an old, neglected cemetery luxuriant with wild vegetation, and were startled when suddenly hatchet-faced and skeleton-like embodiments clad in flowing white abas rose among graves and tombstones. Evidently we were witnessing the resurrection of the dead as we strolled through that necropolis or place of materialized beings during this sacrosanct time of the year.

There was not much commotion during the days, but as soon as the sun set, the noise and the strange, unnerving tootle music started. When we wanted to sleep, these monotonous, whining sounds surrounding us simply would not cease. Every night there was a never-ending hustling and bustling about—the time when they ate and drank to their hearts' content. As far as we were concerned, it was not much of a fast when they were eating and drinking practically all night long—that is, those who could afford to buy food.

In this town, we bought our fare in the native market. We ate a lot of that round, flat, warm bread. Also the native olives tasted different, but good. One night we bought some sausage, hoping that it would make a good meal with the baked loaf. The first bite taught us better. The sausage was so hot that it just about took our breaths away and set our mouths aflame. We gave some to those beggars sitting everywhere at the side of the narrow streets, and they immediately hid it under their jackets as though someone were going to steal this bonanza from them.

"Hast Du das gesehen? (Did you see that?) It looks as though they are scared that we might take it from them again. It doesn't look like the fasting is doing them much good," a startled Klaus observed.

It all was a strange sight—the adobe or stone homes on narrow streets with people of many races and colors (white, coffee-brown and black) milling around in their ancient dresses like the "seraweel," a loose, wide trouser worn by men, or the "kumsan," which are cotton shirts reaching to the ankles and gathered at the waist with a wide sash. "Djellabiat," large, hooded cloaks, serve as outer garments in cool weather. Turbans are often worn by men and leather sandals by men and women alike. The dresses of the women are similar, but they wear in addition the "haiak," which is a body-length cloak covering their heads and their entire faces (except their eyes), according to strict Moslem custom. This is done when they are outside their homes.

There was not much flirting around for Klaus, the Lothario. We could see only fiery female eyes peeking at us through the narrow, open slits which were left across their eyes. It made the girls all the more enticing, because a fellow wondered what was behind those sheets of veiling cloth, especially since some curvaceous forms were revealed at times through all that cover. Our girls, dancing around half naked in the western cities of the so-called civilized world, apparently do not realize this. What is worse than to see old women dressed in shorts or pants tight like the skin of a wiener and their dresses so open on top that a person looks into a deep gulf bordered by dormant, subsiding volcanoes. Weatherworn and shrivelled, they present repelling, loathsome pictures to the onlooker. How much more appetizing were those nice ladies we saw there. When once walking through the court of the palace, I could see hundreds of them milling around, almost running over me.

Interesting too, were the open-air markets scattered all over town along those narrow alleys. At "souks," as they are also called, merchants sold jewelry, clothing, pottery, and food in small, crowded stalls.

FIELD MARSHAL ROMMEL—THE "DESERT FOX"
(Our Return to Rabat)

The following day we returned to Rabat by the same route.

Worlds apart! In these very interesting scenes from Fez, Morocco, one can readily detect a number of different races among the natives. Here vendors line a street which is too narrow for cars. All women are strictly veiled.

"This is the time I've been looking forward to. Now my venturesome plans can become reality. Let's go and look around!" rejoiced Klaus.

But, as is usual, when hopes and anticipations are high, some disappointments follow.

We really must have looked like tourists, for once again Klaus and I were chased down. I level the charge for that on my friend because of his ever-present photo accouterments. To carry such is the best guarantee to be recognized immediately as a sightseer, and it also is the surest way forever to be overcharged and begged or preyed upon wherever one goes. For a long time it had been my policy to conduct myself and dress myself in such a manner that no one would suspect that I was a wayfarer. It already had saved me a lot of trouble and expense. But Klaus was the attraction and I was victimized right along with him.

There were the two boys, between nine and fourteen years old, who literally did not budge from our side. Whatever we said in an effort to get rid of them was greeted or answered with a friendly smile. Their English vocabulary was very limited and they didn't get much of what we told them, nor did we get much of what they jabbered, even though it was plenty. Klaus finally took a picture of them which lingers with us to this day, so the boys are still around.

I recollect vividly the enthusiasm with which the Arabians, especially the better-educated ones of the higher elite, spoke of Field Marshal Rommel. To them he seemed to have been the saviour of their country. They felt he was trying to free them from French colonial rule and they all had greatly enjoyed his "Afrika Korps," its attitude and the treatment they had received. This German "Desert Fox" ranked right after Allah and Mohammed. With us being from Germany, it really brought out their sentiments along this line. I can still see me standing in the Hotel Balima in Rabat listening for hours to one high Arabian government official as he told me more about Erwin Rommel than I had ever heard in all my life. To him, Hitler's biggest mistake was ordering Rommel's demise.

Our time in Africa was nearing the end. In a little less than three days we had seen a lot. Some of the sights would be unforgettable, such as the sweet memories of the old castle walls covered with red blooming vines and the many lush flowers growing all over them. We spent one more night in Rabat and the next day we were ready to leave the second largest continent of this world.

Being then the farthest from our plane rental place in Belgium and our native Germany, we could count it a homeward journey from that point on. During the little time left, we really continued to move along, for in approximately five more dramatic days our trip ended.

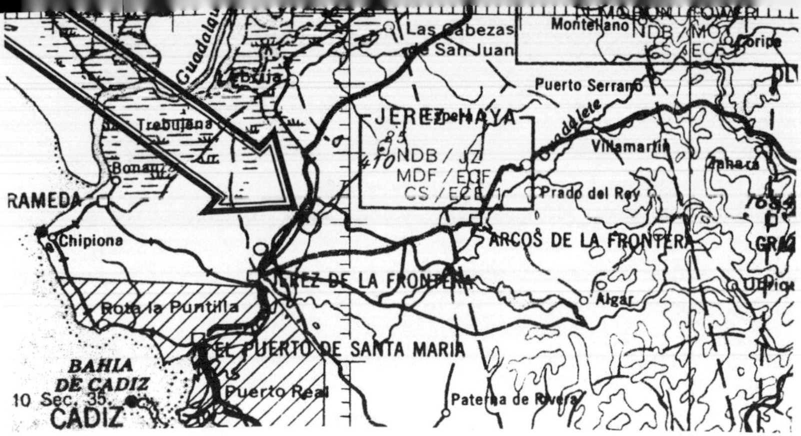

6

Desperate Search for Missing Airport

(The Two-Continent Flight from Rabat, Africa to Jerez-Haya, Spain)

DARTING THROUGH THE AFRICAN CALEFACTION

We were off to a late start. It was about 3:00 P. M. and the countryside was vibrating under extreme heat. This time we used the paved runway and were hardly able to lift off in the seething air rising from a torrid strip baking under a scorching African sun. Our tension was surging as we saw the other end of the runway racing toward us while we were still unable to leave the ground.

Not wanting to run into another Gibraltar experience, which left us with practically empty tanks over the confluence of the Mediterranean and Atlantic until we were miraculously able to reach Africa just in time, we filled our tanks to the brim at Rabat-Ville Airfield. In addition to this, we carried the African keepsakes the "Little One" had pressed us into buying. All of this, in combination with the thin, hot air, was causing us trouble. The "Little One" was taking revenge.

Our Gibraltar nightmare, which taught us not to fly with less than full tanks in this forbidding territory with airports widely scattered, was now having adverse effects. How could we ever win? All our efforts, no matter what we did, seemed futile and to work against us.

What should I do—try to bring the plane to a stop that far down the runway, or keep on going, hoping for the best? I decided for the latter. Like an arrow ready to pierce his victim, we were darting along through the calefaction. Only a few more feet of tarmac for our ground run—already we could visualize a red ball of fire before us.

At the very last moment, finally, finally, our tired, overloaded little bird was winging into the air. An audible gasp of relief spread through the cockpit. It was one of those special moments when one is particularly glad to be alive. We had made it once again. How many more times could we count on it?

"Maybe we will make Seville after all. I like Spain much better than Africa. At least a person can feel at home there, particularly in Seville," Klaus said wistfully.

He had joined this journey strictly for fun and it was still coming through.

Meanwhile, my sentiments were running along much more serious lines.

Perhaps it was good that we were travelling only five more days. Anyhow, we could not have gone on any longer with the physical condition we found ourselves in, upon our arrival back home. The African heat did not help my foot any, and it was continuously getting worse with the pain increasing unbearably. Strong sunshine is particularly bad for recurring osteomyelitis.

With increased frequency, strongly motivated thoughts hit me and seemed to indicate that this journey was more than just another trip. Bit by bit, I began to realize that superior forces were at work to mold me into a different character. By now it was certain that the many bouts with death, the many struggles in strange areas, and all the other difficulties we were facing, were having a profound effect on us. It seemed like we were going through a tough school—an academy of life—which was teaching us lessons we would never forget.

Then I did not really know the magnitude of it all, though at times there was a joyful anticipation of something wonderful and great yet to come. An inner voice called me, occasionally so near and yet sometimes so faraway, which was different, challenging and glorious.

What I also did not know at this juncture was that the outcome would have a tremendous impact not only upon my own life, not only upon the lives of a few people in my locality or even my country, but upon a worldwide scale! More of this later, but for now let's go flying once again.

Well, at least we were airborne! To gain altitude, however, was our next problem. The plane was climbing like an old man ready for a heart attack. It took us the longest time to have at least minimum altitude for a safe conduct of flight. Then we hoped not to hit some airholes or strong downdrafts, again losing our hard-won altitude. Putting the aircraft on direct course to Seville, Spain, we wondered if it were possible to arrive in daylight. With no lights on our plane whatsoever, it would have been out of the question for us to fly at night. No matter what the circumstances—the bird had to be on the ground before dark. With this thought in mind, we found ourselves hard pressed for time. Not even recovered from our last dilemma, Klaus and I were in the middle of the next.

RACING THE SUN

This was going to be a flight which would not permit us to relax for even a single moment. Continuously we worried whether any chance existed to get there in time. The longer the two of us were racing the sun, the more certain it became that we might never make it. The dawdling craft seemed as though it was just hovering and enjoying the scenery.

We were about ready to cross over from the African to the European continent—this time transversing the Strait of Gibraltar from Cabo Spartel, the very northwest corner of Africa, to an area a little east of Barbate, Spain. Up to that point, we again had followed the African coastline, only going north this time.

This area held many memories for us. Only a few days earlier, we came pretty close to feeding the sharks below us with the very substance we are made of.

"Would you like to try another landing at Gibraltar?" I kidded Klaus.

"No, thanks, once was enough! I never want to see that - - - - place again!"

I could understand how he felt about it.

Arriving in Spain, we had to make sure that we were staying west of the large prohibited area which spread across the southernmost tip of that country. Soon after crossing a fairly large lake, Lago Janda, we were flying over the dry southern Spanish countryside with large grape, orange, lemon and almond *cortijos,* or plantations, and their distinguished mansions dotted here and there. Already we passed Medina Sidonia to our left.

Only 24 miles to the west lay Cádiz. Founded by the Phoenicians in 1130 B. C., it is believed to be the oldest city in Europe. This lovely town, situated on a narrow peninsula at the southwestern corner of Spain, is its most significant Atlantic seaport. A mild climate, elegant white houses and clean streets make this place ideal to visit during any time of the year.

Then we approached the Guadalete River at a point about 12 miles east of Jerez de la Frontera. Two hours and 50 minutes of flight were already behind us—195 miles in 170 minutes. It computes into the tremendous and unheard of speed of 69 miles per hour. Intersecting the river, we feverishly tried to decide what to do. Still there was some daylight left. Should we go on to Seville or look for the close-by Jerez-Haya Airport? We decided for the latter.

I turned west in an effort to find that landing strip, supposedly about seven miles northeast of Jerez de la Frontera, according to our map. It was marked as the only field en route closer than our planned destination.

I harbored great misgivings in my mind about the prospect of finding the aerodrome as I was unable to locate or see it on our flight down into Africa. We had passed not very far from that area now in our immediate concern. The closer we got to this region, the greater the doubts that were haunting my mind.

Having made a 90-degree turn to the left, we were now heading west toward the location at which the airport was supposed to be, according to our map. We were still 10 miles from the field but yet unable to see it. Getting closer and closer, finally approaching the area where the aerodrome was indicated, we found none.

We were searching, and searching, and searching. It should have been fairly easy to find–two miles south of a 90-degree river bend, next to a main road and railroad track six miles north-northeast of Jerez de la Frontera. The map showed it to be there, but no matter how insistent the map was, it just "warn't" there!

Again, our only aeronautical charts were the completely insufficient "Carte Aéronautique du Monde" (WAC charts) scaled 1:1,000,000 with the following "ancient" datings: 1946, 1948, 1951 and 1952. We were using two maps on this trip and each carried three different dates. These were references to other charts they were taken from, publishing years, and times the aeronautical information was entered, respectively. It would have been a tough enough job to find the airfield, utilizing a current 1:500,000 map in this unfamiliar territory with upcoming darkness, let alone relying upon our inadequate navigational aids.

Once more, we were at a point of decision! What should we do–still try to make it to Seville, arriving there perhaps late at twilight, or continue our chase? We might find the place very soon while, on the other hand, we might get to Seville in the dark. We resolved to keep looking, in spite of the distinct danger that the airfield had been abandoned, which we were inclined to think.

What now followed was the longest airport hunt in my aviation history. Believe it or not, for a lengthy, tedious 45 minutes we kept up our exploration–and still without result. Our spirits were waning in almost direct proportion to the lowering of the sun and the gas in our tanks. Finally there was no way for us to continue this forlorn pursuit for the elusive aerodrome. Very soon it was going to be dark, and even before that we would be out of gas. Something had to be done–a sobering, fearful thought. There was no more time to waste; we had to arrive at an immediate resolution.

INITIATING EMERGENCY LANDING PROCEDURES

With not much of a choice left, I exchanged my airport quest into one for a suitable place for an emergency landing. A little earlier, I had noticed a grass field for such a purpose, but now I was looking it over carefully. I pointed it out to Klaus and announced at the same time, "I am ready to set the bird in there before the motor conks out."

Klaus requested another chance–one more big circle in the immediate area. Thereupon I flew toward the town, situated only a few miles from the evasive airport, in order to start the search once more from there. While heading that way, Klaus suddenly rejoiced, and called out, "There is the airport!" At this moment I wondered if he were still in his right mind, but quickly I found his statement in the affirmative by double checking. The only reason he saw the grass field on his side of the craft was that there were a number of old German war planes parked there.

If it had not been for these old Junker-52 transports, we would never have found it. Much of the Spanish Air Force consisted of old German war planes, and later the pilots firmly assured us that they were the best in the world. This grass field, without a marked-off strip, looked just like the rest of the countryside and was extremely hard to find, especially since dusk was upon us. After one more quick glance at the field for a windsock and, hopefully, some indicated runway but which couldn't be found, we came in like a sidewinder missile, landing toward the fast-vanishing sun.

As soon as we had landed, Klaus and I spoke simultaneously, "Look at the sun!" and "Look at the gas gauge!" The sun disappearing behind the horizon was already half gone, and the fuel indicators showed absolutely empty tanks.

Our longest flight so far had ended. We had been in the air an interminable three hours and 48 minutes. Until then, the most lengthy flight had been three hours and 14 minutes from Paris to Angoulême. We must really have compressed the gas into the tanks in Rabat! Once more, and in the nick of time, we had made it. Three extremely critical flights in a row lay behind us.

I couldn't help but feel that the Almighty was with us all throughout this endeavor. Time after time we were able to return to the ground safely. Repeatedly, when we came in "On Final" it was another miracle. Many hardened men had become undone or broken apart by a lot less than we had been through so far. So I was thankful for the protection granted.

It was a small wonder that we could not find the airport, for its location on our map was entirely erroneous. Instead of being on the east side of the railroad line as marked, it was on the other side, and in a completely different direction and distance from town. Rather than being a help, the maps were confusing and leading us astray. It almost would have been better to do without them at times, rather than going wrong with false assurances from faulty, misleading aeronautical charts. We continually needed the *compass* I had been talking about earlier.

A warm welcome and comradery at the airport was very comforting and helped us overcome our fluttery condition. Once in a while we could have used a nice experience, especially after we had just been battling so many exigencies, flight after flight, in a seemingly never-ending gamut. Tottering on the brink of disaster had almost become our way of life.

The German planes and the friendly greetings we received everywhere we went in Spain, were a definite result of Spain's past cordial relations with Germany, especially during Hitler's time. Generalissimo Francisco Franco, "El Caudillo," or former leader of Spain since 1939, declared Spain neutral during World War II but clearly favored Germany and Italy. Besides supplying Germany with much-needed mercury and other important minerals, he even sent Spanish "volunteer" forces to fight with the Germans on the Russian front. These sympathies were not without reason. When the Spanish Civil War raged across his country for 32 months from 1936 to 1939, Italy and Germany, sending him military advisers, technicians and aviators, openly supported him as commander of the "Council of National Defense" *(Junta de Defensa Nacional)* at Burgos. When fighting in Morocco with the Spanish Foreign Legion, and a general at 32, he had gained valuable military experience and became Army Chief of Staff in 1934.

France, and Russia particularly, which helped his opponents the Loyalists more than anyone else with military advisers, technicians, planes, ammunition and weapons, assisted the Communists in Spain to gain much power. Communist functionaries and police agents took revenge by committing thousands of political murders. In the beginning of October 1936, however, the Monarchists declared Franco as Chief of the Spanish State. Soon his opposing forces had to move their government seat from Madrid to Valencia, and less than a year later to Barcelona. In early 1939 France and England recognized Franco as the head of the Spanish government. At that time also, the former president of Spain, Manuel Azaña, leading the resisting forces, fled to France, and on March 28, Franco entered Madrid. The Popular Front government was smashed. After this Spanish Civil War, that has been called the opening battle and testing ground of World War II, with many new types of weapons, artillery, tanks and planes receiving their first trials on Spain's battlefields, the land lay desolate and more than one million of its people had died.

Then, for almost 37 years until he expired, Francisco Franco endeavored quickly to bring order, unity and power to Spain through a strong, centralized government. In 1947 Franco was named Chief of State for life, with the right to appoint a successor whenever he retired. Until his end, he maintained a strong anti-Communist policy. He was born in El Ferrol del Caudillo, Galicia, the very northwestern tip of Spain, where we almost found our death over a storm-tossed Atlantic only nine days ago.

Spain's history is very colorful and highly interesting indeed. I was prodded into studying it in particular on account of the exceptionally friendly treatment we received wherever we went. There were old ties of long-lasting friendship we again tasted on our arrival at the Jerez-Haya Airfield at two minutes before seven o'clock that evening.

It was a happy moment that day to retire until *mañana.*

FERIA IN SEVILLE

(Jerez-Haya to Seville)

The next morning, relatively bright and early, we headed back to the airport and left this area, known for its production of the original, true sherry wine. Compared to our other flights, this one was child's play. En route we crossed a large marsh, part of the "Las Marismas" formed by the inland delta and tributaries of the Guadalquivir River, which is the deepest navigable waterway in Spain and flows through Andalusia's olive-growing region. Spain is the world's greatest producer of some of the best olive oil. We enjoyed the exceptionally clear visibility, reaching over 32 miles and more. While arriving over Seville, we marvelled at the many booths and activities at the fairgrounds. Shortly we landed on Sevilla-San Pablo.

While rolling to the ramp, we could see several lines of servicemen standing in formation on the airport with their right hands lifted in a salute to just-arriving honored celebrities, whom all faced.

As soon as we had disembarked, after parking our plane near the beautiful white terminal building with its surrounding palms and orange trees, we were greeted by a most colorful, peppy parade which they had formed by then. The marchers, dressed in official uniforms with a red fillet across their shoulders, red tassels hanging down the side, and golden sashes called "fajas" for belts, were performing drilling maneuvers with ornamental batons. As they marched along, it happened that our craft was standing right in their way, so they had to detour around it. What an ostentation it was to see them pacing ahead with their long, white gloves, decorated uniforms and playing the drums and trumpets.

"I am very honored to see them putting on this fancy parade for us," Klaus said, with an important undertone, and promptly took a lot of pictures of the event so he could brag about it for the rest of his life. Particularly when the column came marching around our plane, Klaus's camera was busily clicking away. Still to this very day, he may be breathing out his treasured secret to some beauty of renown—that he was received with military honors while in Spain!

We both liked to feel important, thinking that this celebration was being put on for us, but unfortunately it proved obvious that some high-ranking government officials were the recipients of that array. Quite a number of fancy limousines arrived on the taxi area and these great personalities in splendid attire were chauffeured away. It was one of those

A lively military parade *(below)* launches our arrival at the fascinating Sevilla-San Pablo airport *(above).* Aromatic odors of blooming orange trees greeted us as soon as we opened the plane doors. The atmosphere seemed to be loaded with pleasant surprises as an Edenic feeling, which overcame us both, indicated.

nice little interludes, adding further piquancy to our trip. Anyway, we included ourselves in the role of honored guests, with the plane, in particular, receiving a special entourage while Klaus was still busy making slides of this scene.

Seville, a Roman center, Visigothic capital, Arab stronghold and royal court, respectively, presents a display of varying styles of architecture, including its tiled patios, fountains, and public gardens, equalled nowhere else in the world. This city, one of the most delightful imaginable and with flowers abounding everywhere, offered us almost 13 hours of unexcelled zest and gusto.

Bullfights and dances with castanets typify Spain to most tourists. Andalusia in this southern portion of the country, has plenty of them.

Much of our time on this second visit was spent at the feria in Seville. What a colorful world which spread her enchantment all over us. During this occasion, many of the rich Sevillians have their own booths set up at the festival grounds. To them it is a must, a part of their prestige, and they don't dare to be missed there. Passing *caballeros* with big *sombreros, chaparajos* (chaps), and tight, buttoned black jackets, and their *señoras* riding behind them sideways in beautiful *faldas* clattering the *castañetas,* added to the glamour. Many *saludos* were exchanged as, thus handsomely attired in elaborate equestrian apparel, they rode their horses down the passageways. We were recognized as *extranjeros.*

There were embellished horse carriages, flagposts and beautifully figured, lamp-studded poles, decorated with garlands and at the same time serving as supports for overhanging wires dotted with colorful light bulbs. Ornamental tapestries, ribbons and flowers were festooned everywhere.

At one time, a stage coach approached on the laterite, drawn by six white horses (three in a team) with heads and necks lined and encircled with the most gorgeous and lush red flowers. The señor, at the same time acting as a coachman, with his flamboyantly dressed wife and daughter on his side, was sitting on the box (outer front seat) of the carriage, holding a varicolored driving whip. The horses were loaded with chimes, representing regular campaniles as they clangorously came ding-donging along. It was a spectacle which caused a stir among the people and kept one spellbound as the fabulous apparition passed.

Such was the fascinating setting when I met the most beautiful girl in all of Spain. Chelo de la Torre was sitting in one of those adjoining festival pavilions with some of her girl friends. Fiery Sevillanas were being danced with much zest. Her attraction was so great that any normal man's eyes would be drawn as by a magnet. I could not resist the temptation to sit down on one of the empty chairs beside her table. She spoke no German and ever so little English, and I at that time spoke almost no Spanish—not nearly enough to converse with such a beauty, and my agonies knew no bounds. What a torture! Finally to find such an Aphrodite, one who likewise was ready and willing to listen to all the lovely words welling up from my heart, and then I had to sit there like a dolt, hardly being able to get one single word across.

The least I could have done under these circumstances would have been to ask her for a dance. This, however, was not possible because of the difficulties with my foot. Every step in one of those fiery Spanish dances would have sent me soaring with extreme pain as if thousands of needles were being driven clear into the marrow of my bone. I didn't dare take this risk and further aggravate my condition.

I could readily see that she eagerly awaited to be asked for a dance; certainly she felt that if we were unable to converse, we could at least communicate that way. It was obvious that she was at a loss to understand why I did not invite her. One after the other melodious dances were played and still we sat there, dumb and like statues. Her eyes repeatedly would flick over to the dance area and right back to me with a longing expression, winking her eyes and her body keeping time to the music. It was plain that she could hardly stand to wait any longer.

I, of course, pretended not to get the message whatsoever, because had I explained to her the reason for not being able to dance, she might have lost all interest in me. Why would a girl in the blossom of her youth be interested in a fellow who was sick at a most inopportune time? She had come there to enjoy life to the fullest during this week of unexcelled gaiety and did not intend to be a wallflower. All of this combined to make my torture nearly unbearable. How I did yearn for a *tête-à-tête*, but such was not my fate.

While I was wondering how much longer she would put up with such an incompetent conversationalist, it looked as though Venus, the Roman goddess of love, intervened and sent along a sympathetic young American from a newly established nearby United States airbase. He asked for permission to sit down on the last remaining chair at this table. First I questioned whether he had come along as a competitor, but, gentle-hearted as he was, he befriended one of the other girls and let me keep my belle. Not only this, but with his good Spanish he also offered to translate for me. That certainly saved the day, and my bubbling over was bearing fruit as I could tell from the smiles and twinkles in Chelo's eyes.

In the city of Don Juan, his spirit had finally gotten hold of me, and I was deeply in love–so much that I almost temporarily forgot the excessive pain in my foot which continued to haunt me. Unfortunately, my visit with this ever-so-enchanting charmer could not last forever. But it brought about a relationship which resulted in extensive correspondence for many years. There were those marvelous postcard-sized pictures I received, full of her alluring appeal. Frequently Chelo also sent wonderful letters and cards of Seville with pleading words to return to Spain to see her soon.

At the time of our meeting in Spain, my private photographer, Klaus, was strangely absent, apparently chasing after some other beauty nearby. That rascal failed to take slides of the prettiest girl splendid Andalusia had to offer. But perhaps it was better that way, because this wolf most probably would have turned out to be an undesired, fierce competitor, particularly since his knowledge of her language exceeded mine. This thought, however, did not trouble me too much, because I was in a position to take quick revenge for such a nasty interference once we were again airborne. With some fast, abrupt acrobatic flying maneuvers, I could bring much distress upon him, resulting in an upheaval of his "innards" similar to the one which brought his romance with the American "knockout" in Lisbon to a quick end.

Following the Holy Week, the Seville Fair is also the time of the Spanish mantillas and bullfights! Leading matadors, who are national heroes, then perform there. During this week, the city was at its glorious best. We did not even have time to watch one of those "corrida de toros." In spite of spending nearly all night at the feria, our 13 hours were slipping by fast.

Around noon the next day, the 19th of April, we were back at the airport and the "in-person" romance with Señorita Chelo de la Torre at the glittering, brilliant fair of showy splendor went into memory and was an element of the past.

SEVILLE TO MÁLAGA

It took us almost 10 days to reach Seville for the first time after we left Ghent, Belgium. This distance amounted to 42.6% of our entire trip. Our return journey from Seville to Ghent via the southern route, 38.2% of

The popular Feria in Seville with all its pomp, color, and pageantry presented that great city at its glorious best during our second visit. Here, in this world-renowned fiesta, spirits are truly as sunny as Andalusia. Arabian horses prancing about with pride, ruffled dresses, passionate flamenco rhythms and the clatter of castanets highlight this celebration. (All pictures on both pages.)

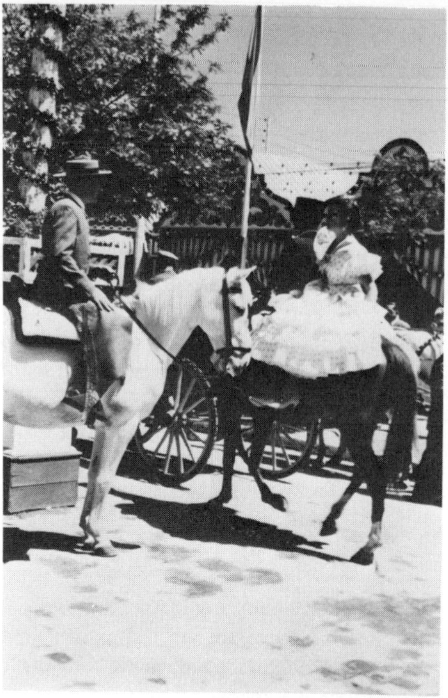

the total and almost as long as the above route, was going to take only a little over three days.

Since Seville lies just at the edge of the main European time zone, one hour later than Greenwich's, we will not include any time difference for our homeward tour. It is interesting to note that Madrid's zone is one hour later than London's. That would make it 1:00 P. M. in Spain's capital when it is only noon in London. This appears contradictory, since Madrid is located almost four degrees west of London and should therefore have an earlier time as the westward-moving sun will have passed London nearly 16 minutes before it reaches Madrid. The sun travels 15 degrees in one hour and that makes four minutes per degree.

So, get ready for a lot of flying, for from now on we are going to be in the air an average of seven hours per day, with still over 21 hours flying time and plenty of incidents ahead. In fact, my log book entries for the 15 days so far ran somewhat more than four pages, while for the last three days alone they amounted to a good five pages, bringing the entries to a total of over nine pages. They are in synopsis style only.

The Seville-Africa portion of our trip figured out to 19.2% of the whole journey and, including this, we travelled thus far a little more than 15 days, or almost 62% of the total distance. *It simply means that from now on we were moving three times faster than we had on the entire trip.* We already had been more than speeding all along, but the marathon which followed required the last of the little strength we had left. With so many emergency calls and being on the go continuously, we indubitably had "had it" by now and were at the end of the line as far as our energy was concerned.

Spain's strange eating times didn't help us along, either. Breakfast usually is served after 9:00 A. M., lunch between 2:00-3:00 P. M. and dinner between 10:00 P. M. and midnight. The abundant use of olive oil in their meals added to the problem. This bad schedule helped to cause upset stomachs for two busy men.

Bien—now, let's go flying again. We are now ready to take off from the Seville-San Pablo Airfield. Our few belongings were quickly dumped into our tail-dragger and off we went around noon. That day's flight was to take us through beautiful Andalusia to Málaga.

Already we had noticed quite a difference between the northern and southern parts of the country. In northern Spain many people were blue-eyed, of fair skin and hair, revealing a Nordic influence. Also the Alpine race of the Caucasoid group is represented in the area. This region—then formed by small Visigoth kingdoms of Aragon, Asturias, Castile, Galicia, León and Navarre—remained Christian during the powerful Moorish invasion from Africa.

Southern Spain, however, revealed a distinctly different flavor. The people were dark-complexioned and of the Mediterranean type. Here, in contrast to the north, with its many deciduous trees, grow mostly lush evergreens. This area was ruled for centuries by the Moors who then had a far more advanced culture than most of feudal Europe. Under their occupation, Spain got more civilized than most other European countries. Granada, which became an independent Arab kingdom in 1238, remained a great center of Moslem learning, wealth, and refinement after all the other Moorish possessions in other parts of Spain had been lost by 1276. Finally its downfall also came in 1492 after Moorish rulers began to quarrel among themselves. Today this region is occupied by the Málaga, Almeria and Granada provinces.

All right, let's wing on to Málaga.

With about one-third of our Seville-Málaga leg already behind us, we then entered the mountains at Moron de la Frontera. In the meantime, we had climbed to 4,000 feet and, without any problems, we were able to clear the range ahead of us. Soon we were crossing Rio Guadalhorce near Alora with Málaga only another 20 miles away. What the Romans first called the "Mare Internum" (or Inland Sea), stretched out before us with promises of further adventures ahead.

The Mediterranean Sea was at one time the greatest water route of the world, and later was given its present name by the Romans which means "middle of the earth." Controlling that sea for about 200 years, they also called it "Mare Nostrum" (or Our Sea). In the ancient world it was the center of life, with numerous glorious cultures growing up along its shores. The Tyrrhenian, Ionian, Adriatic, Aegean and Black seas are all large arms of the Mediterranean, which covers approximately 1,145,100 square miles. It lies between Europe, Asia and Africa. The Strait of Gibraltar, Suez Canal, and the Dardanelles and Bosporus connect it with the Atlantic Ocean, Red and Arabian seas, and the Indian Ocean and the Black Sea. The deepest point, 15,000 feet, is located in the Ionian section. Corsica, Crete, Cyprus, Sardinia, Sicily, and the Balearic Islands are some of the important isles in the "Mare Nostrum." The daring Phoenicians discovered, according to legend, the message "Ne Plus Ultra," meaning "no more beyond," which supposedly was carved into the rocks of Gibraltar. In an effort to gain a foothold for trade in that area, European countries built outposts in the Middle East and Africa. Also, in World War II, a fierce struggle for control of that region developed between the fighting nations.

Spain's hilly shoreline was studded by small, white houses with red-tiled roofs, bordering this pleasantly blue-greenish sea. At some places. that coast was exceptionally rocky. There were also crescent-shaped, sandy beaches, and an occasional lonely fishing boat here and there gave it all an idyllic appearance.

We were touring Spain just at a time when it was hit by bad frosts, droughts causing crop failures and inflation in 1957 and 1958. Certain areas below us seemed particularly arid. Our 93-mile flight took 95 minutes, and early in the afternoon we landed on the Málaga Garcia Morato Airport. It was about five to six miles southwest of town, and we did not

Flying along the idyllic coastline of southern Spain with its inviting beaches and hamlets. The indolent atmosphere and the likeable people make one feel right at home. A far cry from the modern world of intricate involvement.

take the time to visit that center of Spain's sunny Mediterranean Coast with its fine park and harbor. After all, we could see that from the air as we were flying on. After a brief stay in order to fuel up, eat a bite and get the feel of that warm Málaga climate, we were ready to go on.

THE NIGHTINGALE AT GRANADA
(Málaga to Alicante)

We figured we could make one more hop for the day. While taxiing downwind to the other end of the runway, I left the door of the plane open in order to cool down the cabin in the excessive heat. Of course my aeronautical chart had to blow out of the cockpit, and the blast of the propeller carried it all the way back to where we had just come from. We couldn't very well fly without one. Getting tired of all that nonsense, I let the plane stay where it was and cut off the motor.

While Klaus ran back to fetch the map, I lay down on the side of the grass runway, basking in the sun. There was no plane traffic whatsoever, and I thought that it might be all right for a few minutes. It was not okay, however, and soon a car arrived. I was questioned for the reason of the blockade; that was the end of my sunbath. What a pity–no rest again–at the very time when I was able to relax so nicely. At about that time, Klaus returned with the map, and within a few minutes we were airborne.

From then on we continued to follow Spain's Mediterranean coastline all the way into France. First, we enjoyed the view of Málaga with its large bullfighting arena, the harbor with lighthouse and jetty, beautiful buildings, towers, landscaped squares, and adjoining mountains. Being one of the oldest cities in Spain, Málaga is also a renowned winter resort and producer of famed sweet wine.

Many of the homes in the southern part of Spain have flat roofs where people spend the balmy evening hours. Some even live in caves, which are cool in summer and warm in winter, and at times they have electricity and other comforts.

As we continued our eastward flight, we soon saw the Sierra Tejeda and later the Sierra Nevada in the distance to our left. Mt. Mulhacén in the Nevada Range, 11,424 feet high, Spain's highest mountain, and 21 miles off to the north, was an outstanding sight. At about that time, we had the pleasure of starting one of those other fancy 1:1,000,000 World Aeronautical Charts.

As I was unfolding my new flying map I permitted myself to be transported in mind to Granada, the city of fantasy and splendor for a reflective interlude to contemplate life's finer values and beauties. This jewel was located across the Sierra Nevada and directly to the north from where we were flying now.

Also the seat of the identically named province, it was at one time the capital of the Arab dominion and a mecca for its poets and artists. The magnificent Alhambra (Arabic word for "the red"), an ancient Moorish palace and fortress built between 1248 and 1354, stands here and formed their last stronghold against the European Christians. Scholars consider it the finest example of Moorish art on that continent. The chief beauty of the Alhambra lies in the rich decorations covering the inner courts and halls. Plaster moldings interlaced with foliage, and painted with red, blue and gold, overlay the walls and ceilings. Wainscots of green and yellow tile line the lower walls. The floors are marble and the fountains trickle in the delicate courtyards and inner arabesque gardens with lovely trees and flowers. The Court of Lions, with its great fountain is famous and so are the graceful scalloped arches.

The exquisite and pensively melodious songs of the nightingale add to the euphonious charm. She is the queen of the feathered world of singing. So much so, that the finest praise an adoring public could bestow upon the famous coloratura soprano, Jenny Lind, was to call her the "Swedish Nightingale." Her rich, warm voice and remarkable vocal control were unique and of such brilliance that they were reminded of the beautifully sorrowful voice of that greatest artist among songbirds.

This shy singer, mostly at home in deep woods and hedges, is migratory and spends the winters in Africa. From youth on, the offspring surround their father and attentively learn how to polish and improve their melodies and voices. With much perseverance and conscientiousness, they then practice on their own. This elevates them to very special creatures which makes it impossible to confuse them with impostors whose colorful and idle chatter is only an echo of nature. Driven by light and love, their second element is the intuitive premonitory feeling of an inherent artistic talent which keeps them alive with much verve.

The true greatness of an artist lies in the fact that he lifts himself above his gift, does more than he wants to and beyond potentiality, yet still in the realm of its experience feels and frequently conveys something of translunary tendency which cannot be attained.

With much enchantment, the nightingale sings about the transport of love as well as the cares and struggles of life—about its entire sphere of existence. This songster sees nature's ravishing beauties, longingly visualizes the mate it is looking for, and beholds thousands of other attractions of winged life about which normal men have no idea.

She, like us aviators, dwells in upper strata of joys unknown to, or eluding others. Listen to the tuneful dialogue as the male talks to her in his strong, sonorous voice and is answered by her, softly and almost whisperingly. Most likely, he sings about the coziness of the homely life in the nest—the small, poor dwelling. He dreams to be in it, to close his eyes, to be enthralled by its atmosphere. The eggs have opened up, the small ones have come to light and, with unbounded joy, he listens to their first chirps. His presentiments have borne fruit and become living realities. Staying close, he sits on a neighboring branch, seemingly knowing well that his voluminous warble sounds better from that slight distance and will not then disturb the quiet restfulness of the feathered nursery and the tender ears of the new upstarts. From this lofty position he continues to provide melodious support for that lively mystery which develops under the protecting and warming wings of the mother.

You have to hear him in this setting to perceive some of the soaring of a spirit which here again suitably reveals the great hidden God, One Who escapes man's exploration, investigation and research. No matter how much science is laboring, it is only able at times slightly to lift the veil behind which the Almighty stays concealed. "Is it not He," says Linné (Carolus Linnaeus), "Whose shadow I have just discerned?" Moses, after God called to him out of the mountain, saying, ". . . how I bore you on eagles' wings and brought you to Myself" (Exodus 19:4) and ". . . Lo, I come unto thee in a thick cloud . . ." (Exodus 19:9), was warned not to let the people break through to the Lord to gaze lest many of them perish and He break forth against them (Exodus 19:21, 24). Even that great prophet himself could see only His back (Exodus 33:23).

But I put myself into the role of one who closes his eyes and feels the breath of God in the mild, midsummer night which is resounding with the daintily modulated aria of the "Nightingale!"

As, ever so slowly, I was coming out of my meditative mood, I visualized myself still surrounded by the 13 towers of the fabulous Alhambra which rise from a red-brick outer wall that encloses the 35 Edenic acres. From a superb vantage point you can see the Albaicin and also Sacromonte, one of the largest Gypsy cave sections remaining in Europe. With much fire, its inhabitants perform authentic Flamenco dances in cabarets, making up steps according to their mood. Often people form a circle around the artiste and encourage him by singing, clapping, stamping, and shouting in rhythm with the guitar music.

Generalife, the summer palace of the Moorish kings, is surpassed by its magnificent gardens, a maze of countless terraces, grottoes, and pools enlivened by rows of fountains telling us of the love the Moors had for their last medieval foothold in Spain.

If, in addition to this, you stay in one of the great, unusual show places in Spain, like the Alhambra Palace Hotel, built in Moorish style and surrounded by famous gardens, you will have a splendid view of the Sierra Nevada. It all is situated amid Andalusia's lovely mountains and plains, which is known for its sunny Mediterranean climate, fertile farms and production of some of the best fighting bulls in the world.

For quite awhile now I had been engulfed by those thoughts. I was treasuring such moments. They were making life more worthwhile and joyful. In a world drowned by raw commercial materialism, which stamps out anything noble, it is high time that more of us find a renewal of spirit and life by musing about those things which are truly great and uplifting and which carry a breath of eternal value within themselves.

The material gadget I was sitting in had been steadily purring along. New territory was appearing below us. Unfortunately, I had to leave the world of lofty dreams. The plane, the navigation, and other matters needed my attention before we would get entangled by another emergency. But could I truly avoid those situations, even though I was fully alert? Generally not . . .

The Sierra de Gador near Almeria was coming into sight. From there we made a straight shot over the Punta de la Polacra and awhile later we passed the Almazora River. From then on we crossed over the Golfo de Mazarrón and came to the bayside town of Cartagena. Founded by Greeks and cut into a mountain range, it is adjoined by ruined castles on four different hills.

We went to the left of a restricted area surrounding Cartagena and stretching from Cabo Tiñoso to Cabo de Palos. Ever since Cabo de Gata east of Almeria, the coast made a northward bend and then at Cartagena we encountered the next major change in our heading toward that direction.

It would have been the exception to the rule, and too good to be true, to get by on this flight without a hair-raising experience. There was no need for us to have high hopes. About in the middle of the flight, our gas gauge wire in the front tank suddenly dropped all the way. For quite some time it just stayed in that naughty position so that we began to think that our tank had developed a leak, consequently presenting us with fire danger. Klaus uttered, "I guess it is not possible for us ever to make it without agitation!" Finally, and very much to our relief, that crazy wire came up again.

The western edge of the Mar Menor was passed next and then the Segura River. Only 15 miles from Alicante, while flying over the Bahía de Santa Pola, we could see the Moorish-looking town Elche with the largest palm grove in Europe. Then Alicante lay suddenly below us. Now a famous winter resort with lovely beaches, it was founded long ago in the Third Century B. C. by the Romans. The impressive sight here was the vast Moorish Castle of Santa Barbara on a high rocky peak.

We landed around 7:00 P. M. We had just finished the longest flight on our entire journey. It lasted for three hours and 50 minutes, and altogether we had flown five hours and 25 minutes that day.

Here Klaus's attention was attracted by rubber stamps on a revolving stand in the airport management office. Being an apparent collector, he sampled them all and found what he liked exceedingly well. The large, round specimen he selected had a circled and crowned bird with stretched-out wings–possibly an eagle–in the middle field, and the wording "Dirección General De Aviació Civil–Aeropuerto De Alicante" around the edge. As he liked only the particularly fancy types, it met with his visibly happy approval. This one was not being used, but Klaus immediately requested that it also be inserted into his passport for a more distinctive look. In fact, I think he impressed the image on several pages. I, in turn, had the advantage over him to have an imprint not only on my passport, but also in my pilot flight log. Being more sparing because my books were almost full, I used it only once in each.

I was tired and even though I did not look forward to spend another wakeful night, it was good to be lodged once again. We had seen a lot of beautiful Andalusia. All the sights such as the many mountains, rivers, towns, beaches, and the vast Mediterranean, our most steadfast companion for much of the day, in addition to all the piloting, had worn us out.

THE LULL BETWEEN THE STORMS
(Alicante to Barcelona)

We enjoyed the lovely town, but without sleep, I did not know how I possibly could go through another day, even though we were to see much more of Spain's magnificent Mediterranean Coast, including the famous Costa Brava.

At midmorning we took off from the Alicante-La Rabasa Airfield. Sometimes the "Solano," a withering, scorching wind, blows over the coastal plains for two weeks in a row. We were glad that we did not have to battle this east wind. In fact, we had very calm weather. As our plane was pulling up from the field, our eyes took one more sweep over the tranquil Bahía de Alicante. Then, short-cutting across Cape Nao, which protrudes far into the sea, we saw Mount Altana gliding by just to our left. A few minutes later, we were flying over the Golfo de Valencia.

Isla de Ibiza, the closest of the three main Balearic Islands (with Mallorca and Menorca being the other two), is only 53 miles to the east from Cabo de la Nao. Too bad we did not have time to do some island hopping. All together, there are sixteen in the Balearic group. They are an extension of the steep Sierra Nevada range, that after running along the southern Mediterranean Coast extend below sea level and then rise again further east to form this archipelago.

It is a quiet, timeless place, greatly favored by European tourists. Varied recreation, gorgeous scenery, lovely beaches, ideal year-round climate, and comparatively low prices are some of their attractions. At any rate, we were too shot to enjoy them; but, on the other hand, they might have been just the most suitable spot for our overtired bodies to find some much-needed rest.

Then we approached the Júcar River some 24 miles south of Valencia. For some time, and with apprehension, we noticed a layer of clouds and had to start climbing above them. Soon our Aeronca flew along at 4,000-foot altitude, with the overcast well below us. Klaus and I became somewhat worried. Were the clouds going to quit later on, or would they increase? In the absence of a radio, there was no way for us to find out. Hoping for the best, and that the clouds might dissipate, enabling us to land at our destination, I continued.

"Please don't take any chances at this late stage of the game! Being this far down the line, I want to make it home now. I have too many beautiful slides to see them dashed to pieces and too many memories to treasure. I am in a hurry to get home, but not that much in a hurry to end up six feet below the ground! So, be sure that whatever you do is safe."

"Thanks for your kind words of admonishment, Klaus! I know that without them it would be literally impossible to conduct a safe journey. It's always easy to give good advice as long as the other fellow does the job. How about you flying the plane from now on and getting us back? You've been at it for so long with me, don't you know how to fly this bird yet?" I replied.

"No, I couldn't do that. I don't have a pilot's license!"

"Oh, really? You never seemed to be that concerned about paperwork otherwise."

"But now I am very much so. Besides, you've been doing a pretty good–I mean a very good job so far, why not stick with it to the end?"

"Okay, thanks. Why then all that concern, Klaus?" I chuckled.

Very saddening was the fact that we missed a view over beautiful, ancient Valencia, with its many monuments and intriguing buildings of Moorish influence. Fig, pomegranate, palm, almond and olive trees, and hundreds of streams everywhere crossing the rich, surrounding plain, called "Huerta de Valencia," which has Spain's choicest orange and lemon groves, also would have attracted our attention. Flowers grow all over in profusion, and the rich land blessed by a dry, very mild climate, produces several crops each season. The province "Valencia," once an independent Moorish kingdom, is under the almost continuous spell of Spring. Its countryside, like a colorful garden, the sweet scent of orange blossoms, and its gay, costumed fiestas draw the tourists. We did not see much this day of the clear sky for which Valencia is known.

It was rather warm in our cockpit. Flying above the clouds, we were bathed by the sun. I was thirsty. It always seems to be a problem to have enough liquid in the plane to quench one's thirst.

So I suggested to Klaus, "They have some mighty fine oranges growing down there. How about taking a dive through the clouds and sipping some sweet, refreshing orange juice?"

"I like orange juice, but I don't like the dive through the clouds," Klaus grumbled. "It certainly would be nice to have a refreshing drink in a hammock below a tree and let the balmy breeze cool one off while relaxing."

"You won't make any money that way," I teased him, realizing that he was rushing me relentlessly to get back to his business in Hamburg. He was in a hurry-scurry to make more pelf, at the same time endangering our trip needlessly.

While our minds were still lingering with this ravishing Mediterranean garden city amongst canaled rice fields, entranced by bullfights, the unique Battle of the Flowers, and its colorful traditional feasts, our plane had continued to clip through the air and was then somewhere between Tortosa and Cabo de Baña or Cabo de Tortosa with the Golfo de San Jorge ahead of us. Still the expanse below was covered by clouds. Were they going to clear out before we would run our tanks dry? According to our last computation, we had to be over charming Tarragona. The Romans regarded that city as one of the most splendid in existence, and many of their relics testify to this day about its previous grandeur.

Finally, finally, it cleared up slowly. By far the most of Spain's 898 Mediterranean coastline miles lay behind us, including fertile, watered areas which have few crop failures in the Valencia and Murcia provinces. Rice, cotton, onions, tomatoes, beans, and sweet peppers also grow there.

¡Olé! Here we were, coming in for a landing on the Barcelona-Muntadas Airfield. We almost touched down with the wind. It seemed like those Spanish people had a talent for putting the windsocks where they were hard to find. At last we located it, and had a very difficult time alighting in the extremely squally weather. Lately there had been some shifting wind conditions.

Our third longest flight had ended. After being in the air for three hours and 35 minutes, we arrived in the early afternoon.

This city brought back to remembrance one of the greatest seamen and navigators of all time, "Colombo," or Columbus. Self-made and self-educated, he was possessed by the idea of reaching the East by sailing west. Knowing less than a modern sailor in "boot training" about celestial navigation, and with a good compass being the only reliable instrument on board, he cruised by dead reckoning.

When he discovered Cuba, he thought the fleet had arrived at China. As this illustrious adventurer sent his men into the interior in the hope of finding Peking so they could present the Emperor of China with a letter from Ferdinand and Isabella, they found cigar-smoking natives instead. Until then tobacco had been unknown to the Europeans.

When he returned to Barcelona from this, his first voyage across the Atlantic, he was presented by King Ferdinand and Queen Isabella, amid much fanfare and spectacular display, with the titles "Admiral of the Ocean Sea" and "Viceroy of the Indies." Also, the first American Indian was baptized at this occasion.

Christopher Columbus' performances by far exceeded his promises, and no explorer had ever received the extensive royal commitments he had. A spirit of new hope, the attainment of new knowledge and resultant further explorations were spearheaded by his discoveries at the very time when Europe lay under a spell of melancholy.

A replica of Columbus' Santa María, in which he sailed on his first journey toward the Americas, was displayed in the harbor of Barcelona. This most cosmopolitan city in Spain, founded in the Second Century, B. C., is one of the country's largest seaports on the Mediterranean. Many of the interesting general sights mentioned for the other towns are also found here. Pueblo Español is worth pointing out because each building there represents the architecture of a different province.

The lore of southern Spain was intriguing. We thoroughly enjoyed this enriching cultural experience. How tranquilizing, good and much needed it was at that time—*the lull between the storms.*

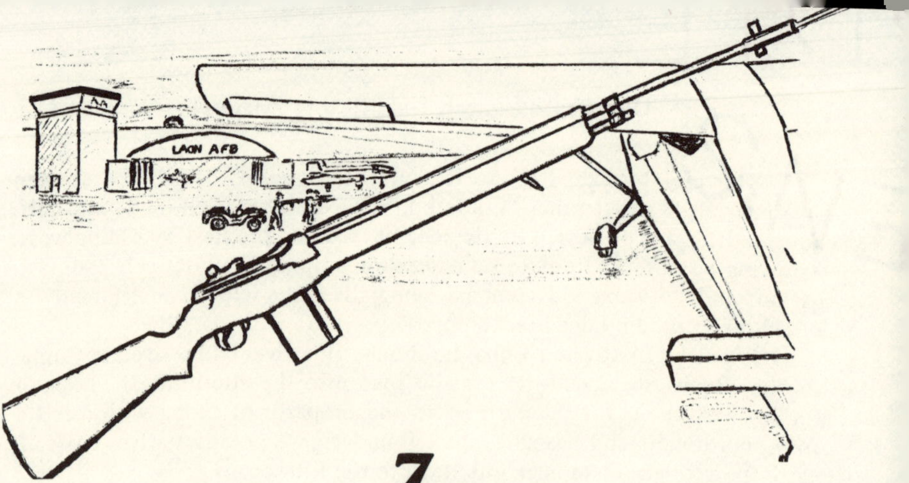

7

An Apparition Leads to a Hostile Encounter

(Barcelona, Spain to Montpellier, France)

After a short stopover to refuel both us and the plane, we again took to the sky. The airport was about eight miles south-southwest of the city, and we were doing our sightseeing in the grandest style by far and the fastest way possible. From the air we saw in minutes what other tourists spend days to see. Our flight continued northeastward along the mountainous Spanish shoreline. Except for the northwest, its coast has few natural harbors. A number of those small, old villages, with clusters of little houses and narrow streets winding through them, passed below us. Since the normal office hours were from 10:00 A. M. to 2:00 P. M. and from 6:00 P. M. to 9:00 P. M., we could usually see a great amount of outside activity when flying over cities in the afternoon.

At Blanes, about 40 miles northeast of Barcelona, we intercepted the famous Costa Brava, which stretches clear to the French boundary line. The particularly beautiful portion between Tossa de Mar and San Feliu de Guixols encompasses 355 curves over 14 miles by car and made flying a "breeze." With our mode of travel, we could take time to enjoy the scenery without worrying about leaving the road at one of those everlasting bends. Many small inns on that charming, unspoiled and incomparable spread of jagged coastline offer supreme comfort, food, and a type of service which you do not find at the French or Italian Riviera, for example. How much we would have liked to spend a few days, at least, in this lovely environment!

About 12 miles beyond Blanes, we ran out of our aeronautical map. The next 45 miles were without any chart coverage whatsoever.

PASSING THE DREADED PYRENEES

Off to our left loomed the gigantic natural boundary line between Spain and France, the Pyrenees, with Andorra, the fifth smallest country in the world, nestled in them. Ranking only second to San Marino in age as an independent republic, its magnificent alpine scenery and fine hotels were enticing us across the 80 air miles we then were from there. The sole country with fewer people is Vatican City. This Papal State, Monaco, Liechtenstein and San Marino comprise the only nations in the world smaller than Andorra.

We were travelling with mixed feelings, even though the absence of an aeronautical chart did not disturb us too much for the time being, as we could easily follow the coastline. Also, we hoped no restricted areas would be in our path, which seemed unlikely because this region was a tourist place.

But while we enjoyed the wild, strikingly dramatic coast below us, we were at the same time wondering what the dreaded Pyrenees were holding out for us in terms of wind. Would some of the prophecies of our pilot friends come to pass, or would we be favored with gentle breezes as was the case when we passed north of them from France into Spain some 13 days earlier? Already gusty blasts had raised warning flags in our minds as to the safety of passing this colossal mountain chain that day.

By then we were approaching the Gulf of Rosas on our last stretch through Catalonia's year-round playground with its rich, walled cities, castles of grandeur and partly ruined fortresses. Our new map coverage started at a latitude of 42° north, just about two miles south of where the river Ter enters the sea.

We crossed over Cape Creus, the north boundary of the lovely Gulf of Rosas, which formed a crescent-shaped coastal basin. Immediately to our northwest was a giant prohibited area which, jutting out into the ocean, ran along the French-Spanish boundary line for over 70 miles. We didn't mind staying out over the ocean a number of miles to avoid that restricted territory, for in this way some distance was obtained from at least the worst winds near the Pyrenees.

"Better tighten your seat belt," I cautioned Klaus as an added safety measure. "You never know what is ahead, we may as well be prepared."

I followed suit immediately. To be jammed suddenly against the ceiling with your head is not a pleasant experience and often leaves one with long-lasting neck injuries. It is hard to fly the plane under those circumstances.

Strangely, but happily, we for a change hit a good day in this area. When flying toward this forbidding range, we had tailwinds which helped us to gain instead of losing altitude. It was not very windy southeast of that mountain chain.

Well, the great moment came, and we were leaving the chatoyant land of the once-mighty Spanish Armada—this former "Mistress of the World." From Palafrugell, Spain to Lake Bages south of Narbonne we flew almost generally on a north course. The Pyrenees were being passed, and while flying away from them northward, we encountered headwinds. They had changed in the meantime. This again gave us lift rather than downward pull and also presented us with smoother wind conditions.

With relative ease we managed that other dreaded portion of our journey. It seemed odd, but the areas we were warned against, and which appeared loaded with inherent dangers, treated us rather mildly, while nearly all other territories we did not fear, got the best of us.

Isn't that just like life? How many times the things you have feared the most have never come to pass, while things you never even dreamed of really harassed and tormented you! This teaches us not to worry, especially since most of it is being done about the wrong things. At the same time, we will be happier and healthier for it.

Well indeed did the great Nazarene utter these profound words, "But seek ye first the kingdom of God, and his righteousness; and all these things shall be added unto you. Take therefore no thought for the morrow: for the morrow shall take thought for the things of itself. Sufficient unto the day is the evil thereof" (Matt. 6:33-34).

Now we followed a relatively straight stretch of coastline with many sand dunes, river inlets, lakes, bays, and a few little towns scattered here and there. After a while, our direction changed again to the northeast as we kept curving around the Gulf of Lions. Soon we passed the only significant port in this region, the man-made harbor of Sète, and two more big lagoons to our left. Exactly three hours after we left Barcelona, Spain, we pulled into the Montpellier Fresjorgues Airfield five miles southeast of Montpellier, the capital of the Mediterranean Province of Languedoc.

On our combined flights for the day from Alicante, Spain, the wind had shifted three times. We had flown an unexcelled six hours and 47 minutes. There had been a few flights in the five-hour range, but nothing like this, and it was to remain unsurpassed for the rest of our trip. Even the next day, with only 17 minutes less, we would come mighty close to it. Can you believe what I was like, when I fell into bed that night?

The next morning we were sorry that we did not have time to do some sightseeing, for there were museums and beautiful gardens in this town; also King's Garden, founded by Henry IV, the oldest botanical garden in France, and the famous university situated in the old fortified monastery.

LEAVING THE MARE NOSTRUM
(Montpellier to Chalon-Sur-Saône)

After another sleepless night for me, we were back at the Montpellier Fresjorgues Aerodrome. This would be the second longest flying day on our entire trip. Also, it was going to be loaded with more calamities than any other on our journey. It seemed like we were leaving a relatively quiet, peaceful Mediterranean environment, a region that treated us in a rather exceptionally friendly manner, for an ordeal which would make a "badaud" faint. Apparently we were presented with the "Grande Finale." *Alors!*

By midmorning we were winging out of the Montpellier Fresjorgues Airfield, and with this, away from the Golfe du Lion. The Languedoc, Lyonnais, Burgundy, Champagne, Ile-De-France, Picardy, and Artois provinces were yet ahead of us. They would be travelled over next on our flight home.

Flying first between Nîmes with its vast, ancient arena and baths, and Arles with its giant, aged amphitheater and pagan burial grounds, we were entering a large treasure house of old Roman city remnants. Numberless antiquities are spread throughout this region between Marseille and Lyon. The landscape is adorned by such places as historical Avignon, Orange, and Valence. Fortified towns, pictorial resorts and hilltop castles are scattered everywhere.

What a sight! This gorgeous hilltop castle shows Europe at its foremost splendor.

Looking back once more, we said good-bye to the Mediterranean Sea whose guests we had been for so long and which had afforded us with one of the most pleasant flying experiences anywhere on our trip. We also gave a farewell to the Rhône delta with its large swamp areas, Lakes Scamandre, Vaccares, and Berre, and the many lagoons bordering the sea glistening in the sun behind us. We were rapidly heading north over the charming Rhône River with its many small and larger islands and deep valley bordered by the Cévennes to the west and Alps (Maritime, Cottian, and Graian Alps) to the east.

"Some of our flights along the southern coasts of Spain and France actually have been the only halfway decent flights we have been having on this trip. True, there were problems, but nothing to be compared to the rest of the journey. Too bad that we didn't spend more time in that beautiful area," Klaus suddenly said in retrospect and with apparent prognostication.

"Too late now, why didn't you say something along this line sooner?" I frowned. Somehow I couldn't help but get a sneaky suspicion that it was fear all along which prompted him to rush me. Apparently he had only used his business as an excuse. At this time I felt like opening the door and dumping him for such selfish behavior. He had been letting fear get into our way and mess up a "once-in-a-lifetime" trip for both of us. As an added comfort more perilous ventures were ahead.

It seems odd that we did not continue our journey to the Riviera, which runs from Hyères, France to La Spezia, Italy, and includes the Côte D'Azur (meaning "azure coast") in eastern France, with its many steep cliffs, sandy beaches, and small harbors. There the Alps keep cold north and east winds away, and mostly balmy Mediterranean breezes soothe the area. An ancient Roman highway preceded today's roads along that shoreline bordering a deep blue sea. This coastal region is studded with orange trees, palm groves and brilliant tropical flowered gardens. Even pomegranates, bananas and dates are raised there.

Our present position was only 88 airline miles away from that world-famous territory. We were too worn out to add further miles to our trip, and that overcrowded place, with visitors coming from everywhere, did not interest us much anyway. We had been there many times before and knew it well. Klaus and I just saw a different part of the Mediterranean Coastline and, to us, much more beautiful without those throngs of people and the many tourist traps and inflated prices.

I still remembered the time when I even was charged for the fork, knife, spoon, plate and napkin, in addition to the already high price for the meal, consisting of cooked, wizened macaroni and a few slices of raw, only partially ripe tomato. They called it a "user fee," as they were so gracious to let us eat the already outrageously expensive meal they served, with those utensils. Maybe we should have fallen to with our hands more cheaply, but this was not allowed, being against good manners. I wondered whether we next would be charged for the air we were breathing!

A long time ago I learned that the best places to avoid are the highly advertised tourist areas. By the time you get there, you are disappointed from the very start, for they usually do not measure up to the things you have read or heard. Your neighbor who visited them last won't tell you the truth because he wants you to be jealous of him for having been at such a fancy resort. He figures that if you knew the score, you would just smile at the sucker he had been.

Also, it is hard truly to enjoy any beauties of nature—if there are any left—when everything is crowded with screaming, carousing people from everywhere who suddenly have been thrown out of their natural element and now, out of gear, do not know what to do with themselves. In addition to this, the natives are usually unfriendly in such regions because they have grown tired of those species, and since their only interest is to get that other buck from travellers, the prices are grossly overinflated.

But go to localities you know little or nothing about, and you will find friendly folks, low prices and scenery in a tranquil environment which will leave you spellbound. I have experienced this various times in my travels all over the world.

Who, for instance, heard much about the spots we had seen on this wild escapade? With few exceptions, like dashing into some famed tourist haven and running into people like the "Little One," we were treated with utmost hospitality and amiability. You can throw a lot of money to the wind, come home tired, nervous and broke, or spend little money and really have a genuine "ball." If, in addition, one knows how to make himself well liked by the natives, by trying to understand their languages and customs and appreciating them rather than wanting everything his way then he will reap many extra benefits and also be a better ambassador for his own country. Let's not be ugly Americans, or whatever, but instead win friends with genuineness and understanding cordiality. If you want things the way they are at home, then it is better to stay there. When travelling, a person should be interested in getting acquainted with different customs, landscapes and races. This is the beauty of variety.

While we reflected about those things, our plane had passed the large Durance River which, coming from the Alps to the east, joined the Rhône just south of Avignon, seat of the Popes from 1309 to 1377. Also behind us lay Orange, whose Roman Amphitheater, built in the First Century, A. D., is the most perfect example surviving from the Mediterranean culture, and accommodates 10,000 spectators in performances still being given in the summertime, and also Valence, with its Romanesque Cathedral of St. Apollinaire. Lyon, a capital of gastronomy and the world's silk industry, was coming up next.

Less than 100 miles to our right, one of Europe's highest peaks lifted to the majestic height of 15,781 feet near Italy. About 60 miles to our southeast, near Grenoble, was the deepest known cave in the world—the 2,485-foot Gouffre Berger.

As we passed Lyon, we enjoyed the view over the Fourvière, the center of the city in Roman times, the lately excavated Roman Theater, the Basilica of Notre Dame de Fourvière, a place of pilgrimage, and the Place Bellecour, with beautiful Louis XVI façades surrounded by flower beds and fountains. We had travelled more than two-thirds of the way to our next fateful destination.

So far we had been cruising along rather comfortably in calm weather. The flight through the beautiful Rhône Valley was pleasantly reposeful—the lull before the storm, so to speak. At Lyon we left it. All the way from the Mediterranean we had followed this river, which starts in the Rhône glacier in Switzerland and flows through Lake Geneva on its way to France. After dumping glacial clay there, it turns clear blue when resuming its course. Then we continued along the Saône River, which is connected by canals with the Moselle, Marne, Yonne and Loire rivers.

We landed at Chalon-sur-Saône Champforgeuil, without a map, early in the afternoon. The very peaceful flight above the serene valley of the Rhône at an altitude of 4,000 feet had lasted almost 3½ hours. We spent only 1½ hours at the airport of this bustling Burgundy town with its centuries-old Cathedral of St. Vincent.

But now hold on—the next flight really tested my operational control of the plane. About 20 miles north of Lyon we were left without a chart. This represented a break of coverage for about 138 miles, as each chart extends over two degrees in latitude.[1]

It was a very unpleasant situation, as we did not know whether we might run into prohibited or restricted areas. Also, it made landings a risk, as we had no aeronautical information on the airports. Without being able to navigate from a map, it was, of course, hard for us to find our way. Our problem along this line must have resulted from the unavailability of that particular chart. We had found ourselves in this situation before, but it was only over a short, easily navigable stretch. Furthermore, what would we do if we ran into bad weather? How could we find the closest alternate airport—or any aerodrome, for that matter?

"GRANDE FINALE"

(Chalon-sur-Saône [Champforgeuil] to Couvrons)

It was midafternoon when we took wing for a destination as far north as we could possibly get. We were presently less than halfway through the area for which we lacked any aeronautical coverage whatsoever.

[1]The distance between two parallels, one degree apart, is about 69 statute (land) miles. Since the earth is not a perfect sphere, the length of one degree latitude varies from 68.7 statute miles near the equator to 69.4 close to the poles.

Some road map apparently had to do for that stretch, and we thought that our next stop would be Châlons-sur-Marne, slightly south of the 49° latitude, almost due east of Paris. It did not work out that way, however. Everything on this trip was going to be different from our plans.

The trouble began from the very start of this flight. Were we, after all the things behind us, still going to suffer shipwreck so close to the end of our journey? Was all the fighting for a safe homecoming and the preservation of our lives going to be in vain? Even today, it sends chills up and down my spine, when I think of how close we came to a crack up.

Fences Race Toward Us

Our tanks had been filled completely. We wanted to get as far as we possibly could before darkness set in. As we initiated our take-off roll on the short, hilly grass field, the many molehills and the great heat of the day didn't help much, either. Again and again, the plane took a jump and promptly settled back on the poor, calamitous runway. Another bound and another sinking onto the disastrously bumpy landing strip. On this uneven, grassy terrain, the aircraft was just not able to develop any speed, and loaded as we were, we would descend through the thin, hot air after every leap like a punctured kite. Already the fences, enclosing the airport, came racing forebodingly toward us. Obviously we could not afford many more gambades, if any, or we would sit in a ditch after smashing through the fence, possibly catching fire. Each successive fruitless hop of the plane brought a sickening, sinking feeling to our hearts. Was this the end?

There, one more vault, and the exhausted little bird, scarcely hanging in the air, barely cleared the fence, tragically ready to drop down for the last time. I think our prayers that day carried us through, defying the diluted, thin, hot air; the rough, impossible aerodrome; the gross weight of the plane and the insufficient length of the runway. It requires a much longer take-off roll to clear a grass field than a paved runway, let alone the molehills and all the other limitations we had. In fact, long grass, sand, mud, or snow can easily double the distance.

Air Battle

Well, after all, we were airborne, and no sooner through with the ground bumpiness than the air battle started. Even though the mountains had been tapering, it was rather choppy. The visibility continued to decline. This, in combination with a dull uniformity of the landscape and the absence of an aeronautical chart, really made navigation everything but a lullaby. As if this were not enough, immediately after our departure we noticed a rapid increase of the oil temperature to an unheard of 178° Fahrenheit. This excessive degree of heat had been unsurpassed on our entire trip, even in the African calefaction. In addition to this, the oil pressure sank to 30 kg/cm^2. The combination of all of that was quite a humdinger.

"I guess we have had it too good lately. Everything has to cave in at once," gasped Klaus.

I was too busy to answer. The situation was serious and needed my full attention.

I was ready to turn around, but how we hated to go back to that disastrous strip. As I levelled out and sincerely entertained the thought of a wing over under these stultifying conditions, the gauges all went back to normal again. The strenuous take-off roll on that bad field with the resultant laborious climb out in such heat and the lower speed of the plane during this time; apparently had caused the difficulty. Also, the load had a lot to do with it, and we evidently added too much oil to the engine.

If you think that was really something, then listen to this!

Eighty minutes after our ill-boding start, crossing the 48° parallel, we found ourselves under aeronautical map coverage again. About 2½ hours of flying without a proper chart ended. We had quite a time finding our location. In fact, I sincerely do not know to this day whether Klaus ever knew our position. He thought he did, but what soon transpired proved otherwise. Once you are lost over a monotonous countryside, it is rather difficult to reorient yourself, especially under declining weather conditions and other odds.

Lost

Our present outdated map was scaled 1:500,000. The navigational line we had pencilled on it, leading to the Ecury-sur-Coole Airport about five miles south of Châlons-sur-Marne, was superseded by another, this time in red, and about 14 miles to the west of the former. The red line gave a slightly different heading from the black one. By then, it seemed that we were really vagabonding around. Maybe, in the mad dash to get home fast, we had decided to make this slight course alteration in order to reach a destination quite a bit further north from the one we had planned. Heaven knows. My memory leaves me at this point, but not in what followed, for this I shall remember with crystal clarity the rest of my life. It made too great an impression.

What we were heading for then is still a mystery. The true course went between three civil aerodromes—Athies Field, about 4½ miles east of it, another rumored airport drawn in by pencil between our line and Athies, and yet another one about 2½ miles west of our plotted course and a little farther to the north. All of them were near Laon.

In a daze, and getting wing-weary, we were cruising over the Province of Champagne. All looked about the same, except Klaus who was really sweating by now. There were rivers, patches of trees, towns and villages, railroad tracks, small hills, and more rivers. Weaving through the countryside like veins through a body, they gave it the much-needed lifeline of moisture and humidity, bringing refreshment. It all looked so neat, but it was not that way in our cockpit. There was utter confusion and timorous feelings were running rampant. Some time ago we crossed the much-remembered Seine which had saved our lives at the outset of our journey. Were we going to stay in trouble clear to the very end—throughout the last leg of our trip? We hoped not! Hopes and realities do not always run parallel, however.

We assumed that Troyes had passed, and kept feeling our way like a man in the dark. A little later we felt that somewhere in the haze was the meandering Marne and the City of Reims which sustained daily bombardment for almost four years during World War I and where, on May 7, 1945, the Germans signed their surrender.

At this point we likewise were about ready to sign our surrender.

In its beautiful Cathedral of Notre Dame, almost all the French kings were crowned. It is one of the most magnificent Gothic structures. Reims also has France's most important wool market and leads in the manufacture of champagne.

Now hold on some more. To make a long story short, we will get right into the grotesque middle of it. If what I am writing now seems to you characterized by ludicrous or incongruous distortions, I don't blame you. Let me assure you that every word of it is true and factual. Here we go.

Under the Clash of Machine Guns

Somehow we had managed to make it to what our map showed as the Couvrons Airport about 20 miles south-southeast of St. Quentin. Fatigued by prolonged difficult, hazardous flying, I was ready to end the day as I anxiously looked forward to landing. But what we saw when we approached the airfield staggered our imagination. Did we see a phantom? Did our overtired, overtaxed minds play havoc with us by producing an illusory mental image before our very eyes? Were we having visions? Could it be real? After wiping our eyes as if under a veil, we still had the same apparition.

A giant United States Air Force base with miles of runways came in sight. Modern structures and building complexes everywhere enveloped the countryside. This was what our map showed as a civil aerodrome—one of the consequences of being able to obtain only grossly outdated aeronautical charts. What a wingding!

Certainly we couldn't land there; that field we knew was going to be taboo for us. When I expressed this feeling to Klaus and considered going on to look for another field, I met with immediate mutiny on board. "Go down," the exhausted fellow traveller gasped—"It is another emergency landing!" Our fuel was getting *very low,* darkness drew close, and I realized that this was exactly what I had to do.

Trimming the plane for the landing configuration, I entered the approach pattern. "Watch out for red signal flares," I hollered to Klaus, but to him it didn't seem to make much difference one way or the other, as long as we landed. That was all he was interested in at this crucial point.

What came next might sound like an "Aesopian fable." As I approached the colossal runway of this mammoth air base, I felt like a mosquito lighting upon an elephant. No red rockets were fired. No signal flares were sent off–in fact, no lights whatsoever were received. God bless that kind tower operator who, willingly or unwillingly, shed his grace upon us on the evening of that forlorn and cataclysmic day.

Being in a hurry to get down before they might flash red lights at us, I landed fairly early on the endless runway. Our closest taxiing exit seemed to be miles away, and it took our wee tail-dragger forever to roll, roll, and roll–all the while powerful jets had to be kept in the air, unable to land because of our forming such a formidable obstruction.

Finally we could turn off, and slowly–ever so slowly–cautiously and apprehensively we approached the apron and parked our plane. We thought the worst was over, but the "encore" was yet to come!

As soon as our craft had "screeched" to a halt, three automobiles speedily arrived on the scene. Heavily armed white and colored military men came rushing out with a clash and their machine guns already trained on us. The showdown had commenced.

Even though we didn't feel like it at that time, the whole situation was laughable because of the absurdity and ridiculousness involved. We definitely had not come to take over or shoot up the base. Nevertheless, it was obvious that we were out of place and not very welcome. After a day like this, a better reception than that on our arrival had been hoped for. Here we were, worn, torn and dead tired, and surrounded by antagonism and hostility. Barely had the two of us survived the day, and then found ourselves in these incompatible circumstances. What a deal! One could understand them–after all, they had their orders. But could they, or at least their commander, sympathize with us? We had fought for weeks, every day had been another battle, and all we wanted was peace, harmony and some smiling, friendly faces.

Immediately after opening the doors of our plane, we sat with raised hands in the face of those cold, threatening steel barrels. Exiting the same way, still confronting the menacing battery of automatics with uplifted hands, we tried to make it perfectly clear that we came with peaceful intent.

At once the interrogation started. They wanted to know why we had landed there, where we came from, where we were going, who we were, and so on. All the while, Klaus and I trusted they would perceive eventually that we were the most peace-loving people on earth, just thankful that such a nice, plush landing pad had been provided for us.

In the meantime, the commander had arrived and was being briefed about the latest developments after his subordinates saluted him and stood at attention. With a smile, one of his armed men told him, "This *thing* was landing here!" I guess that must have been obvious to the commander. We had not materialized as spooks to startle them, nor did we drive into the base, but possessed real wings on our flying machine and could aviate indeed.

At a later time we learned, this was the first time a civilian aircraft had landed in the history of that air base. That fact, and particularly the tininess of our bird, appeared to them illogical and inconsistent. In their eyes, we were a whimsical, bizarre visitor—or like one from Mars!

We had landed at the Headquarters of the 38th Air Base Group (USAFE) of the United States Air Force, APO 17, USAF.

At the Nerve Center of An International Warning System

Next, they hauled us off to the tower. There, at the air traffic control station room, we marvelled over the impressive array of what appeared to be small rectangular boxes about 7" x 3½" in size which, in great number, lined the walls. In the middle of each of them was a button and below it were the names of nerve centers around the world. These panelled walls apparently served as part of a global warning system. If something should go sour anywhere, a confluence of air power and related military forces could be set into motion by the depressing of some of those buttons at this strategic global Air Force center.

We felt quite honored to be taken to such an interesting place. Soon, though, we found out that there was a reason why they took us there. The commander asked the air traffic controllers why they didn't signal us not to land, upon which they said, "WE DIDN'T SEE THEM!" Apparently we were too small for them to notice. They had been used to the big, powerful jets which kept them briefed on their position via radio.

No one had looked for that lonely little bird which suddenly had touched down at the beginning of the gigantic runway. To them it had come out of nowhere that hazy evening. Possibly God veiled their eyes, for our heavenly Father knew that we were at the end of our rope.

While the questioning was proceeding in the tower room, Klaus, like a buffoon, with his mischievous humor at the wrong time, said, "It looked so comfortable and we came down." He meant, it was such a nice runway, so we landed. Instantly I sharply elbowed him, hoping the air force personnel would not see it. With nearly closed lips and clenched teeth, I hissed at him, "Shut up!" I didn't want or need any more trouble for the day than we already had and still faced. Having quite a sense for jocularity myself, I couldn't enjoy it at that moment. They were planning to send us off again, and I was longing for a way out of this predicament.

First, though, we were charged the equivalent of $3.00 in landing fees. To this day I have two copies of the receipt from this air base, which reads as follows:

HEADQUARTERS
38TH AIR BASE GROUP (USAFE)
UNITED STATES AIR FORCE
APO 17, USAF

22 April 1958

Received from Hans Jurgen Schneider, Passport No. 1612/52 the following: Landing Fees 1260 Francs (Maroc) and Parking Fee 420 Francs (French).

ROBERT E FRITTS
Major, USAF
Base Operations Officer

It was rather expensive for us. We had never paid that much for landing such a small plane. After this, we were ordered to leave. It would have been suicidal. The sun just disappeared below the horizon and it was impossible for us to go on to another field. We were at our wits' end; it was simply too much. At this awful moment I had to find a way out. A keen plan was conceived and forthwith executed.

"Contact!"

I climbed into the craft after I informed Klaus (in German) of my intentions, and shouted, "Contact!", upon which he *bravely tried* to start it by pulling through the propeller. We did not have an electric starter and had to handcrank the plane. While pretending to start the motor, I merely left the contact switches in the "off" position and it, of course, would not start. Once again, I enterprisingly yelled out, "Contact!", and again Klaus *courageously* turned over the propeller.

One of those smart alecks then looked through the open door, but as if bracing myself against the instrument panel, I held my hand mostly over the area which was occupied by the ignition switches. Of course, again the motor did not catch. "When the engine is warm, we have starting problems," I told the officer, and his men standing around thought it was funny.

By this time the sun was gone, so I mentioned to him that it was illegal for us to fly on then, and without lights on the plane we could not do so anyhow. Also, the Belgian validation issued on my German pilot license was not good for night flying. Lastly, the commander gave us—or was literally forced into giving us—permission to let the bird roost there for the night.

Then everybody turned friendly and offered to haul us in their bus to the next town so we could find accommodations for the night. Gladly we accepted and, amongst a bunch of servicemen, we rode to town. They offered to pick us up in the morning on their way back, and again we agreed joyfully.

Our last horrifying, lengthy flight had a dramatic ending. Altogether we had been in the air that day 6½ hours, and survived a lot of bouncing and searching around with much trepidation and consternation. Our second longest volational day of the entire journey had ended and we rolled into bed like logs.

SURROUNDED BY JET FIGHTERS

(Couvrons to Niergnies [Cambrai])

Bright and early the next morning, the 22nd of April, we were back at the airport. What was this day going to bring? It certainly had a sensational beginning. When we arrived at the American military field, all kinds of people galore were milling around us, almost like ants in an anthill. A photographer took many pictures of us in the tower and at the plane. We had to pose for him in front of our craft, seated inside looking out of the open doors, and what have you. There was a journalist or stenographer who wrote down our entire travel story, which Klaus eagerly passed on.

I was not too happy about it. Making preparations to immigrate to the United States, I feared that all this ado would cause me trouble along that line. Even though we meant no harm to anyone, I wasn't so sure what they would make out of it. I didn't want to run into difficulties with my proposed project and told them so. They quickly brushed aside my fears, telling me that they wanted to publish the entire story about us, the trip and the strange, uncommon visit at their base in their air force journal. We requested a copy, but unfortunately never received one from them. When writing this book about 19 years later, I initiated an extensive worldwide search for this article and received the following interesting responses.

On August 23, 1976 the Department of the Air Force, The Academy Library, USAF Academy, Colorado wrote:

> Dear Mr. Schneider:
>
> In response to your letter of 5 August 1976, requesting information on your emergency landing at the 38th Air Base Group installation in France on 21 April 1958, we do not find that we have any information on this incident. We checked the *Air Force Times, Air Force Magazine* and the *Army, Navy and Air Force Journal* for that time and came up with nothing.
>
> We also called Mr. Gilbert Campbell and asked him if there was something specific he was thinking about, but all he could say was that it sounded familiar.

We are sorry we cannot be of help to you.

Sincerely,

/s/ Mrs. Evelyn Myers
Chief, Reference Branch

On August 24th, 1976 the Department of the Air Force, Washington, D. C. wrote:

I regret to inform you that the Headquarters of the United States Air Forces in Europe does not have any records concerning Mr. Schneider's "experience" in 1958.

We have contacted the Office of the Chief of Air Force History, also, without success. We are awaiting an answer from the Albert F. Simpson Center at Maxwell Air Force Base, Alabama, which is researching your request at this time.

We will be in touch with you when we have an answer from the Simpson Center.

Sincerely,

/s/ Richard E. Stevenson
Major, USAF
Chief, Magazine & Book Branch
Public Information Division
Office of Information

Then, a letter sent to us on the 25th of August, 1976 by The Albert F. Simpson Historical Research Center, USAF, HO R, Maxwell AFB, Alabama finally brought us the much-desired article with the following note:

Attached is the only item we could locate on the incident you mentioned. This is taken from the Laon Air Base newspaper, the *Laon Sentinel,* 1 May 58. The photographers and journalists you mention in your letter certainly included personnel from the base information office and photo lab, and they may have been the only ones there. It is possible that the US newspaper in Europe, the *Stars and Stripes,* carried something on the incident, and we suggest you contact that publication to determine this. The *S&S* may have been the "Air Force Journal" you mention.

/s/ Benjamin B. William, Colonel, USAFR

I was very happy to receive the extensive write-up about the incident in the *Laon Sentinel.* This article is reproduced on pages 137 and 138 of this book. We give our thanks and credit to The Albert F. Simpson Historical Research Center of the USAF for their fine and successful research in this matter.

U. S. Air Force... Guardian of Freedom

Laon ☆ Sentinel

PRÊT VOLONTÉ CAPABLE

Vol. IV. — Nº 18 Laon AB, France 1 MAY 1958

Klaus G. Rügge, Hamburg, Germany and Hans Schneider, of Bielefeld, Germany wave a friendly goodbye to Laon Air Base. The pair of German civilians landed their small plane here last week during a flight to Brussels, Belgium.

TWO GERMAN CIVILIANS MAKE UNAUTHORIZED LANDING HERE

The base Air Police Sabotage Alert Team got an unexpected opportunity to test their effectiveness on 21 April when an unidentified aircraft landed here.

The plane, a small, civilian, two-seater, Piper-Cub-type touched down on the base runway at 1830 hours and before its pilot could cut his engine, the Air Police Sabotage Alert Team, had completely surrounded the craft and its occupants. The Air Police team was heavily armed with the necessary weapons when they swooped down on the unexpected, unsuspecting pilot and co-pilot.

The occupants, two German civilians, were detained at their aircraft until Captain Robert Blickenstaff, Airdrome Officer, arrived. The French Liaison Officer, Commandant (Major) Jean Claude Faure, who had also been called to the scene arrived with base-assigned French Gendarmes and an immediate search of the plane was instigated.

Klaus G. Rügge, of Hamburg, Germany and Hans Schneider, of Bielefeld, Germany identified themselves to base authorities and were escorted to the base Provost Marshal's office for interrogation.

Here, after showing a 1950-52 map which listed a landing field near Laon, and explaining that many landing fields in Europe are co-occupied by civilian and military alike, they launched into the explanation of their "unauthorized" landing at a military airfield.

Mr. Rügge and Mr. Schneider were on the last leg of a three week vacation which took them to Morroco, Spain, Portugal and various parts of France. They began their trip from Brussels, Belgium and were on their way back to Brussels when approaching nightfall dictated that they land in this vicinity.

According to Mr. Rügge, the word "surprise" fails to express their feelings concerning the "reception" they received upon landing.

After satisfying proper base authorities that they were more or less the victims of circumstances, the twosome was escorted to the main gate. After spending the night in Laon, they returned to the base, where an escort from the Air Police squadron met them and accompanied them to base operations.

At base operations, after answering a few more questions, they were accorded the facilities of the base weather station where they decided on their final flight plan from here to Brussels. Upon payment of landing and parking fees, Mr. Rügge and Mr. Schneider were escorted to their aircraft and allowed to complete their flight to Brussels.

Just prior to taking off, Mr. Rügge said, "We'd like to thank everyone connected with this incident for the fine courtesy with which we've been treated. Those security boys had us surrounded before we stopped rolling and if we had been up to something, they surely would have foiled our plans. We certainly apologize for any inconvenience we've caused."

Major Edward A. Redler, Base Provost Marshal, commenting on the incident, stated, "This has been an excellent test for the men on the Air Police Sabotage Alert Team and I'm very pleased with their outstanding performance. They have shown by their action in this case that their training was worthwhile and I'd like to congratulate them on a job well done."

Back at the base the hurly-burly eventually ceased, and we were ready to press on. Amongst a lot of aircraft activity, we rolled almost forever on that endless taxiway to our run-up area. Having gone over our memorized check list, including the testing of the controls and the magnetos, we moved toward the runway with our eyes on the tower. After being given the green light, we took off at 10:55 A. M. amid heavy jet traffic. Once again we were on the wing.

While so slowly humming along, we suddenly heard a boom, increasing to a deafening roar, and were surprised to see a formation of five jets surrounding us, one above and two on each side. With a speed which made our bird look like it was hovering in the air, they blasted by with nearly ear-shattering thunder, bidding us farewell with a short, final escort. They had become our friends, and we shall never forget that token of companionship they presented to us during our final minutes in their airspace. Perhaps all the jet traffic when we left was partly caused by their desire to leave in time to give us this, their last salute. Moments like these added immeasurably to our trip.

The visibility was still terrible, and our exclusive navigation consisted of contact flying along railroad tracks. After travelling for almost an hour, we made a brief stopover at a big, old German-built military airfield to fuel up. As I remember, there was either no fuel suitable for our plane at the United States air base, or they were not allowed to sell it to us. When we landed in Niergnies, our tanks must have been down to the last drop. Including the two latest flights, we were airborne a total of four hours and five minutes without gassing up. The longest time we flew so far without refuelling was on our Málaga to Alicante, Spain flight. Now that was exceeded by 15 minutes. We apparently figured on a shorter flying time between the two last airports, but the poor visibility forced us off our straight "true course" line and added unwonted miles to our flight.

THUNDERING INTO ACTION
(Niergnies to Lille Lesquin)

Again we felt the familiar surge of pride in our aircraft as we taxied to our take-off position. The "enormously powerful" motor, with its 65 horsepower thrust, was ready to thunder into action. After clearance, I pushed the throttle forward and instantly we felt the smooth force of acceleration.

Shortly after noon we were in the air. Once more we struggled with the same poor old visibility and obscuring mist on our 45-minute skip over the flat Artois Province from Cambrai to Lille. After a heavy rain shower, however, the weather improved. It was a day of brief flights. Very close to home, they were our final hops. Our three-quarter-hour Lille stopover, apparently necessitated by custom procedures, was our last stop in France. There were no check-out facilities at Cambrai. Gasoline-wise, we could not have made it all the way from the air base to Lille, so we had to do some hedge-hopping that day.

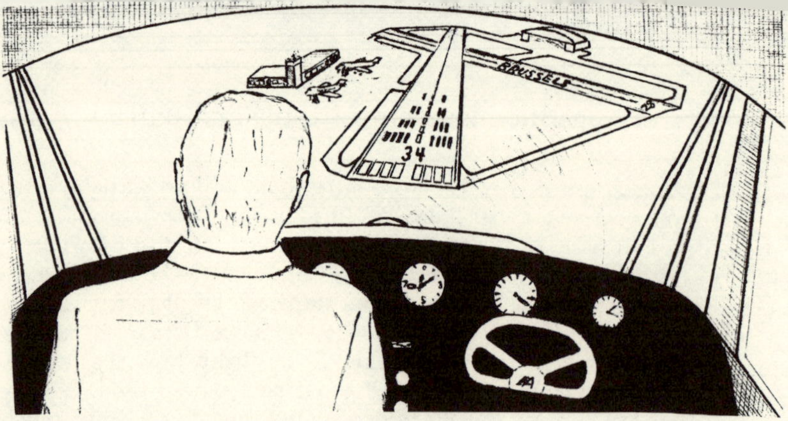

8

Our Bird Returns To Its Roost

(Lille, France to Ghent, Belgium)

After this other short stopover, we were back up in the air viewing the "Old Bourse," which is an outstanding example of 17th Century Flemish architecture. Also, the masterpiece of 18th Century military construction, the Citadel, afforded an interesting sight. With this, we waved goodbye to Lille and a few minutes later to France, as we crossed over into Belgium, the plane's adopted home country.

Soon Ghent was below us, the city where the Treaty of Ghent was signed on December 24, 1814, ending the War of 1812 between England and America. John Quincy Adams was one of the negotiators present. This treaty marked the beginning of a period in which Great Britain and America preferred to settle their disagreements peacefully.

The city is built on little islands at the junction of the Lys and Schelde rivers, and is Belgium's second largest inland seaport. Famous for 200 bridges, the older part with narrow streets and medieval houses, the 14th Century Belfry, and flax and cotton mills, Ghent was quite an entrancing place as the "terminus" of our trip.

NEAR MISS

When nearly completing this last leg, or "grande finale," of my journey with Klaus, I felt like an old, worn-out soldier returning from battle.

With our destination at hand, everything within me started to relax. Surely nothing would go wrong at this late stage. The slight carelessness almost became our downfall, for when coming in for a landing and leaving "base" for "final," I almost stalled and crashed on this last turn of the trip.

Overtired and extremely weary, I had not permitted the plane to keep enough speed to the degree that conditions required for controlled flight could be maintained. Many factors were suddenly converging into a most critical and exigent situation.

When entering the traffic pattern, paralleling the runway too closely, I first reduced the airspeed. Then, rolling the plane to the left, I initiated a steep bank in an effort to go from "downwind" to "base" leg and "final approach" in one tight turn. This big angle of bank placed a much greater load on the wings, which now had to produce lift equal to the weight of the airplane plus the resulting centrifugal force. It increased the stall speed considerably and brought the same right up to my present velocity. At the very moment while executing this 180° "pivot" during intended descending flight, I overtrimmed at that unfortunate time, and rather than reducing, the angle of attack enlarged right to the "burble point," making it now an "angle of stall." An onset of plane vibrations suggested that the air had broken away near the upper trailing wing edge and, spreading forward, was now forming vortexes or whirlpools on top of the entire airfoil.

We were at the very brink of plummeting to our doom. To lose an airplane in the low altitude of a final landing configuration is one of the most dangerous flying calamities which ends nearly always with death. That close to the ground, the pilot usually does not have enough time and opportunity to recover the craft and prevent it from diving into the ground.

Jumping back one more time into alertness and action, I immediately reapplied full power, pressed the plane down with the elevator control, and lessened the degree of bank. Instantly the plane recovered its safe flight configuration, moving back into a functional airspeed operating range.

As soon as the worst was over, I broke this latest news to listless Klaus, who already knew that something was "fishy." "While you tried desperately to avoid a smash-up, I noticed your clenched teeth and a reddening of the neck," he asserted.

During many close calls in the past 2½ weeks, a nervous compatriot learned that this meant imminent danger. But—as was the case with me—he couldn't imagine that something might go amiss in these concluding moments of our trip. Klaus, tuckered out and languished as well, didn't recognize to the fullest extent how near we came to the decisive *"coup de grâce."*

Without a go-around, I was able to bring in the Aeronca for a smooth landing on the St. Denis Westrem Field in Ghent at 2:32 P. M. on the

22nd of April, 1958. This last flight took 47 minutes. We had completed our circuit and were back at our starting point.

Tall, lantern-jawed Klaus lost 50 pounds on this 18-day escapade, one-third of his former weight. He looked like a starving, emaciated East Indian with his remaining 100-pound flyweight and sunburned hatchet face. At an average, the poor skeleton-like fellow had been divested of nearly three pounds per day and was quite a cadaverous sight. Would the heavy-set, overweight ladies please stand in line as the next candidates! What an interesting, thumpingly quick way to knock off some of that blubber! We cannot promise, though, to bring back what is left!

IN RETROSPECT

To endure what we had gone through, and to fly the plane under all kinds of crazy conditions which required all the tenacity, attention and diligence we could possibly summon under such physical handicaps, was really more than humanly bearable.

There are times when a person does daring, reckless things, seemingly playing with fate, but still believing that everything must go all right. When later looking back, one shudders and wonders why such a crazy venture was ever undertaken. What brought it about?

Maybe the motivating forces came from childhood days. Then at times I would stand at the edge of a mountainside or cliff and see the birds carried on updrafts for hours, rarely flapping their wings. I felt they had unfair advantages over us men to be able to fly, and desired to be as free as they. If only I also had wings to glide down that mountainside and then at the bottom of the valley I would level out and sail speedily along for a while until I decided to soar up again.

My limitless crave for weightlessly drifting along over nature's bounties went so far that I even constructed a pair of wings when yet very young. They were made of thin cardboard, wood lath and strings. These did nothing further beside prolonging my state of being airborne only slightly when jumping into semi-gliding flight from as high a hill as I could find without breaking my legs. It was hardly enough to satisfy me.

I needed to become a pilot of real planes. Then I could watch a beautiful sunny, silvery earth gliding by beneath. I imagined how wonderful it must be to live joyfully and colorfully as an airman in a different, exciting sphere. Up there I could be far removed from everyday strife, tumult and pettiness of ordinary mortals. The landscape would look so clean, refreshing and harmonious from those heights: no noise besides the gentle hum of the small engine, no blowing of car horns, no red lights, no police cars running you down, no exhaust fumes, trash or gross pollution. A sparkling planet at its best primordial state, just like far out on the ocean. It would be food for the soul. The wind conditions, the cloud formations, and the sunset would never be the same in this world of everlasting changes—man's last frontier.

Now I had conquered this realm. As if by sudden and wondrous tintinnabulation, it had announced itself upon my very life. A universe of a crescent moon and silvery stars in crystal clear, lonely nights only accompanied by the gentle purr of the motor. Once in a while an isolated glimmer appeared below me like the mirroring of a star. Then there was the radiant reflection of myriads of glittering city lights on the wings above me, nearly blinding my eyes. Many other happy and treasured memories, of flying in tinted ever-changing cloud valleys toward the setting sun with a seemingly more beautiful and alluring land beyond, haunted me–just like the siren call of the wilderness, always drawing the explorer back and back again. I, like an eagle scanning the countryside from way above, would always feel the pull heavenward–to the chatoyant and iridescent domain of flight.

KLAUS RETURNS TO HAMBURG

Klaus, not being able to share these deep thoughts, was different; he did not dilly-dally around. He picked up the rest of his baggage from my car and apartment after we had returned to the bustling town of Kortrijk (Courtrai), with its wide, tree-lined streets, near the French border, and in the center of Belgium's linen industry where I was studying and working at that time. Before I knew it, Klaus was gone. He, this time indeed, remembered his promise given at the outset of our journey in Paris, France, and took the next train and went back home. One of the most exciting and unbelievable 18-day flying ventures in modern aviation history had come to a safe end. Our "grand total" of this journey was 32 flights, with 54 hours and 54 minutes in the air. Excepting added local sightseeing jaunts at various fields, it ran to 25 flights with 52 hours and 49 minutes.

GRIMBERGEN

(Ghent to Brussels)

The next day, the 23rd of April, in the early afternoon, I ferried the plane in a solo flight back to its home port, Grimbergen, in Brussels (Bruxelles), Belgium.

Here, 28 days earlier, my eyes beheld the Aeronca Chief for the first time when Mr. Ricart gave me my check-out ride in it and only 20 days earlier I had chartered it at this base. The elopement with my little, much-treasured friend had lasted two-thirds of a month–a relatively very short and yet seemingly so long time. With all the experiences gathered and all we endured, it seemed as though we had been gone for an eternity.

Still on April 23rd, in mid-afternoon, I took one of my friends, Jules Van Moer, on a sightseeing flight over Belgium's stately capital. During 40 minutes of circling around, we enjoyed the fine parks, boulevards, public squares, Royal Palace, Grande Place with its exceptionally beautiful

Lfd. Nr. des Fluges	Datum 19.58 Tag	Monat	Flugzeugführer	Begleiter	Flugzeug-muster	Zulassungs-Nr.	Zweck des Fluges
434	4	4	Schneider	Klaus Rügge	Aeronka Chief	OO-LEM	Ferienflug
435	5	4	"	"	"	"	"
436	6	4	"	"	"	"	"
437	7	4	"	"	"	"	"
438	7	4	"	"	"	"	"
439	7	4	"	"	"	"	"
440	8	4	"	+1	Jodel D-112	EC-ALX	[illegible]
441	8	4	"	+1	"	"	"
442	8	4	"	+1	"	"	Kunstflug
443	9	4	"	Klaus Rügge	Aeronka Chief	OO-LEM	Ferienflug
444	9	4	"	"	"	"	[illegible] 9-4-58
445	9	4	"	"	"	"	"

Lfd. Nr. des Fluges	Datum 19.58 Tag	Monat	Flugzeugführer	Begleiter	Flugzeug-muster	Zulassungs-Nr.	Zweck des Fluges
446/48	11	4	Schneider	—	Aeronka Chief	OO-LEM	Landungsübungen
449	11	4	"	+ Freundin von Klaus	"	"	Rundflug
450	11	4	"	Klaus Rügge	"	"	Ferienflug
451	13	4	"	"	"	"	"
452	13	4	"	"	"	"	"
453	14	4	"	"	"	"	"
454	14	4	"	"	"	"	"

Plastered with exotic stamps from a string of foreign nations, these logbook entries reflect about 4000 miles of perilous air travel.

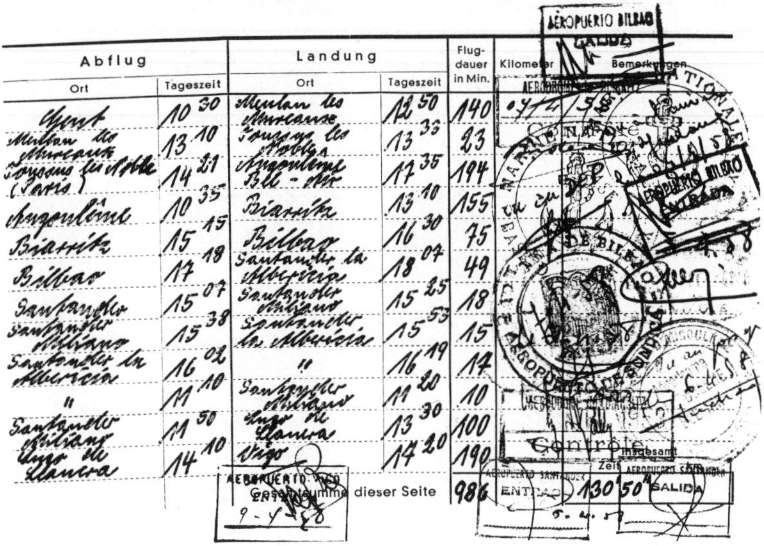

Abflug Ort	Abflug Tageszeit	Landung Ort	Landung Tageszeit	Flugdauer in Min.	Kilometer	Bemerkungen
Ghent	10^{30}	Meulan les Mureaux	12^{50}	140		
Meulan les Mureaux	13^{10}	Toussus les Nobles	13^{33}	23		
Toussus les Noble (Paris)	14^{21}	Angoulême Bel-Air	17^{35}	194		
Angoulême	10^{35}	Biarritz	13^{10}	155		
Biarritz	15^{15}	Bilbao	16^{30}	75		
Bilbao	17^{18}	Santander la Albericia	18^{07}	49		
Santander	15^{07}	Santander [illegible]	15^{25}	18		
Santander [illegible]	15^{38}	Santander la Albericia	15^{53}	15		
Santander la Albericia	16^{02}	"	16^{19}	17		
"	11^{10}	Santander [illegible]	11^{20}	10		
Santander [illegible]	11^{50}	Lugo de Llanera	13^{30}	100		
Lugo de Llanera	14^{10}	Vigo	17^{20}	190		
		Gesamtsumme dieser Seite		986	Insgesamt Zeit 130' 50"	

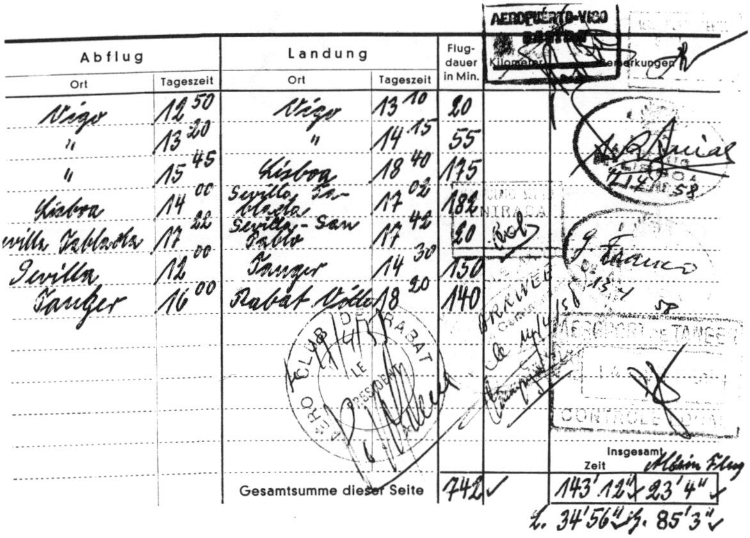

Abflug Ort	Abflug Tageszeit	Landung Ort	Landung Tageszeit	Flugdauer in Min.	Kilometer	Bemerkungen
Vigo	12^{50}	Vigo	13^{10}	20		
"	13^{20}	"	14^{15}	55		
"	15^{45}	Lisboa	18^{40}	175		
Lisboa	14^{00}	Sevilla Tablada	17^{02}	182		
Sevilla Tablada	17^{22}	Sevilla-San Pablo	17^{42}	20		
Sevilla	12^{00}	Tanger	14^{30}	150		
Tanger	16^{00}	Rabat Ville	18^{20}	140		
		Gesamtsumme dieser Seite		742	Insgesamt Zeit 143' 12"	23' 4"
					L. 34'56"	S. 85'3"

On the bottom of the next two pages are the flights I logged with Rudi Lehmann. Read the tragic story in Chapter 11.

Lfd. Nr. des Fluges	Datum 19 58 Tag	Monat	Flugzeugführer	Begleiter	Flugzeugmuster	Zulassungs-Nr.	Zweck des Fluges
455	17	4	Schneider	Klaus Krügge	Aeronca Chief	OO-LEM	Ferienflug
456	18	4	"	"	"	"	"
457	19	4	"	"	"	"	"
458	19	4	"	"	"	"	"
459	20	4	"	"	"	"	"
460	20	4	"	"	"	"	"
			Flugzeitberichtigung des Fluges von Barcelona				

Lfd. Nr. des Fluges	Datum 19 58 Tag	Monat	Flugzeugführer	Begleiter	Flugzeugmuster	Zulassungs-Nr.	Zweck des Fluges
461	21	4	Schneider	Klaus Krügge	Aeronca Chief	OO-LEM	Ferienflug
			Berichtigung der Flugdauer von Montpe... na				
462	21	4	Schneider	Klaus Krügge	Aeronca Chief	OO-LEM	Ferienflug
463	22	4	"	"	"	"	"
464	22	4	"	"	"	"	"
465	22	4	"	"	"	"	"

Lfd. Nr. des Fluges	Datum 19 58/59 Tag	Monat	Flugzeugführer	Begleiter	Flugzeugmuster	Zulassungs-Nr.	Zweck des Fluges
466	23	4	Schneider	—	Aeronca Chief	OO-LEM	Überführungsflug
467	23	4	"	Jules van Meer	"	"	Rundflug
468	7	8	"	Alfred Schneider	Aeronca Champion	OO-TWH	"
469	10	1	"	Lehmann	Piper Tri-Pacer	N7605D	Testflug
470	11	1	"	"	Comanche 250	D-ELAC	Überlandflug
471	11	1	"	"	"	"	"
472	11	1	"	"	"	"	"
473	11	1	"	"	"	"	"
474	11	1	"	"	"	"	"

Abflug Ort	Tageszeit	Landung Ort	Tageszeit	Flugdauer in Min.	Kilometer	Bemerkungen
Rabat Ville	15^{10}	Jerez-Playa	18^{58}	228		
Jerez-Playa	10^{50}	Sevilla-San Pablo	11^{59}	69		
Sevilla-San Pablo	11^{45}	Malaga	13^{20}	95		
Malaga	15^{05}	Alicante-La Rabasa	18^{55}	230		
Alicante	10^{30}	Barcelona	14^{05}	215		
Barcelona	15^{20}	Montpellier Fréjorgues	18^{20}	180		
nach Montpellier		"	18^{32}	12		
		Gesamtsumme dieser Seite		1029		Insgesamt Zeit 160'21"

Dirección General de Aviación Civil — Aeropuerto de Alicante
Aeropuerto Jerez — 17-4-58
Aeropuerto Sevilla — Salida — 18-4-58
Aeropuerto Sevilla — Entrada
Aeropuerto Sevilla — Salida
Aeropuerto Alicante — Entrada — 19-4-58
Aeropuerto Alicante — Salida — 20/4.58
Aerop. Barcelona — Entrada
Aerop. Barcelona — Salida
Aérodrome de Montpellier — Contrôle — Vu au passage le 21/4/5-

Abflug Ort	Tageszeit	Landung Ort	Tageszeit	Flugdauer in Min.	Kilometer	Bemerkungen
Montpellier	10^{35}	Champforgeuil	12^{55}	140		
le Champf.	12^{55}	"	13^{55}	60		
Champforgeuil	15^{25}	Couvrons	18^{35}	190		
Couvrons	10^{55}	Niergnies	11^{50}	55		
Niergnies	12^{15}	Lille Lesquin	13^{00}	45		
Lille Lesquin	13^{45}	St. Denis Westrem	14^{32}	47		
		Gesamtsumme dieser Seite		537		Insgesamt Zeit 169'18" km 23'4"

Aérodrome Chalon-sur-Saône Champforgeuil — Contrôle — Le 21 AVR 1958
Landed L.H.C.N. 1735 21 APR 58
Aérodrome de Lille-Lesquin — Contrôle — Le 22/4.1958
Union Aéronautique du Cambrésis — Terrain de Niergnies — Cambrai — 22-4

Abflug Ort	Tageszeit	Landung Ort	Tageszeit	Flugdauer in Min.	Kilometer	Bemerkungen
Gent	14^{03}	Brüssel	14^{40}	37		
Brüssel	16^{10}	"	16^{50}	40		
"	10^{03}	"	10^{16}	13		
Teterboro	15^{15}	Teterboro	15^{40}	25		
"	10^{30}	Flushing	10^{45}	15		
Flushing	11^{05}	Dutchess Co.	12^{15}	70		
Dutchess Co	12^{25}	Teterboro	01^{20}	55		
Teterboro	04^{15}	Flushing	05^{45}	90		#1662
Flushing	05^{50}	Teterboro	06^{10}	20		
		Gesamtsumme dieser Seite		365		Insgesamt Zeit 175'23" km 23'41"

Aéroport Bruxelles Grimbergen — 23 AVR 1958

U.S. FLYING TIME: 4'35" 34'56" 116'46"

gabled Guild Houses and the Exposé or 1958 World's Fair grounds with the interesting and unique Atomium. It was that Fair's symbol, and represented the atomic make-up of a metal molecule enlarged about 200 billion times. The highest sphere of the giant structure housed a skyline restaurant, and the others contained exhibits from the various countries, including Belgium.

We landed on this windy, squally day late in the afternoon, and it was the last trip I ever took with that plane. I returned to Kortrijk (Courtrai), packed my belongings, quit the apartment, and returned with my Volkswagen to Bielefeld, Germany, where my parents lived.

ARRIVING HOME SICK

I reached home on the 24th of April, one day before my birthday. They had sweated a lot during my crazy venture, wondering if they would ever see me again. No one was home when I arrived. Hearing them coming in the evening, I sneaked into the foyer and stood there in the dark with my African fez on my head, ready to surprise them. When they put on the light, they got the shock of their lives. Just skin and bones, that red fez on my head and my brown color made me look like a Moroccan. Their joy was great, but they instructed me that I must not frighten them like that again—they conceded that it was hard to recognize me any more.

I started my birthday party the next morning by staying in bed, utterly sick. It gave me time to think.

I also had lost a lot of weight, while struggling without sleep for many nights. Suffering for so long with that unbearable, persistent pain in my foot, I could not even remember when I had been in the "land of nod" last. Truly, I had taken a heavy toll. I mustered all the little strength which was left during the latter portion of the trip and arrived home entirely exhausted and half dead.

It was a formidable and herculean task to fly the plane for such lengthy periods, day after day, in strange and mostly difficult territory. The strain of travel and lack of slumber during much of the trip aggravated my condition to such an extent that after arriving home, my foot soon broke open. As a result, I was bedridden for one quarter of a year. Not until three months later had I been able to cure it, return to normal life and walk again.

This sickness helped to bring about a *marvelous surrender*—very different to the one at the United States Air Force base. Then it was to earthly but now to heavenly powers.

Conditions throughout the entire trip already had spearheaded what was presently being finalized.

PART III

ON FINAL WITH THE ULTIMATE

The following two chapters are dedicated to those gallant souls who, despite all the degrading influences of ever-increasing institutionalism, are determined to keep an undimmed eye and keen sense for that which is unusual, uplifting and challenging, raising man out of the ordinary humdrum of everyday existence.

Some books leave us free and some books make us free.

–Ralph Waldo Emerson

And ye shall know the truth, and the truth shall make you free.

–John 8:32

9

The High Calling

The setting was perfect.

Just a short while ago I had returned from a once-in-a-lifetime odyssey which left me greatly humbled in spirit and afflicted in flesh. My self-reliance and philosophy of life, as well as the trust in my own strength and understanding, had received severe jolts.

To top it all, I was now sick in bed suffering with tremendous pain.

My desperate inquiry about life's ultimate purpose had been greatly stirred by what was just behind me. Now I had time to pursue this all-important search. It was not going to last much longer. God, in His infinite mercy, intervened in a most unique and providential way.

There had been a long quest for truth. My studies had engulfed myriads of subjects. Psychology, philosophy and the religions of mankind were among them. Diogenes, Aristotle, Immanuel Kant, José Ortega y Gasset and a host of other intellectuals attracted my attention. Many nights I spent in the circle of friends, likewise studying philosophy and other complicated matters, in fervent peruse of man's problems and apparent answers.

With finite minds we tried to solve infinite issues. When, at times, we thought that we had solved one problem we wound up with 10 new ones instead. Actually we were travelling on an ever-widening road without end. Soon, I had to agree with the Greek sage that *the more we know, the more we realize how little we know.*

Not in vain did Diogenes teach that man ought to be free from all desire for pleasures and material things. He felt that honor, riches and good birth were artificial and empty objects and could not help man to live a virtuous life. At times, while carrying a lighted lantern through the streets of Athens, he would lift it up to strange people's faces saying, "I am looking for an honest man." Once Alexander the Great visited Diogenes who was sunning himself at the tub he used for shelter and said, "Ask any favor you wish." Upon this the shaken world conqueror was told, "Then I would have you stand from between me and the sun." When pirates captured him he told them, "I know no trade except how to govern men," and pointing to a rich Corinthian he continued, "Sell me to this man, he needs a master." That Corinthian took him as a teacher for his sons.

Diogenes was different. I couldn't help but be distinctly impressed by such characters. It was for that very reason that I did extensive research on the lives of Gautama Siddhartha (Buddha) and Mahatma Gandhi for instance. For a number of years I was a disciple of Buddhism and Yoga. In the latter I desperately tried to train my consciousness for a state of perfect spiritual insight and practiced its system of exercises as part of that discipline. There seemed to be great power to those beliefs. Yogis were doing feats unknown to the Christians I had met.

I therefore thought that there was more delegation in those Far Eastern religions. Meanwhile I had also devoured Ralph Waldo Trine's book, *In Tune with the Infinite.* Its content left me reeling with enthusiasm. For the first time I had found some literature which reflected my way of thinking more closely than anything I had read before. I underlined so much material that when I was finally through reading it, I could hardly find an unmarked page.

By now I was sure that a golden thread was weaving its way throughout all the religions of mankind. It was up to me to pick out whatever I liked best and what suited me most among all of them. This is exactly what I did. At this juncture I really was a lost case as far as the cause of Christ was concerned. From what I could feel and see, I certainly had more depth and spiritual knowledge than the Christians around me. What an indictment against the lives of the nominal followers of the Nazarene—I just couldn't find those who were truly empowered and motivated by Him, similar to the ones who had *turned the world upside down* (Acts 17:6).

This strengthened me in my belief that I had found truth and therefore saw no need to search further. I was just as blinded and self-righteous as the scribes and Pharisees whom Christ solemnly condemned in one of His most scorching sermons ever preached (Matt., chapter 23).

It is true, I had noticed that my experimenting with all those various religions only brought me to a certain stage and then left me stranded there. Time and again I found my road to final victory over man's passions and desires blocked by an iron gate. There were things which I knew were intolerable in the life of a saint. The fanciest promises and claims of all of these man-made beliefs did nothing further to break down the obstacles I had run against. Each and every one of them were unable to move me through the sound barrier—to pull me into that realm where the ultimate spiritual inspiration flows and where true and mighty supernal victories were going to be won.

At this instant I would like to warn you, the reader! One of the most dangerous situations to be in, is to be caught up and entangled with some of these ideologies of man. How often you have heard someone say, "I don't care what he believes, as long as he is sincere." What a foolish statement this really is. The followers of Communism and Adolf Hitler were and are for the most part utterly sincere. Does this mean that they have found the truth? Indeed not. They are sincere all right, but they are sincerely wrong. The Bible speaks of those who even had a zeal of God, but not according to knowledge (Rom. 10:2). In Proverbs 1:7 we read: "The fear of the LORD is the beginning of knowledge: but fools despise wisdom and instruction." Truly, real wisdom and knowledge only comes from God (2 Chron. 1:10).

There is a great difference between the learning and understanding of man and God's wisdom. Anyone can acquire a lot of human ideas by reading plenty of books others wrote and by spending much time in the institutions of learning. This way you will really get far! Scientists have pointed out the fact that if a man spends his entire lifetime studying just one specialized subject, he will only know 1/2000 part of that one specific field at the end of his road. Think of it! That's all you can know, even though you study from the time you are able to learn until the day you die! What a humbling thought. This is why truly well-educated people are rather meek. They realize that the more they delve into things, the more yet unexplored matter comes into sight. The half-educated are the ones who have an air of brazenness about them, thinking they carry the world by its tail. I sincerely doubt that even at the end of the journey, we will understand 1/2000 part of one field as those who made that research tackle the problem again from the finite spectrum. It is impossible for them to have a complete view of the entire range of complex involvements.

Has it ever dawned upon you that anyone who relies on worldly wisdom actually sits in a merry-go-round? Human knowledge is based on the faculty of external or self-perception exemplified by the functions of the five principal senses (hearing, sight, smell, taste and touch). We learn and judge from the experiences we make with those senses.

When a child is first born, it is a *tabula nova* (a new writing tablet). The first impressions in its young life are the strongest. Increasing practice and background as he grows up carve deeper channels into his mind. This is why our milieu is so important. Then, when it falls down and hurts its knee, the child knows that healing will take place. Why? Because mom said so or because of a previous similar encounter. This assumption is derived from previous experiences and things learned. Therefore, let me stress once more that worldly knowledge depends on our senses.

The trouble, though, is that in many cases our senses are actually lying. They often convey false images or impressions. If a blind man hears a horse gallop in a radio broadcast, he would tend to believe that it is happening right there. If your eyes follow railroad tracks into the distance, they seem to run together. I heard of tests performed on criminals who were blindfolded and told they would be bled to death. After their arms were pricked by a needle, warm water was slowly being run over them. This created the sensation of losing blood. The criminals died and after examination it was revealed that they died from loss of blood. A movie was made at the site of an airplane accident. Three witnesses, who were also present, were asked for their account. When the movie was being shown, it became evident that the reports of all three witnesses were different and wrong. Their senses had played havoc with them.

This should be sufficient to show that our senses are very unreliable, to say the least. Just as unreliable, therefore, is the knowledge you have gathered with them. The only reason why we see the world as we do, is because our eyes work on a certain frequency. If they were to work on a different frequency, we would see something completely different. Most people live in a world which is strictly relative.

Furthermore, what has man's great intellect achieved? It seems that the more sophisticated we get, the more destruction we bring upon ourselves. Take Germany for an example: a nation of great thinkers and scientists which wound up with two world wars within decades.

Now, my whole former world came crashing down around my head like a house of cards. It took a combination of many dangerous flying bouts of such magnitude as you have read to tear me from the clutches of these synthetic traditions and traps.

UNDER THE CROSS FIRE

Here is how my final surrender came—a surrender of a temporary in exchange for a beatific, eternal world. I was living in Bielefeld, West Germany. Franz Brinkman, an evangelist who had come to that town, was holding a large tent campaign. One night I decided to attend his meetings. I had not come out to learn, but to argue and find fault. Yes, I was seeking wisdom, but I didn't think that I could find it there. I was just like the Greek men of old of whom it is said, ". . . and the Greeks seek after wisdom" (1 Cor. 1:22). At the end of the meeting I went forward to converse with the man. While listening to him, a lot of questions came to mind. Now was the time to fire them at him, one by one. Bluntly I started out, "Why are you so narrow minded? You preached Christ, but no word was said about any of the other great founders of religions. How about Buddha? He lived approximately 500 years before Christ and taught almost the same thing! How about Kant, Aristotle, Ortega y Gasset and all the rest of the great thinkers?"

The challenge was on. The evangelist drew the sword. Not one made from iron, but the sword of the spirit. With eloquence he declared: "Christ sent me not to preach the gospel with wisdom of words, lest the cross of Christ should be made of none effect. For it is written, I will destroy the wisdom of the wise, and will bring to nothing the understanding of the prudent. Where is the wise? where is the scribe? where is the disputer of this world? hath not God made foolish the wisdom of this world? For after that in the wisdom of God the world by wisdom knew not God, it pleased God by the foolishness of preaching to save them that *believe.* For the Jews require a sign, and the Greeks seek after wisdom: but we preach Christ crucified, unto the Jews a stumbling block, and unto the Greeks foolishness; but unto them which are called, Christ the power of God, and the wisdom of God. God has chosen the foolish things of the world to confound the wise; and God hath chosen the weak things of the world to confound the things which are mighty; And base things of the world, and things which are despised, hath God chosen, yea, and things which are not, to bring to nought things that are: That no flesh should glory in his presence" (1 Cor. 1:17-29).

There was a man who knew the scriptures, who could recite vast portions of it. His voice came through, clear like a trumpet—he did not make an uncertain sound.

"Where are the ancient founders of man's religions at this time? Where are the past wise of this world now? They were buried or burnt and are still dead. However, Christ not only came, was crucified and entombed but arose and presently intercedes for us on high! He lives on, and is the same yesterday, and today, and forever (Hebr. 13:8). Come to Him and you will be saved," he thundered.

A man of strong convictions, he made no bones about what he believed. His face took on a beautiful radiance as he continued, "Tell me about another book like the Bible. One containing that much prophecy of which much has been fulfilled already. One consisting of at least 66 books written by many different people throughout the span of centuries, and yet they all agree. One book dovetails with the other and, in fact, one strengthens the other. What greater proof do you need that the Bible was written by holy men as they were inspired by the Spirit of God? Know this first, that no prophecy of the scripture is of any private interpretation. For the prophecy came not in old time by the will of man: But holy men of God spoke as they were moved by the Holy Ghost (2 Peter 1:20-21)."

Was this it, the very thing my heart has been yearning for all these years? Was this going to give me the freedom I was seeking in flight—one I felt the birds have by being able to fly? I desired to be as free as they. Was this message going to wing me toward the setting sun with a more beautiful and alluring land beyond? No, it couldn't be. The teachings of Buddha, for one, were too beautiful to do away with. Before I could build up any more resistance, the next blow struck.

"Buddha taught that 'we are sad because we thirst for things and finally become the slaves of them. *Desire for possessions prevents us from attaining knowledge and insight.* Only the desire for goodness, truth and salvation is praiseworthy. One must practice self-control, humility, generosity and mercy and cultivate a heart of love that knows no anger, that knows no ill will. Hatred does not cease by hatred at any time; hatred ceases by love.' True, one who examines these teachings cannot help but see the similarity to the Christian teachings in some aspects and how many of its adherents do fall short of those qualities.

"But here comes the catch! When Buddha set forth a pattern of self-righteous teachings in saying 'that by destroying evil desire, we may become free from sorrow and since we have the freedom to make our own choices, *we can escape from the bondage whenever we will,'* we find him absolutely on false ground scripturally, for we read in Romans 9:16: 'So then it is not of him that willeth, nor of him that runneth, but of God that sheweth mercy.' When you become a Christian, then you are not going to strive any longer in your own strength, but you simply become the tool in the Master's hand. You are then the executing agent of His power.

"There are things which are too great to describe in words or to behold with your eyes. 'But as it is written, eye hath not seen, nor ear heard, neither have entered into the heart of man, the things which God hath prepared for them that love him. But God hath revealed them unto us by his Spirit: for the Spirit searcheth all things, yea, the deep things of God' (1 Cor. 2:9-10). But that Spirit of God can only effectually work within you if you become quiet before Him and sit down at the feet of the Master. 'For thus saith the Lord God, the Holy One of Israel; In returning and rest shall ye be saved; in quietness and in confidence shall be your strength: and ye would not' (Isa. 30:15). 'And the work of righteousness shall be peace; and the effect of righteousness quietness and assurance for ever' (Isa. 32:17)."

"The last part sounds good," I replied. "I learned about the need for quietness and peace in Yoga. Many times I have gone to quiet locations and tried to make my mind a blank for hours and even days. At times I felt an euphoric state of being, just like floating in the air with beautiful music enveloping me. Yes, I think I know what you . . ." This was as far as I got. Once more the preacher's sword took over.

"You are like the people who had been lost sheep: their shepherds had caused them to go astray, they had turned them away on the *mountains:* they had gone from *mountain to hill* (they went lower and lower spiritually), *they had forgotten their resting place. All that found them had devoured them* (Jer. 50:6-7). You are following the wrong shepherds—they are nothing but robbers and thieves. Come to the *One* who was willing to lay down His life for the sheep (John 10:11)."

By now I was reeling under the spiritual cross fire put out by one man. What had I gotten myself into? I came to argue and not to be shot at.

I couldn't let my emotions get the better of me—no, certainly not now. So, I argued with him to the end. I did not understand the simplicity of the gospel.

With a prophetic connotation he concluded, "But they that wait upon the Lord shall renew their strength; they shall *mount up with wings as eagles; they shall run,* and not be weary; and they shall walk, and not faint" (Isa. 40:31) and pointing upward he finished, "I can not convince you, the Almighty up there has to do it."

The evangelist had given me much time. I was very hard-headed and, sad to say, at the end of the lengthy discourse, still not converted.

Approximately half a year later, I conducted the crazy flying venture you just read about. Truly, I was then mounting up with wings as eagles. It was in God's providence to put me through those trials and tribulations in order to capture me finally and bring me into the haven of His rest.

SURRENDER

When I returned from that journey and was laid up on the sickbed, Manfred von Gerkan suddenly visited me. He was living in Bremen. Manfred had been a good friend of mine for a long time. He was a supervising architectural engineer, smart, of noble peerage and, above all, a fine Christian.

"Do you remember what that evangelist at the tent meeting in Bielefeld told you?" he asked me.

"What evangelist?" I replied. I had long since forgotten him. "You'd better be more specific. I have met and conversed with so many people, that I cannot remember one from the other most of the time."

"Don't you remember Franz Brinkman? You and he had a long talk together at the end of his meeting."

Now it dawned on me whom he was talking about. "Yes," I said, "I remember him now. What about him?"

"Here is what he told you," rejoined Manfred. "Let's say you fell into a pit. You are trying to make it out of there on your own, but fail. After awhile Gautama Siddhartha passes by the edge of that depth and you cry out saying, 'Please, please, help me to get out of this hole!' At this point Buddha explains to you what you can do to get out of that pit. 'Put one foot here and one foot there and you will slowly make it out of there,' he says. Then, as you desperately try to follow his instructions, you slip and fall back to the bottom, maybe even breaking your back. 'I told you what you can do, now I am unable to help you any further,' admits Buddha at this time and leaves. There you lie with a broken back and in pain, more miserable than ever before.

"A little while later comes yet another person. This time, the man of Nazareth. Again you cry out, 'Please, please, help me, oh Jesus Christ, to get out of this mess I am in!' Instantly the Nazarene steps to the edge of the pit, stretches out His hand and, healing your broken back, pulls you out of there. Who do you think helped you?"

"You mean the evangelist told me that, and I could not understand it? Thank God you remembered. He must have put it into your mind at this moment so you could help me. How marvelous! That's it!" I cried out in great excitement.

I felt as if thick scales were falling off my eyes. How foolish I had been! Suddenly I could understand what Christ meant when He said in John 14:6, "*. . . I am the way, the truth, and the life: no man cometh unto the Father, but by me.*" I could also understand what He meant when He said, "Verily, verily, I say unto you, He that entereth not by the door into the sheepfold, but climbeth up some other way, the same is a thief and a robber. But he that entereth in by the door is the shepherd of the sheep. Verily, verily, I say unto you, *I am the door* of the sheep. *All that ever came before me are thieves and robbers . . . . I am the door:* by me if any man enter in, he shall be saved, and shall go in and out, and find pasture. Therefore doth my Father love me, because I lay down my life, *that I might take it again.* No man taketh it from me, but I lay it down of myself. I have power to lay it down, and *I have power to take it again . . . .*" (John 10: 1, 2, 7, 8, 9, 17, 18).

There it was! My, what a rich diet. How ignorant I was all these years. Could anything be clearer? These passages made it plain that I had been following thieves and robbers all that time. There was *only one way, one truth and one life, and that was Jesus Christ.* Not only did He put Himself into the veil of flesh so He could reestablish a personal contact with man, not only did He die, *but He rose again and sits presently on the right hand of power* (Matt. 26:64, Mk. 14:62).

Who of the other prophets or founders of mankind's religions ever claimed that they would immediately rise again so they could intercede for us? Who of them laid down their lives for my sins and yours? Who of them were born contrary to the laws of nature? What a difference between them and HIM. Here He is, Jesus Christ the same yesterday, and today, and forever (Hebr. 13:8). When He came on the scene of this world He lived in poverty and was reared in obscurity. He did not travel extensively. Only once did He cross the boundary of the country in which He lived—that was during His childhood when He was in exile in Egypt.

He possessed neither wealth nor college education; yet the profoundest wisdom of men has never equalled His teachings. The people said about Him: "Never man spake like this man." His relatives were inconspicuous and uninfluential, apparently having had neither training nor formal education.

In infancy He startled a king; in childhood He puzzled the learned professors, for His wisdom was of God. In manhood He ruled the course of nature, walking upon the billows of water as if they were pavement, defying the laws of gravity, and hushing the raging sea to stillness. He healed the multitudes without medicine and made no charge for His services.

He never wrote a book, yet in nearly all the libraries of the world there are some books that have been written about Him; one could not hold all. He never wrote a song, yet He has furnished the theme for more songs than all the song writers combined. He never founded a college, yet all the schools put together cannot boast of having as many humble students as He has.

He never marshalled an army, drafted a soldier nor fired a gun, yet no leader had more volunteers who have, under His orders, made more rebels stack arms and surrender without a shot being fired. He has worldwide authority. He is honored by some kings and heads of government. At His command men are willing to lay down their lives. His kingdom has no boundaries and it cannot be defeated.

He never practiced psychiatry, yet He has healed more broken hearts than all the doctors far and near. While once each week the wheels of commerce cease their turning, and multitudes wend their way to so many worshipping assemblies trying to pay homage and respect to Him, every day humble Christians around the world, meet Him face to face as they read and inhale His word in their daily worship at home and wherever they are.

The names of the proud statesmen of past empires, such as Greece and Rome, have come and gone; the names of the past scientists, philosophers and theologians have come and gone; yet He lives on, His name abounding more and more. Though time has spread more than 1,900 years between the people of this generation and the scene of His crucifixion, yet He lives. Herod could not kill Him, the devil could not seduce Him, death could not destroy Him, the grave could not hold Him, and even demons obeyed Him. He fed the hungry multitude with a boy's little lunch and broke up funerals by giving back life to those who were dead. He left heaven and all its glory and chose the life of the common people. He was rich, yet for our sakes He became poor. How poor? He was born in a cattle shed. He never owned a house or property and had no place to lay His head. He rode on a borrowed beast, although most of the time He travelled on foot. He died on a cross for the sins of others, wearing a crown of thorns. He was buried in another man's tomb. It is His death that makes us joyful, for He conquered death by rising from the grave the third day as He said He would. He is now at the right hand of power and will very soon come again in the clouds of heaven. He will come as King of Kings, and Lord of Lords with ten thousands of His saints in great glory, and He will take His followers to be forever with Him. Then He will judge the world righteously and every knee shall bow to Him and every tongue shall confess to God indeed. His friends shall be glad on that great day, but His enemies will seek a place to hide.

He is the Comforter of the sorrowing, the Hope of the dying, the Redeemer of people from every nation. He is the only One Who can satisfy the soul and give an everlasting life of blessedness to others.

So He stands upon the highest pinnacle of heavenly glory, proclaimed as God, acknowledged by angels, adored by saints and feared by devils as the living Christ, our Lord and Saviour.

There is a Book which tells about Him. In this Book you read about the condition of men, the intentions of God, the way to salvation, the punishment of sinners, and the blessedness of the believers. The teachings of this Book are holy, its commands binding, its stories true and its regulations untouchable. Read in that Book to be wise and live accordingly to be a saint. It contains light to lead you, admonitions to keep you, and consolations to give you strength. This Book is the map for the traveller, the staff of the pilgrim, the compass of the pilot, the sword of the warrior, and the banner of the Christians. Here the paradise is going to be reestablished, the kingdom of heaven is at hand, and hell awaits the wicked. Christ is the main subject of this Book from Genesis to Revelation, our redemption its purpose, and the glorification of God its ultimate goal. This Book should engross our hearts, be absorbed in our thoughts, and lead all our steps. Read it slowly, prayerfully and under His guidance! It is a fountain of wealth, a river of joy. It has been given to you for your life; it contains the highest responsibility, gives rewards for the greatest and smallest works, and condemns all those who do not act according to its content. This BOOK, written by holy men under the direct inspiration of God, is called "BIBLE." From the beginning to the end it speaks about this unique GREAT AND GOOD SHEPHERD I have just described.

Christ helped me more than any other friend could. He freed me from the bondage of sin; He has given me His peace. My life has been changed because Christ lives in my heart.

Truly, in the face of *so much* overwhelming evidence of genuine salvation, I could no longer be indifferent to that INCOMPARABLE SHEPHERD. I already had wasted too many years. How empty life really had been without Him who alone knows how to satisfy a hungry soul.

Have you ever felt a tugging in your heart for something which can truly gratify, for something real and lasting, something wonderful . . . peace and happiness? It was put there by its Creator, the One Who made your heart and, therefore, only He knows what we need and can truly fulfill these desires. Christ planted that longing in our souls so it will pull us along *until we enter His harbor of peace.*

He invites you to come to Him and accept Him by faith. Wherever you are, whoever you are, Christ will receive you; He will become your perfect Friend and Saviour. He will forgive your sins and change your heart. "If any man be in Christ, he is a new creature: old things are passed away; behold, all things are become new." (2 Cor. 5:17.) He is the ever-perfect One, the bright and morning star, the only One Who can satisfy the soul and give everlasting LIFE to those who do not have it but want it. Therefore, accept Him as your Redeemer today, for at this time the incomparable Christ is still standing at many a heart's door, seeking complete admission. His Word says: "Behold, I stand at the door and knock; if any man will hear my voice and open the door I will come in to him, and will sup with him, and he with me." (Rev. 3:20.) Also, "there is none other name under heaven given among men, whereby we must be saved." (Acts 4:12.) The Lord Jesus Christ is the greatest gift ever given to the world. He can be yours. IS HE? "Believe (give yourself up to Him) on the Lord Jesus Christ and thou shalt be saved." (Acts 16:31.) "For God so loved the world, that he gave his only begotten Son, that whosoever believeth in (clings to, surrenders to) him should not perish, but have everlasting life." (John 3:16.)

All my striving, all my craving for adventure was nothing else than a sidetracked search for *life's ultimate.* I could see the jigsaw puzzle was being fitted together. My life had not been a bed of roses by any means. But now I could understand that the dark fibers were just as necessary as the threads of gold and silver in the pattern He planned.

MY BACKGROUND

I was born in Breslau, Germany in 1935. The years of my early life were blessed with many of the world's comforts. The estate of my multi-millionaire industrialist father provided many of the luxuries most only dream about. There were a fleet of cars, large landscaped gardens, luxurious fur coats, maids, gardeners and gala dinners for the social elite with beautiful music accompanied by my mother's powerful coloratura soprano.

This utopia did not last long, however. Life was getting rough as the Second World War began to spread its fury over my homeland. Soldiers were taking over our playgrounds and turning them into forts. There was the howling of sirens, the sound of flak and the flash of exploding bombs reddening the night sky as air raids were blanketing our territory with increased frequency. Shortages became widespread while a misled populace continued to defend a vanishing empire with desperate courage. We never knew whether we were going to see another day.

As I witnessed the collapse of the entire world around us—my father's fortunes, the monetary and political system, the nation and even society itself, I came to see the frailty of man's achievements. It taught me early not to rely on gadgets and knickknacks. Therefore, it is very hard for me to understand why the American people pay so much attention to all those cheap commercial gimcracks. Kickshaws wherever one looks. A world of make-believe. Men everywhere feeding on empty husks, as they struggle year after year to find peace and contentment where there is none. It is not surprising that we see the empty, hurried looks most people have. Only a few wonder what life is all about and the hereafter amid all this frantic shuffle to get temporary gratification. But how can one find true enjoyment unless God gives that individual the capacity to look for and find satisfaction in the worthwhile things of eternal value?

Well did the seasoned apostle Paul write to the Corinthians, "For our light affliction, which is but for a moment, worketh for us a far more exceeding and eternal weight of glory; While we look not at the *things which are seen,* but at the things which are not seen: *for the things which are seen are temporal; but the things which are not seen are eternal"* (2 Cor. 4:17-18). Our bodies, our eyes are passing and therefore the materials we see must of necessity also be mortal. Secular eyes see terrestrial things. So take your eyes off an earth that is visible and temporal and put your attention on eternal matters. You cannot see the Almighty, His Spirit, His love and the eternal world. By letting God's Spirit work in and through your life, you are taking hold of lasting values. Then you are laying up treasures in heaven, where neither moth nor rust doth corrupt, and where thieves do not break through nor steal (Matt. 6:20).

My life was definitely being channeled into that direction. An existence of physical suffering, privation and simplicity followed as I grew up under the rule of two dictatorships. After World War II the part of Germany where I lived was taken over by Communism. I spent five years under its terror regime.

It was not easy for us children to hear the nightly cries of women as they were being raped by brutes. Our teeth were slowly decaying in the absence of dental care or even toothbrushes. Fortunate people were searching the countryside and forests for whatever food was available, but large numbers of highwaymen made it very risky to try to visit even a nearby farmer in an effort to obtain some food.

Picture yourself, for a moment, under the following circumstances which took place in Communist-occupied territories. Let's say it occurs right now.

The general populace has been subdued and taken care of. The more resistant subjects are forced to attend sessions from early in the morning until late at night seated on narrow slats. Gruelling questioning takes place as half-starved, tortured persons just dragged from dark cells and now blinded by bright spotlights, attempt to give answers to a continuous bombardment of questions by the merciless inquisitors. "Wrong" answers bring retribution upon the hapless victim in the form of having his head thrust into a pot containing human excretion until he expires. Another method is the driving of wooden or metal spikes up the nose of the doomed person until the brain is pierced through.

A crowd has been gathered by force. A number of people (dissenters and God-fearing persons) are led upon a platform at the side of that square. Two men comprising an execution squad are already waiting there with large knives to chop off the heads of the victims which then fall into a large basket. While this is in progress, the throng is asked to applaud, cheer and smile. You are one among the many persons in attendance. Many government functionaries and a sizeable police force in civilian attire dispersed throughout the crowd watch the actions of all present. Anyone observed who does not rejoice about the proceedings by clapping and smiling will be executed when the meetings resume the next week.

Children dressed in white robes are lined up and marched past the platform where the executions are taking place. They are told to dip their hands into the blood and wipe it onto their robes. Prizes are awarded to the children with the most bloodstains on their garments.

Others are dragged off into bitter-cold concentration camps. You are placed in a small, watertight room struggling to stay alive as icy water floods it so that you could breathe only by standing on tiptoe. How long do you think you will last? Nearby, a fellow citizen is buried with only his head left above ground. A large glass bowl enveloping the head is set into position with rats enclosed. The rats then slowly but relentlessly gnaw the helpless victim to death.

After reading this, you probably appreciate more the freedom we still have left in our country. Above all, you may want to take an active part in the fight to maintain liberty. And the best way to do so is to present the King of all true freedom and liberty, which is to live and preach the gospel of Jesus Christ.

Conditions were so bad that also we had to search the forest for edible foods in order to survive. Schools and churches were closed; there was no formal schooling or religious worship. Christians met secretly. The hay and stubble were burned but the gold came through the fires of persecution purified and refined (John 17: 20-23).

When I was finally able to come to West Germany, I had to work hard to make up for lost schooling. Years of study in the various secular and spiritual subjects of man's suppositions and work in various secular jobs came next. And *then* came the flying venture which changed my ambitions. It was during this trip that I realized God was speaking to me. All along, my unique life had been a preparation for the High Calling but now I felt an absolute dependency upon Him. Something broke within myself during this journey and something new rose like a morning star in my heart.

Throughout many years I *thought* that I had found what I was looking for, but now I *knew*. In John 6:44 we read, "No man can come to me, except the Father which hath sent me draw him: and I will raise him up at the last day." It was all by His grace. He had been drawing me all along. I was coming out at the top of the mountain. It had been a long, arduous trail. I had brought the problems upon myself. Instead of reaching out and allowing the Master to grasp my hand and pull me up to the pinnacle, I had gone around and around the mountain trying on my own. I could not see the top from below. Trees and other obstacles were hiding it from my view, so I had failed in my search. But He, the great Creator of the universe, knew where the summit was and brought me up there quickly. And, oh, what a wonderful view there was on top of that peak! How great to see the entire panorama laid out before you as you scan God's great country from above. It seems as though you understand the Lord better when you can look down upon His creation, just as we had done so many times from the plane. But then my eyes had been closed.

The religious and philosophical leaders I had followed theretofore gave me sets of rules, intricate regulations and vague theories to abide by in order to work my way to a better state. All these complex and high-sounding ideas gave glory to their promoters rather than help to their followers. I remembered now how Christ said in John 7:18, *"He that speaketh of himself seeketh his own glory:* but he that seeketh his glory that sent him, the same is true, and no unrighteousness is in him."

I had read the New Testament many times when I was afflicted with sickness and pain and laid up in a hospital bed, but only now through the illumination of His spirit could I catch the true meaning. "Howbeit when he, the Spirit of truth, is come, *he will guide you into all truth: for he shall not speak of himself;* but whatsoever he shall hear, that shall he speak: *and he will shew you things to come"* (John 16:13). Look at the promoters of cults in America today! Are they not all interested in building up their own organizations, their own names? Again, Jesus said in John 8:50, " . . . *I seek not mine own glory:* there is one that seeketh and judgeth."

It was the most wonderful day in my life when I was born again. The world took on a different glimmer. The grass looked greener, the birds sang more beautifully. The whole creation seemed to radiate a peace and harmony unknown to me before. This is why I feel sorry for those who want to see the world without this new pair of eyes. They are missing more than they are seeing. I experienced what the Psalmist meant when he cried out, "Thou wilt show me the path of life: in thy presence is fulness of joy; at thy right hand there are pleasures forevermore" (Psalm 16:11).

Soon I was to receive a commission in this new realm God had called me into which was to carry me through nearly 100 countries around the world.

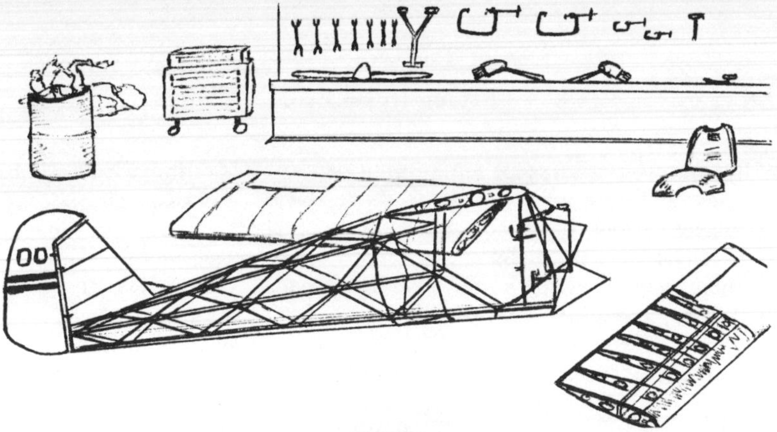

10

That Was Flying

I could not forget that little bird of mine, though. Again and again, my tender thoughts returned to the 18-day flying odyssey it had bravely endured with us and, other than playing a little trick here and there, the craft really never let us down entirely. By God's grace it stuck with us to the end.

REVISITING GRIMBERGEN

Three and one-half months later, on August 7th, not very long after I had recovered, I revisited Grimbergen while on a business tour through Belgium with my father. I wanted to see my little winged friend. But what did I see when we arrived there! I nearly wept! There, much to my disgust, the mighty challenger of the continents lay like a bird plucked of its wings and feathers. It was all dismantled, displaying only a naked, unimpressive, pitiful-looking fuselage. I meant to show my father that proud little bird of renown, but was unable to impress him much with what he saw. With a big smile, he asked, "Were you the ones who brought back the plane in that condition?"

Certainly our brave little fellow sufferer did not deserve a fate like this. Seeing it there so helpless and torn apart, it struck me how many times on the trip we could have ended up just like it. All of a sudden, the highlights of our now past flying adventure rolled like a fast-moving film in front of my eyes once more.

There was the time when we were hopelessly lost in the "soup" over Paris. Then those terrorizing hours when storm signals were fluttering so wildly that no person with a minimum of moral discrimination could fail to understand their unmistakable warning. It was a day of total crisis, when we tottered between life and death on our flight around Cape Finisterre, the northwest corner of Spain. Bitter winds, approaching hurricane velocity, then swept over the entire area. These gales, screaming with fury and filled with foreboding, whipped to tatters the storm flags flying above our every realm of that day's life.

It was followed by the red rocket shots and signal flares at Gibraltar resulting in a thirsty bird heading with forlorn hopes over the deep waters to Africa—a moment of penultimate disaster as we saw the end of our flying coming on apace. Then came the sudden dive toward the depths of the Atlantic when I fell asleep at the controls off the shoreline of Morocco; not to forget the evenings when we initiated emergency landing procedures after a fruitless 45-minute search for an airport at Jerez Haya and "conquered" that strategic American Air Force base in France . . . and to transcend it all, finally the day when the effect of these experiences resulted in the most glorious change of my entire life.

It was more than I could take. Wiping across my forehead and shaking myself, I dashed out of the hangar. Quickly I chartered an Aeronca Champion—the closest type to my beloved one I could get. With this, I took my father on a brief ride over Brussels World's Fair this sad and yet so blissful August morning, and left for good—never to return.

My destiny was fixed. Soon I left Europe altogether! My *new life* was to start on a *new continent.*

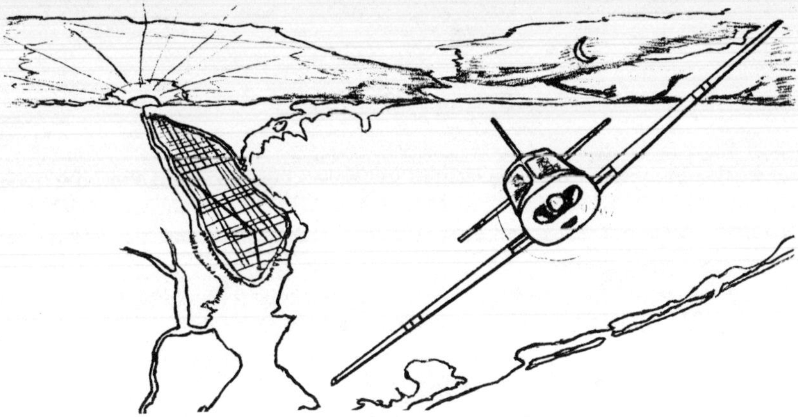

11

Rudi Lehmann's Last Flight

It was late afternoon on a sunny January day in 1959.

Rudi Lehmann and I sat at the controls of the beautiful Comanche 250 as we were circling approximately 10,000 feet over New York City.

"This is the distance I enjoy being from any large town, particularly one like New York," I said, marveling at the sight spread under us.

"I had to make this high altitude flight to check my physical shape before I leave on this transatlantic venture. I am particularly concerned about my heart," replied Rudi as he kept monitoring the instruments. "I don't anticipate any problems. I've been across this pond before. Altogether 73 times as pilot in command of big commercial airliners. But to do it with this little 'one engine job' is going to be different. I reckon it will take me about 30 hours to make it there; so I need to install a number of additional tanks. Then let's hope for the best that the engine won't quit and that I won't fall asleep–I will be the only one on board."

"Eh! It sounds like you need me along," I exclaimed hastily. "That's something for me again–exactly the type of thing I am always looking for." There was another flying adventurer. It would be so much more fun to travel with him than it was with scared Klaus who always left you at a loss what to expect next of him–whether he was going to hang with it or leave. But this stocky little former Lufthansa Captain was tough and ready to move. One could tell that he knew what he wanted and he was not about ready to dump an unfinished project.

"I already notified the German television network and they are going to film my arrival over there. It means $1,250.00 and that will help along to meet my expenses. I will also realize a good profit on the sale of this plane. It's a good combination!"

"Well Rudi, how about it? Should I join in and help you?" I insisted. After all, I could give him the treatment Klaus gave me when I fell asleep off the shores of Africa. Being a pilot myself, I could also help him fly the plane while we took turns in catching some sleep.

"Not this time. I need all the extra space for additional fuel. But I'll return for more planes. They will be twin engines and can accommodate us both. Then we can make it a joint venture." Soon I was to learn that this decision saved my life. Evidently God had something more in store for me.

"I'll tell you what," I returned. "Let's utilize both trips. When you come back to pick up the twin engine, I will accompany you on that flight. Then we will purchase a German ocean-going yacht and sail it across the waters to the U. S. There are good markets, especially in the Caribbean areas and Florida where we can realize a $10,000 gain on the boat alone. Then in turn we'll purchase the next plane over here and keep on in that order. I have the knowledge we need because I attended the High Sea School in Bremen where I learned such matters as astronomic navigation, the sea lane marking systems and all the rest."

"Good idea—that's what we'll do," he said in short businesslike fashion, as if we had just decided on some ordinary matter. However, I knew he meant it. He realized the relatively low purchase price, good workmanship of German boats and the fact that they successfully crossed the Atlantic were going to make it a profitable venture. The lack of aircraft industry in Germany so soon after the war rendered the sale of American-made aircraft lucrative over there, particularly when he saved the high shipping expenses by ferrying them himself. At the same time, these undertakings were adding to our interesting life style and flying as well as sailing experience. We could combine other sidelines with it, such as the making of movies and the writing of documentaries.

While we were fully engrossed in discussion, we didn't notice how time was quickly slipping away from us. Rudi was cutting back the motor power and trimmed the plane for descending flight which hastened the sunset. The western horizon was bathed in a pinkish-reddish gleam. The presence of an already fairly high crescent moon silhouetted against the dark-red clouds added to the gorgeous display of colors. Our conversation was subsiding at the emergence of this fantastic wonderland all around us and it ushered in a hushed silence. While we continued to bank toward lower flight levels, our wings were pointing toward crystal clear stars hanging like little lanterns in the night firmament. At times it seemed as though these heavenly objects were near enough for me to grasp. Continuously all things appeared under different perspectives—what a dreamy wonderland.

I was now praising the great Creator Who had become my Saviour. How elated I became when I realized that the Almighty Who made all this had not long ago become very personal in my life. I was just assimilating the greatest sermon my mortal ears could ever hear. "The heavens declare the glory of God; and the firmament sheweth his handiwork. Day unto day uttereth speech, and night unto night sheweth knowledge. There is no speech nor language, where their voice is not heard. Their line is gone out through all the earth, and their words to the end of the world . . . ." (Psalm 19:1-4).

At this moment it was hard for me to understand how anyone could possibly be so narrow-minded as not to recognize the Infinite and without Whom they would not exist. Again I had to think how His Word speaks of the glory of these heavenly bodies. "There are also celestial bodies, and bodies terrestrial: but the glory of the celestial is one, and the glory of the terrestrial is another. There is one glory of the sun, and another glory of the moon, and another glory of the stars: for one star differeth from another star in glory" (1 Cor. 15:40-41). I was now under the influence of many glories. It was good to know the Father of glory (Eph. 1:17) for some day I shall appear with Him (Col. 3:4).

The sight below us was fascinating. Long lines of lights were outlining the streets of Manhattan and Times Square. Some of the world's largest ocean liners, the Queen Elizabeth, Queen Mary and United States, were in New York's harbor under full illumination. It was just more than I could take and stay silent. All these mighty impressions were playing an overwhelming tune on the strings of my soul. I felt as though I were set aflame. How could I keep all that joy to myself! It was impossible—I had to share it and Rudi was the logical choice.

To top it all and create a near explosion within me, two Bible verses flooded my mind. "Whosoever therefore shall confess me before men, him will I confess also before my Father which is in heaven. But whosoever shall deny me before men, him will I also deny before my Father which is in heaven" (Matt. 10:32, 33). By now I was certain about the next course of action. I was to witness to Rudi Lehmann.

I did not have to search for words. The inspiration was flowing too heavily. "Here you fly but for a season; soon these joys, as well as your life, will all have passed. Let me introduce you to the source of all eternal bliss . . . ." I could proceed no further.

Rudi broke in abruptly. "I am not at all interested in religion," he flashed, and continued to puff on his freshly lighted cigarette more nervously. "It's not my bag."

His sudden change of mood stunned me for an instant. "Neither am I, but I am interested in Christ, the living Saviour," I meant and should have said, but for fear of losing his friendship I didn't. I also was afraid that it would have spelled an end to the transatlantic ventures we had planned. I didn't want to see all of this smashed and stayed silent at this crucial moment. It was a fateful decision, and I came to regret it the rest of my life.

Darkness had settled upon the metropolis as we were now coming in "on final" at Flushing Airport. It was nearly impossible to differentiate the runway lights sandwiched between an ocean of brilliant city illumination. Gusty winds gave us a bumpy approach. The plane suddenly dropped as we hit several airholes. It almost caused us to strike the buildings below.

After a short stopover, we city-hopped and soon landed at Teterboro Airport, a large general aviation facility in New Jersey, not far from New York City. Altogether we had flown about 4½ hours this January 11th. Today's IFR high altitude flight had great variety. We saw the Atlantic Ocean, mountains, lakes, rivers, and giant cities at daytime, twilight and night and occasionally even sliced through an isolated cloud.

I was still sad that I had not acquainted my friend with the *brightness of God's glory* (Hebr. 1:3). I was thinking of a passage where it says, "For all flesh is as grass, and all the glory of man as the flower of grass. The grass withereth, and the flower thereof falleth away:" (1 Peter 1:24). I did not have the slightest idea that this verse, as well as the only statement I made in witnessing to him, was truly prophetic.

I saw Rudi once more in Manhattan before he left. He had invited me to a crazy movie. It was hard for me to sit through it. At the end he said, "I figured it wasn't a bad investment of my money to buy the tickets. I saw several dead people for every cent I paid." I could not share his philosophy, but it was a fitting description of that film. Two days later he left. He took to the sky for the last time, leaving for good . . . never to return.

I was waiting for the letters he had promised me. But there were none. Finally I wrote. An immediate reply from his wife informed me that he had died on this, his final journey. I was shocked. As soon as possible I visited Teterboro Airport and talked with the manager of the Piper aircraft office. With a serious face, he briefed me on what had happened. "Mr. Lehmann could not leave the U. S. They had just passed a law forbidding single engine planes to cross the Atlantic. He had to fly to Canada so he could leave from there. On his trip up, an ice storm rent him from the sky. Forced to make an emergency landing, he was smashed to pieces. His gold cigarette lighter and watch were all we found. His SOS was his final message to the world."

Whereas I was shocked before, now I was stupefied. The words of Ezekiel, the prophet, entered my mind with sudden violence: "AGAIN the word of the LORD came unto me, saying, Son of man, speak to the children of thy people, and say unto them, When I bring the sword upon a land, if the people of the land take a man of their coasts, and set him for their watchman: If when he seeth the sword come upon the land, he blow the trumpet, and warn the people; Then whosoever heareth the sound of the trumpet, and taketh not warning; if the sword come, and take him away, his blood shall be upon his own head. He heard the sound of the trumpet, and took not warning; his blood shall be upon him. But he that taketh warning shall deliver his soul. *But if the watchman see the sword come, and blow not the trumpet, and the people be not warned; if the sword come, and take any person from among them, he is taken away in his iniquity; but his blood will I require at the watchman's hand."*(Ezek. 33: 1-6).

"Oh Lord, forgive me," I cried. It seemed as though my prayer froze on the ceiling of that office and dripped down icily on my back. It was clear to me this forlorn day, that the *blood of Rudi Lehmann* was on my hands. God had given me a clear opportunity to witness to him and I had worried more about losing his friendship and missing out on ventures than seeing him come to the Lord. There would never be another chance for me to talk to him. Rudi was gone–gone for good. I had trouble holding back my tears. "Thank you, thank you for telling me what happened," I stuttered feebly and left.

This experience was instrumental to channel me into God's great harvest field. That day I made a vow to God. "Lord, if You ever again give me an opportunity to witness to a soul, and I hope You will, I shall not any longer worry what man may think or say. My only concern will be what You think and say so that I may one day hear the words *well done, thou good and faithful servant"* (Matt. 25:21, 23). I couldn't have been more sincere. I felt relieved after this vow. I could breathe easier, and apparently God was pleased with my response. Very soon I was to find out that *witnessing* to men everywhere would become my way of life!

While visiting Germany shortly afterward, I was able to testify to Rudi Lehmann's French wife, who lived in Hamburg with her two little children.

12

Wandering in the Wilderness

It was a hot August day in New York. The air, sandwiched between the skyscrapers, was vibrating—and so was I! Soul-searching events had thrown me out of my former orbit, and I was now being hurled into a new realm yet unknown to me.

A wandering in the wilderness followed. Later it became evident that I was being led in a similar way to Moses. He was learned in all the wisdom of the Egyptians (Acts 7:22) for the first 40 years of his life. The next 40 years God led him through the desert so he could forget it, and then the last 40 years the Lord could use him.

True, my sapience had received severe jolts! But a time of flushing out the *old* and gloriously filling in the *new* had to come next. An experience not very different from the one Paul made when he did not confer with flesh and blood to receive a greater revelation of the Son, but went into the desert of Arabia instead (Gal. 1:16, 17). Then, after quite a period of time in direct contact with the ONE Who moves heaven and earth, he could say, "But I certify you, brethren, that the gospel which was preached of me is not after man. For I neither received it of man, neither was I taught it, but by the revelation of Jesus Christ" (Gal. 1:11, 12).

For five months I travelled without taking up residence. During this time I spent only $160.00. There were a lot of visits to national forests, parks and monuments. For quite awhile I followed the skyline drive along the Appalachian Mountains. During the nights I slept in the open or in the car. Usually I camped away from people. I could draw closer to God in the great quietness I so much enjoyed. While watching the starlit firmament through the open sun roof of my vehicle, I would fall asleep serenely. In the morning, just before sunrise, the melodious chatter of the birds woke me up. Soon the sun was casting its warming rays of light in little beams through the trees. Autumn had arrived and the varied-colored leaves, like myriads of tiny lamps, were reflecting much of the sunshine and setting the forest aflame. A beautiful setting for my early morning prayer and study in His Word. I felt so happy that I joined the birds in a rejoicing song.

In some ways I lived almost like the deer. Nature provided much of my food. For lengthy periods of time, I saw no people whatsoever. Every so often my journey brought me through a town where I usually met some of the friendly Southerners who invited me to their homes. Nearly always I felt inspired to witness to these dear people, and I know that often a great impact was left behind.

I remember one night I pulled into a Smoky Mountain National Park Campground. I was led to camp beside the only other people present. Very tired, I was ready to rest for the night. But soon the old couple invited me for the evening meal. Since they seemed to be nice folks I accepted.

It was not very long before we started to talk about spiritual matters. I will never forget how the old gentleman painted a wonderful and enlightening picture of a true believer versus a make-believe. I can still hear him explain, "If you do something wrong as a genuine Christian, the Spirit of God convicts you and it will be hard for you to relax until you repent and ask God for forgiveness. David did so after he had grievously sinned but God called him, '. . . a man after mine own heart, who shall fulfill all my will' (Luke 13:22). He forgave him, though David had trouble the rest of his life, reaping what he sowed. But if a person, after his profession of faith, continues his old ungodly life without feeling guilty, something is wrong. The Spirit must not dwell in that individual. This is the difference I see between real and fake Christians."

Our fellowship around the fire continued for a long time. At the end he asked me, "Do your parents know what kind of a son they have?"

There were numerous experiences along such lines. I particularly remember how God began to keep me from erring. Whenever I fell into temptation, my body would start to shake as if I were freezing to death. In that condition, I was literally unable to speak a word, and this helped me greatly to stay away from sin. My wilderness experiences brought me into such a closeness to my Heavenly Father that I treasured an almost continuous dependence upon Him. In fact, I was now so finely tuned to that Higher Power that I became very sensitive toward the forces of wickedness.

Big cities, for one thing, started to affect me in a negative way. Most people in those centers of population are concerned with material rather than spiritual matters. Many of them actually have outright thoughts of evil and practice it as well. Our brain emits waves according to our sentiments. These many emissions of mostly low morals from a town then form trunk lines which reach for quite a distance. If you are sensitive toward spiritual influences, you will feel these currents when yet a long ways from town. Many a time when coming from the wilderness and driving toward a big city, I have felt very depressed–almost like a lid was being clamped down on my head.

All this was interspersed by spine-tingling episodes, such as diving among swordfish and barracuda off the east coast of Florida. One diver nearby sighted some sharks so close that he first thought they were submarines. Upon surfacing, he was ready to faint. The shock left him temporarily namby-pamby. There were so many wholesome excitements, that I am unable to describe most of them in this volume. I will endeavor to do so in my forthcoming book which will feature my life story.

13

The Great Commission

Time had been flying. About five months after my departure, I arrived in New Orleans, Louisiana. It was to be a short stop, but God determined otherwise. I stayed there about a year and a half. Apparently I had strengthened sufficiently spiritualwise during my wandering in the wilderness that I could take it. Now it was time to work among people for a season. It started with commercial work, but the Lord had other plans. I soon became a fiery witness unto this city, distributing hundreds of thousands of gospel tracts all over. Many sermons were preached in the middle of town on Canal Street, in the French Quarter and in parks. It was from this place that I conducted my campaign all over Latin America and the Caribbean areas. But before that, something happened which decidedly determined the course of my life from then on.

For many weeks I had been praying and fasting. Usually I wouldn't eat nor drink for periods of three days. I didn't know then that a person needs liquid while he fasts. It is possible to live without food for many weeks. But without water for any such length, a person will soon die. At times I became so weak, I could hardly raise up after resting. I had symptoms of dehydration in that heat. The climate there is such that it is claimed, "If you can stand it in New Orleans, Louisiana, you can live anywhere in the world." Providentially I interrupted this extensive fasting period every three days or so. It may very well have saved my life, because then I also took liquid.

There was a definite reason for withdrawing to this ascetic lifestyle. About two years previously I had been born again. Christ had become my Saviour, yet I still served two worlds at times. I knew it was not possible for a dedicated Christian to do so. Christ said in Matt. 6:24, "No man can serve two masters: for either he will hate the one, and love the other; or else he will hold to the one, and despise the other. *Ye cannot serve God and mammon."*

The reason we have so many unhappy Christians today is that too many of them are halting between two opinions (1 Kings 18:21). They serve God a little and then the world a little and so on. It's like driving a car by stepping on the gas a bit and then on the brake a bit, and so forth. It will wear out any vehicle in a hurry. That kind of life will exhaust you as well. It is the very reason why so many formerly fine Christians ended up in insane asylums. *The only way to be really happy is to be centralized in God's perfect purpose for your existence–in what He wants you to do.*

I became increasingly aware of this, and *now needed to know God's complete will for my life.* It was the very reason for my extended time of fasting. I was tired of dabbling around. Already I was doing much more, by the grace of God, than most Christian people ever endeavor, but it was yet child's play. I needed to break through the sound barrier fully. It had to be clear-cut. Either for the world or for God all the way. No in-between muddling. No stumbling in the twilight. It had to be all out for either side, and I knew it was going to be for God. I came this far–there could be no return into the mess of the world. No desire manifested itself to be compared with the dog which turned to his own vomit again; or the sow that was washed, to her wallowing in the mire (2 Peter 2:22).

Once the disciples asked Christ why they were not able to cast out the devil from a lunatic boy (Matt. 17:14-19). Jesus replied, ". . . Because of your unbelief: for verily I say unto you, If ye have faith as a grain of mustard seed, ye shall say unto this mountain, Remove hence to yonder place; and it shall remove; and nothing shall be impossible unto you. *Howbeit this kind goeth not out but by prayer and fasting"* (Matt. 17:20-21).

Clearly, I was doing the right thing. If in no other way, by prayer and fasting it was going to be done! The problem was not that God didn't want to answer me, but rather that I wasn't in the right condition before Him to hear His answer. Prayer and fasting was going to bring me into this closeness with God. "If ye abide in me, and my words abide in you, ye shall ask what ye will, and it shall be done unto you" (John 15:7). From John 1:1 we learn that the Word was God. "In the beginning was the Word, and the Word was with God, and the Word was God."

Plainly, the Word and, at the same time, God were not as yet sufficiently implanted in me. However, all this was changing quickly now. While fasting, praying and searching His Word almost continuously, the last countdown had come! I was readied for the take-off which was to send me soaring all over this world.

The deciding divine signal came one night during the fast. I had just cut off the light and gone to bed. Then the vision struck. As far as I remember, it was the first one I had in my life. A Bible appeared before me upright on its spine. Slowly the book was opening and 2 Tim. 4:5 distinctly entered my mind twice, summoning me for a definite commission. I whispered to myself, "This is strange, I don't know what that scripture says, but I will look it up in the morning." Immediately the Lord compelled me to rise, put on the light and read the passage. With wide-open eyes I read the amazing scripture, "But watch thou in all things, endure afflictions, *do the work of an evangelist,* make full proof of thy ministry."

What could be any clearer than that? For quite some time, I had felt God was going to use me in a kindred capacity. However, I had to be sure of my calling. Whatever it was, I wanted to obey. Whether to be a pilot, teacher or in some type of other commercial work or in the ministry—I desired to be centered into His perfect will. Only then could I expect His full blessing, protection and provision.

Already I had endured a lot of afflictions through the years. More was to come as I was now launching out in the work of an evangelist, making full proof of my ministry. Nearly endless crusades circling America and the globe followed. In the next chapter you will read how the trail to the pinnacle of His heavenly glory led me through valleys of the shadow of death and over quickening mountain tops. Afflictions, necessities, imprisonment, tumults, watchings, fastings and labors were among my steady travel companions.

If Paul had to approve his ministry in such a way (2 Cor. 6:3-5), how much more would it also have to apply to me. "Endure afflictions," was part of my commission. Soon I learned how to be abased and how to abound. One day in prison, the succeeding day in the mansion of a king. I understood that both experiences were needed to humble and encourage me. How well I could now fathom the words of the great apostle Paul, "I know both how to be abased, and I know how to abound: every where and in all things I am instructed both to be full and to be hungry, both to abound and to suffer need" (Phil. 4:12). Yet, when I think of all the miracles He bestowed upon me during those trips, I never cease to marvel. Also, the way I was provided for makes me think of David when he cried out, "I have been young, and now am old; yet have I not seen the righteous forsaken, nor his seed begging bread" (Psalm 37:25).

So, at this juncture, accompany me on my first extensive international evangelistic tour. Taste some of the highlights and distresses such a life presents!

PART IV

WINGS OF ADVENTURE

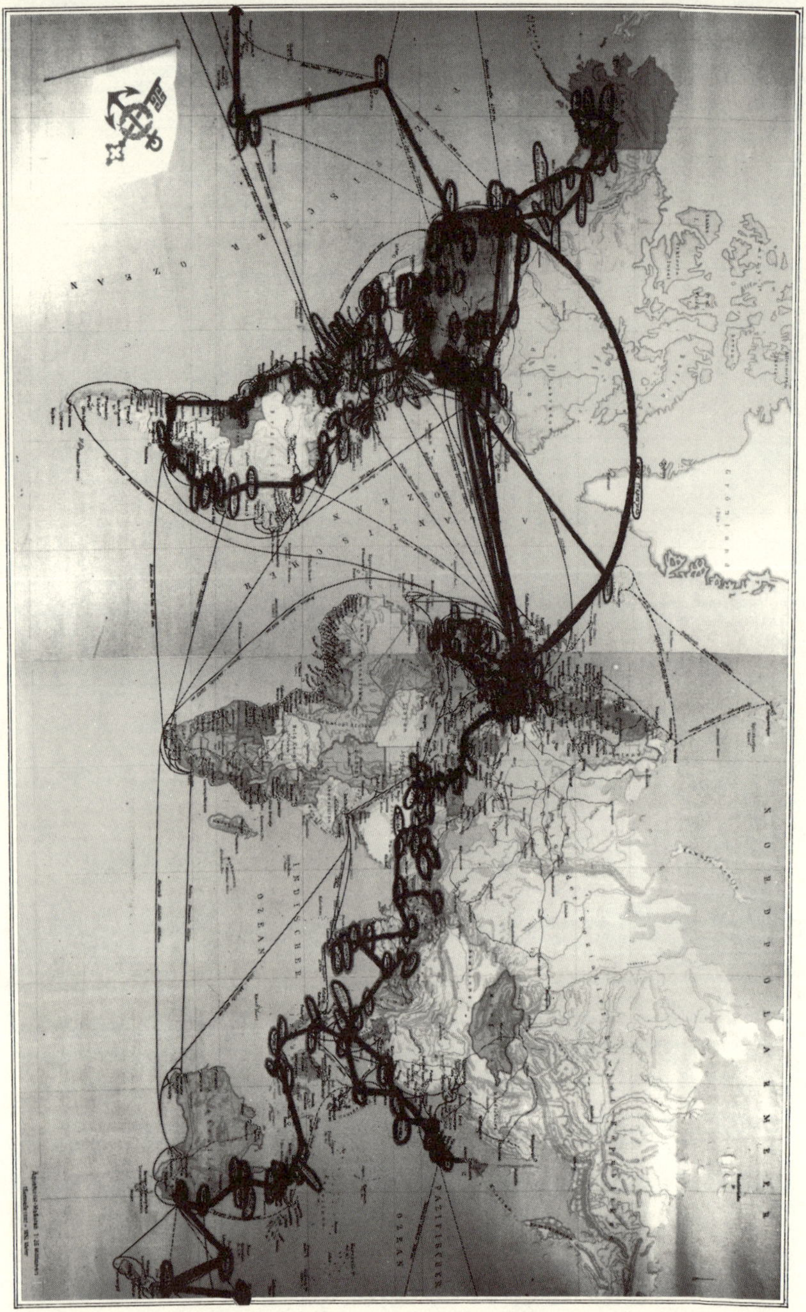

IN SEARCH OF EXCITEMENT . . . AND THEN IN FULFILLMENT OF A COMMISSION. A globetrotter's mappery! The journeys of Hans J. Schneider who logged more than one-quarter million miles in air travel alone, equivalent to 10½ times around the earth. He encountered country and people in nearly 100 nations while straddling the world in many years of continent-hopping.

14

Come Travel with Me

Almost continuous preaching campaigns came next. In keeping with the general tone of most of the book, I will now present you with some of the adventures I experienced. Because of their great number on account of my frequent travels, I can only pick a few isolated cases within the framework of this volume.[1]

CARIBBEAN, CENTRAL AND LATIN AMERICAN JOURNEY

While on an extensive crusade to the Southern Hemisphere via the Caribbean area, around South America and on the way back through Central America, I ran across a number of interesting and dangerous encounters.

Detained in Caracas

Toward the beginning of the trip, I had the unpleasant experience of being detained from leaving Caracas, Venezuela, because my name was on the prohibition list of the custom authorities. I did not have much hope

[1]The complete story of my unique life will be relegated to another forthcoming book. Watch for this autobiography, which I am sure you will enjoy. It will probably be published by World Wide Publishing Corporation also. You may find the address in front of this book. Many people are awaiting the arrival of my life story. Pray that I will be greatly inspired as I write.

for exiting the country. Tanks on that particular day were lined up on the street to the airport. People talked about another revolution.

I knew from others' experiences that if I were not allowed to leave as planned I might never be able to do so. My eyes glanced over to the airport ramp to see whether the Pan American plane scheduled to depart at 12:00 o'clock noon was still there. It was only a few minutes before that time.

Once again, I cried to the Lord to help me in this new predicament. When you travel a lot or live an exciting life, you have plenty of occasion to learn how to pray and expect answers from God. This time I needed His help *right then.* His answer came in a most unusual and different way than I had expected. Airliners have to leave on time. If they are delayed, it causes them great expense. People miss their connections to fly on with another plane. Pilots are under pressure to count the minutes. Only an Almighty can cause them to delay departure for one passenger.

But the captain left the cockpit and came back to the custom counter to see to it that I would be permitted to go. I suddenly thought of the old passport in my possession and showed it to the authorities proving that I had never visited Venezuela before. The impossible had happened! It was a relief as the Pan American airliner took off *15 minutes after 12:00* with me on board! I still remember with thanks the intercession of the pilot of that plane, who I hope will read this book and write me.

Up to this day I have never found out why my name was on that list, whether it was someone else's name or whether it was entered under the pro-Communist Betancourt government on account of my anti-Communist stand in the United States.

Die Grüne Hölle (The Green Hell)

There are still vast wilderness areas in South America, such as the Matto Grosso and Amazon territories in Brazil; in fact, most of that continent is settled only along the coastlines while the inner regions are practically vacant.

Once, while spending time in Belém at the Amazon, I met a German globetrotter who had been living for some years in Peru's capital. He had crossed the mainland travelling from Lima to that giant stream; then he followed it and spent much time visiting some of the Indians, such as the Jaguars, who were practically untouched by civilization. In his possession was a stack of highly interesting photographs. One pictured him standing in the Amazon among the piranhas while he wrestled with an anaconda. Another showed this brave adventurer under the strangle hold of such a serpentine monster as he held its head in a secure grasp beside the mighty river.

"Watch when the *bore* comes in!" he said. "Several walls of water nearly 15 feet high then rush upstream with a roar that can be heard about

16 miles away. For the last 400 miles, until it enters the ocean, the Amazon River drops only 1/8 inch per mile. When the tide enters, the current in the river mouth is, therefore, reversed.

"At times the river is so wide that one cannot see the opposite shore. The current from the huge 150-mile-wide mouth of the Amazon can be seen 200 miles out at sea."

One evening, while lying in hammocks at one of the native hotels in Belém, we were both caught up in an interesting conversation about life in the jungle. I mentioned that I had read books about the "green hell" and how people who had experienced that type of life were always drawn back until they finally would disappear from civilization altogether. I asked, "Do you find that to be true?"

He confirmed it by saying, "I keep being attracted to the primitive regions. Already I have been thinking about making other extensive wilderness journeys and expeditions such as to the Matto Grosso, a place which I heard about as being one of the great wild areas of this world."

"What do you feel is the challenge of the jungle?"

He said, "The uncertainty of life," and continued, "For instance, you travel by canoe down the stream overhung by subtropical fauna (trees and orchids), with colorful birds and monkeys playing overhead, but you never know what will appear around the next bend. Alligators, dolphins and giant turtles are common. There is a constant changing of scenery beyond every river curve, past every bend of the trail. You continuously have a different, beautiful view and no two scenes are alike. There is the confrontation of new animal life and perhaps meeting some natives along your route; also, the uncertainty of where to spend the next night and the challenge of picking and finding your next meal."

I had to think about our *65 horsepower over Europe trip* and all the suspense it held.

He also related the experiences of one Danish explorer who had become lost in the South American jungles and who, 35 years later, had been found living with an Indian wife. When asked by the European expedition that met him whether he wanted to return to civilization, he replied with a definite "NO!" When asked whether he had need of specific items, if he wanted to have or see certain things, his only request was, "Give me a Danish newspaper so I can bring myself up-to-date as to what has happened during the last 3½ decades." Most people who have had a chance of practical comparison between a civilized and a pioneer-primitive type of life have sealed their remaining days with a preference for the latter. My encounters with the South American wilderness were very enjoyable.

One of the most delicious and refreshing drinks I ever found while travelling, was in Rio de Janeiro. Here's the recipe: Take one avocado, cut it in half, remove the stone and then take out the "meat" with a small

Among the Jaguar Indians *(upper left)* in the Amazon region of Brazil. Exploring the Amazon River by canoe *(lower left).* Enswathed by a gargantuan anaconda *(above).* These serpentine giants grow to a length of more than 30 feet, unapproached by any other South American snake. They kill by wrapping their coils tightly around the prey, choking it to death. These monsters also can inflict deep wounds with their many teeth by biting. Some have even been known to attack large mammals. The unusual ability of their jaw bones to stretch far apart, and their throat and body to expand considerably, enables them to swallow and hold animals much larger than their heads. Also called *water boas,* they often swim in rivers.

spoon and put it in a blender. Add honey or sugar (whichever you prefer) and milk, blend and drink.

Agonies in Rio

While spending time in some of the major metropolitan areas of Latin America, I had a few unpleasant experiences. While in Rio de Janeiro I wound up with a stolen wallet, watch and clothing. The wallet contained much of my money and most important papers. This all happened while I was swimming at the Copacabana Beach. I had asked some people next to me, "Please watch my belongings." They promised to do so.

Panoramic view of Rio de Janeiro, Brazil—a place of many unpleasant memories.

When I returned from a five-minute swim in the ocean, I found that they and my things were gone. A medical doctor, whose acquaintance I made there, took me to a police station where they recorded the theft. I was told, "Do not fret, this happens every day. Just the other day $2,000 was stolen from an American on that beach." What a nice consolation!

After extensive paperwork, but no help, I ended up in a taxicab. The medical doctor lent me some money which took me to the center of Rio de Janeiro. There I was unloaded wearing the only belongings which were left, namely, an old pair of shoes, a decrepit straw hat and, of course, my bathing suit. Conspicuous in that very unique uniform, I had an instant audience! There was quite a crowd around, smiling at me and thinking that I was rather a funny individual. I, however, was not much inclined for jokes. This time I was sped on my way by a police car, which brought me the rest of the way to the hotel. To the amazement of the administrative staff, I arrived in that unusual outfit. Needless to say, I brought my stay in Brazil to a quick end!

Before I left the land of thievery, however, I had a real session of prayer. "Please, Heavenly Father, convict this filcher's heart and make him return these absolute necessities for my trip," were some of the words I cried.

Unfortunately, I did not have enough faith to linger to see what would happen and left the next day. This lack of trust in the power of prayer resulted in severe hardships throughout the rest of the long journey. It was hard to continue without the items which were stolen.

By the grace of God, I was later able to board the plane on my last leg of the trip from the Yucatán Peninsula to Miami. Very unusual, because I didn't have the needed papers. I still can hear the customs officer of the large Floridian airport say, "You either need an Alien Registration Certificate or a visa, and you have neither one. It is impossible for me to readmit you to the United States of America!" and with this he left. For about half an hour I stood there lonely and forsaken. I did not have enough money to fly to another place. What could I do? In my distress I cried to God, my everlasting help in trouble. I prayed about the entire time he was gone. When he finally returned, I said, "Won't you have mercy on me? Today is my birthday!" He took my passport, entered *waiver of visa,* and I was readmitted to the USA! Hurray, what a day! Exceptional indeed. "Thank you, Lord," I whispered softly as I passed through the customs barrier.

For some reason, my supplication to God in Rio de Janeiro was not forgotten. It seemed as though my faith for an answer after all this time increased as the days went by. Finally, six months after the pilferage, I decided to write to the American embassy down there to see if some of my things were returned. Their answer took a long time, but when it came, my papers were included. Though my money, watch and clothes were not returned, I did receive the most important items. Again I thanked God for answering my long-ago prayer.

In the Cockpit of a Comet High Above the Andes

There were, however, numerous joyful experiences such as the traditional Latin American hospitality at the homes of many dear people and a spectacular flight in the cockpit of a Comet jet from Buenos Aires, Argentina, to Santiago, Chile. I will never forget the dramatic view of the cordillera (Andes Mountains) past Mt. Aconcagua. What a sight to behold from the cabin of this Comet airliner! Finally the pilot reversed the turbine thrust as the mountain chain came to an abrupt descent on the west side and the plane started to plummet like a rock. The ground literally rose to meet us.

Soon afterward came a journey by train, boat and bus to Cuzco and Machu Picchu, the famous ruins of the former Incan Empire. To have seen the accomplishments of that great culture is unforgettable. On the way we

Cusco, Peru *(above),* capital of the once mighty Inca Empire which stretched 2,500 miles from north to south. Situated at 11,440 feet above sea level, it served as a ceremonial center, with many palaces, temples and government buildings. Here stood the Temple of the Sun, which gleamed with gold and precious stones. A huge fortress called Sacsahuaman *(below)* guarded Cusco. The Inca built walls without mortar. Large stones fit so tightly that a knife cannot be inserted in the joints. Actually, 20,000 men labored 30 years to shape and position the rocks of the fortress—some weighing more than 100 tons.

Fabulous Machu Picchu *(above)*, lies 8,000 feet high, amid towering Andes Mountains. This deserted Inca city, discovered in 1911 in the Peruvian wilderness, still baffles historians who find no clear record of its origin or the reason for its abandonment. The great Pyramid of the Sun *(below)* near Teotihuacán, Mexico, covers a larger area than Egypt's Great Pyramid. Once used as an altar and observatory, it is 217 feet high.

crossed Lake Titicaca on a steamboat which was packed in on muleback and then assembled. The highest large navigable lake in the world, it reaches an altitude of 12,507 feet. Ruins of an ancient city are submerged in the 600-foot deep waters.

ARCHAEOLOGICAL WONDERS OF THE WORLD

Much of the Bible is a historical account. Maybe partly because of that, I have become very interested in archaeology. During the years I have done a lot of research in this field. Now it was of utmost importance personally to see some of the ancient sites I had studied about.

Still today as a person travels over the face of the earth, he will find many traces of the past splendor of other once-mighty empires. So I visited the remnants of the great Mayan Empire in Central America, especially the lost city Tikal in the Peten Jungle of Guatemala and Chichen Itza as well as the Uxmal ruins on the Yucatán Peninsula of Mexico. I also saw some of the few remaining evidences of the Aztec Empire in Mexico as well as many national monuments and national parks in the United States which contain remains of the diverse Indian cultures of this nation which reached their zenith in the Mesa Verde civilization during the 10th to 12th centuries.

Further great sights visited later were the magnificent Borobudur, one of the world's greatest Buddhist sanctuaries, and the ninth-century Prambana temple near Djogjakarta, Indonesia, as well as the impressive ruins of Angkor Thom and Angkor Wat near Siem Reap in Cambodia. (Pictured in Chapter 18, "Circling the Globe.") These remains of Angkor rank with the greatest tourist attractions in the world. The architectural miracle of the Angkor Wat Temple with its 200-foot towers and many more ornamental monuments, palaces and temples which cover 60 square miles, were constructed by Khmer warrior kings between the 800's and the 1200's. Angkor Thom, their ancient capital, is surrounded by an eight-mile-long wall. The outer ones of the Bayon Temple at the center of this five-square-mile city are beautifully decorated in detail with bas-reliefs and carvings depicting Khmer life and Hindu scenes. The 150-foot main tower is surrounded by 50 smaller ones.

Students of archaeology find some of the world's most fabulous treasures on the intricately decorated and carved ruins. Only within the last century were these fantastic jungle-covered remnants discovered. Even those priceless remains were not left untouched by the recent *international monopoly capitalist*[2] wars. These money-hungry warmongers have no

---

[2]Monopoly capitalism, also in control of Communism, is against free enterprise. Read the shocking, eye-opening truth about how these international cartels manipulate America and the world on pages 78-83 and 122-127 in my book, *Timely and Profitable Help for Troubled Americans.* See order form in back of book.

respect for cultures which express individualistic achievements in the various nations. They want everything internationalized, monopolized and standardized. Just remember what happened to the Chinese civilization after the Red take-over.

Also many ruined as well as standing temples and palaces in India were on my itinerary. A lot of beautiful frescoes could be seen in Ceylon.

Other awe-inspiring places were Palmyra in Syria; the Baalbek (Heliopolis) of Lebanon which contains remnants of one of the most famous and oldest acropolis in the Middle East; the "lost" city of Petra, "a rose-red city half as old as time," in Jordan; the Goreme Valley (site of Troglodyte dwellings inhabited by early Christians) in Turkey; the many traces of the Roman Empire in Italy and the age-old pyramids of Egypt containing royal tombs for the pharaohs.

I have marvelled many times as I examined the great constructions performed by relatively small men and realized the unbelievable energy, manpower and workmanship that went into those architectural wonders.

Many were built to *unknown* gods. If pagans could put forth that much energy to serve them, how much more should we Christians enlist in an active life for the *living God.*

Truly the history of mankind has been a spectacular one. The remains of these magnificent constructions present a stark contrast to our world of today; just as much contradistinction is seen when one compares the strong, industrious, independent and noble-spirited pioneers of a few years ago with the tax-oppressed, pleasure-loving, subservient wage-earner slaves of today.

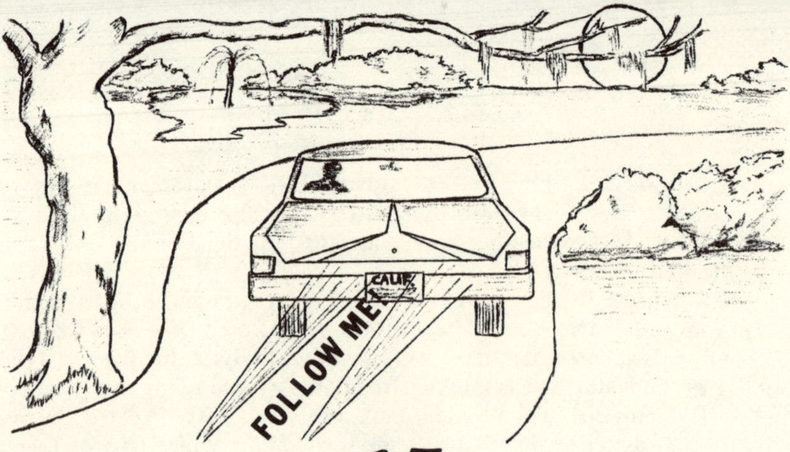

15

The Call to California

Once more the scene is set in New Orleans, Louisiana. I had been given a direct commission, and my first exhaustive foreign missionary tour lay behind. Other calls for service were coming in. Where to go next was the question. I prayed, "Lord, show me the way."

Again, I partially fasted and, during a period of a week or two, I went through the entire Bible. So far, there were portions I had never perused before. I wanted to read the whole Book to be fit for proper service. A few watermelons here and there gave me the needed strength and I actually gained weight. I studied God's Word from about 4:00 or 5:00 A. M. to 11:00 P. M. and up to 1:00 A. M. every day.

One afternoon, I took a friend to a park and shared my most beloved verses in the entire New Testament with him. After this, we drove all over that area in search of an illuminated fountain I had seen earlier. It was unsuccessful, and the wild-goose chase wound up in a dead-end road. I was glad to find a car there, and asked the driver for the fountain. Upon this, he replied, "Follow me and I will show you!" As his vehicle pulled in front of me to lead the way, my car lights blazed upon a California license plate. A flash went through my mind. *California!* One of the places I had been invited to in the ministry. There it was! *Follow me and I will show you*–suggestive of Christ's words, ". . . Follow me, and I will make you fishers of men" (Matt. 4:19). The fact of searching for and finding the fountain reminded me of two other verses: "For the Lamb . . . shall lead them unto living fountains of waters . . ." (Rev. 7:17) and ". . . I will give unto him that is athirst of the fountain of the water of life freely" (Rev. 21:6).

To someone else, all of this might have been a coincidence. To me it was clear, as God confirmed to my heart that *California* was calling. Little did I know at this time how many doors were going to open there and that within less than a year I would speak in about 250 meetings, including radio and television interviews.

Now join me once again on another decisive journey. I put the few belongings into my VW bug and said good-bye to New Orleans. Another one-half year wandering through the wilderness followed as I headed for the open country. What a joy to leave that big city behind.

As I travelled down the highway, many Bible verses were reverberating in my mind. My extensive study of the Word was already rewarding me. ". . . I am the God of thy father, the God of Abraham, the God of Isaac, and the God of Jacob . . . ." (Exo. 3:6); "I am the LORD thy God, which have brought thee out of the land of Egypt, out of the house of bondage" (Exo. 20:2); ". . . the LORD thy God is with thee whithersoever thou goest" (Josh. 1:9); "I, even I, am the LORD; and beside me there is no saviour" (Isa. 43:11); " . . . the glory of the LORD shall be thy rereward" (Isa. 58:8); " . . . and thou shalt know that I the LORD am thy Saviour and thy Redeemer, the mighty One of Jacob" (Isa. 60:16) were some of the scriptures which surged through my mind.

The glory of God fell upon me in such power that I just couldn't stand to sit in the little car any longer. I stopped, jumped out, and headed for the trees along the roadside. There I lifted my hands to the sky and held a revival meeting all by myself. Day after day I travelled as He led me. I practically never knew where I would be the next day, but I was sure that it was going to be another adventure with God. I moved across the land just as we read in Rom. 8:14, "For as many as are led by the Spirit of God, they are the sons of God." For weeks and months at a time, His abiding joy and presence were upon me. I now tasted the difference between the miserable existence in this world and the glorious life in Christ!

16

The Art of Exciting, Purposeful and Wise Travel

FIELD TRAINING

On my way to California followed a number of interesting experiences during the six-month trip throughout the entire portion of the United States west of the Mississippi. There were frequent hikes in high-altitude country with practically no or very little equipment. Often I hiked 20 to 30 miles per day. When losing directions, I applied some of the methods which are mentioned in my book, *Timely and Profitable Help for Troubled Americans,*[1] and they always brought me to safety. At that time, I was travelling alone and had to rely upon God and myself to survive any predicament encountered. I learned during this period how much a body can actually endure if properly trained.

I strongly recommend that you are in good physical condition for the times ahead. It certainly would be very helpful if you train your body through such activities as extensive hikes, hunting, swimming and temporary outdoor life, including supplying your own food from nature, so you

[1] It can be obtained from this publisher. See order form in back of book.

will be able to endure adverse circumstances. The advantages of living at your homestead in the open country as I do,[2] will give you a chance for many of those exercises in your daily activities.

I also learned how little nourishment the body actually needs for health and strength. I ate very sparingly and there were many days without food, yet I kept on at a stringent pace.

SHARPENED SENSES WARD OFF A MUGGING

You will also find as you live a natural life such as the early frontiersmen did, that your senses become sharpened and you develop what some call a "sixth sense." Then you are capable of hearing noises other people do not and to sense dangers they might be trapped right into.

Once, while sleeping in my car at a gasoline station in what later turned out to be a slum area in Sacramento, California, I was aroused by a natural—or shall I rather say supernatural—warning signal. I was resting on the right side of the car (a Volkswagen "bug") in a sleeping bag. A tremendous racket abruptly woke me up. It sounded as if a large window of a giant store had been shattered by rocks and thousands of glass pieces were falling on the pavement. I know that God created this noise in my mind so I would be alert in time to prevent a calamity.

Upon awakening I sat up, looked toward the left window which I had open and noticed a fellow standing there ready to break in, making a good surveillance of all the things in the car. I kept my eyes on him. Suddenly he recognized me, turned on his heel and took off. While following the man, I saw him vanish underneath a bridge among bushes. There was no doubt that he had evil in mind.

Had I not been stirred from sleep in time, I would have only noticed him as he was in the process of breaking into the car. Any resistance on my part at that point would probably have caused him to react violently. He might have shot or hit me over the head in order to avoid immediate apprehension. My Heavenly Father may very well have saved my life that day.

Many times while travelling by plane in foreign countries, I slept during the night on airport benches, below a tree out in the open, or in some garden patch with my head on my small suitcase. This way I would be awakened immediately if anyone tried to disturb it. Over and over I have been roused by just the slightest approach of danger.

FIERCE ENCOUNTERS ON THE WESTERN FRONTIER

There were other challenging experiences, such as close calls in the form of threatened attacks by a bull moose, buffalo and grizzlies. Common sense and wilderness experience always aided me in these circumstances.

---

[2]This lifestyle, its advantages and how to set yourself up in it, are described in detail in *Timely and Profitable Help for Troubled Americans.*

Once, while in the high mountains in California, I could hear a cracking behind me as I warmed myself by a campfire at night. Knowing that I was in bear country, I kept all the food items relished by them in a way that would minimize odor and accessibility. This precaution helped me to rest that night, but a near neighbor found his food chest and supplies completely demolished and saw his camp almost torn apart.

The adventurer-author at his mountain homestead ready to leave on a bow and arrow hunt in his "back yard."

ADJUSTMENTS

Any person who travels in this manner for an extended period will soon lose interest in returning to a monotonous routine, unpleasant environment and dull job. My journeys were instrumental in changing my entire way of life. I thank God that there are so many lifestyles available to an individual, limited only by one's imagination.

If you have any desire at all to feel like a human being again, you may want to exchange the caged life in a big city for one in the open country. For helpful, comprehensive information along this line, read the LIFESTYLE PART in my book, *Timely and Profitable Help for Troubled Americans.*

While making an initial transition from an urban setting to a wilderness-type life, you might have adjustment troubles. If you have any drawing by nature at all, you soon will become accustomed to your new surroundings, feel so much at home and be joyful and happy in it that a return to a stereotyped and artificial city life would be nearly unthinkable. At the end of all your resettlement and adjustment problems, you will find that the effort was well spent, even though you might nearly faint along the wayside in the process.

It reminds me on a strenuous climb to the top of Mt. Whitney where I gazed at the splendid view and, looking back on my day of labor and troubles, exclaimed that it was worth it all.

HITCH YOUR WAGON TO A HIGHER STAR

If you are overwhelmed, dear reader, by the many difficulties you are in, consolation may be found in the following:

Once, while on a hike into Grand Canyon, I made a journey through the various geological periods. As the river carved away on the crust of this earth, it exposed different layers deposited during centuries, representing the many ages of mankind. As I hiked, I truly lost a perspective of time; that is, the time we figure in, and I thought of the incalculably minute problems which seem so big.

Personally, I like the desert because it gives me an aloofness to things. My experience has been that if I have troubles and need answers, a multitude of different advice would be obtained if a number of persons were consulted. In the peaceful desert surroundings, however, I can receive definite, individualized, inspirational answers which hit home.

What is more beautiful than to be all alone out there at night? No mosquitoes, no flies to molest you, no noise, no traffic to interrupt the tranquility of a crystal-clear night. The mild temperature is just perfect. Not too hot, not too cold, but exactly right. Barefooted, and in light clothing, you walk for miles through the soft and relaxing sand, bathed by the silvery moonlight. Almost bedazzled, you traverse an argent mirror resplendently aglow by glistening myriads of gleaming sand grains.

Roaming the great American wilderness far from turmoil and confusion. A radiant moon over Glacier National Park makes me dream of higher things in life. This serene setting offers a great contrast to the crowded, noisy places in this world.

What a way to feel alive, to get inspired, and to know that you are here for a purpose—for a greater mission than may have been realized. It's a state most men in the *zoo* of their man-made environment, called cities, know nothing about. Occasionally I fly over some large town and see people below me dashing and rushing about like ants in a mad scramble. They are sorely vexed in their pursuit for temporal things. It reminds us of the passage in Luke 10:38-42, ". . . and a certain woman named Martha received him into her house. And she had a sister called Mary, which also *sat at Jesus' feet, and heard his word.* But Martha was cumbered about much serving, and came to him, and said, Lord, dost thou not care that my sister hath left me to serve alone? bid her therefore that she help me. And Jesus answered and said unto her, Martha, Martha, thou art careful and troubled about many things: But one thing is needful: and Mary hath chosen that good part, which shall not be taken away from her."

Finally you lie down and rest on the wasteland's soft floor. Your eyes scan the vast expanse of the nightly firmament irradiated by the sparkling of numberless glittering stars. What a sermon! It was out in the mountains and deserts where I learned some of the greatest lessons. We need to live a balanced life of quiet periods interspersed with times of sharing and giving out. Only a battery which is recharged every so often will be able to start the big and powerful motor when it counts. Again Jesus Christ set the example (Matt. 14:13, 23; Mk. 3:7, 9, 13; 6:31, 46; 11:19 etc.).

Whenever I withdraw into solitude after a busy time in some big city, I find that it takes me awhile to simmer down. During the first day or so I may not get much out of reading the Bible. There seems to be no genuine grasp of its contents. My mind, under a heavy influence of the impressions and activities it just escaped from, is still cluttered by trivialities. Then, after a few days, a great peace envelops me afresh, God's Word takes on a new meaning and I can hear His voice within me saying, "This is the way, walk therein!"

17

On Eagle's Wings

Let's consider another aviator, the eagle, for a moment. From this large, strong flier who soars at great heights, surveying the country with keen eyes, we can learn some wonderful lessons. Having long been considered as a symbol of power, courage, and freedom, he lives in lonely mountain regions. A pair builds its eyrie on top of tall trees or on the edge of a high cliff and will not tolerate another in the same territory. The tremendous flying power, swiftness, adroitness, and great striking force with wings and talons (claws), in short, its unrestrained, wild energy issuing forth from his flashing eyes, turned blood-red in anger, make it the most formidable enemy of the animal kingdom. When its sharp penetrating voice is heard during raids, the panic-stricken game flees to hiding places. The antelopes press their little ones protectingly against the steep cliffs. A scared flock is in uproar. Another shrill whistle and with folded wings the fierce hunter nose-dives into the middle of the confused herd. Within seconds, two tenacious claws pull its victim into the air. A golden figure of an eagle was used by the Romans to represent strength, skill and bravery.

It was the *inner voice* I wrote about in the beginning of Chapter 5 which caused me to study and observe the life of an eagle. This bird and I seemed to have so much in common. That soarer's life was different, challenging and glorious just as that voice within me!

An eagle egg was hatched in a chicken coop. The little bird scarcely felt at home. It didn't like the menu, took no interest in scratching around the yard, and couldn't understand the clucking. It was the oddball among them all. Slowly, with wings growing stronger and bigger, it was getting ready for something greater than fooling around in the chicken pen. This king of the air was created to soar the high heavens in freedom of flight. Eking out a dull and miserable existence, it noticed one day a huge shadow sweeping over the place as the hens scattered in sudden fright. A voice rang out, "Sonny, what are you doing down there? Come up higher!" That call from the sky sounded just right. Quickly flapping the wings, an enthused fledgling took to the sky, joining mother for a life it was born for. It was destined to be free, enjoying God's splendor from on high.

Too many people are digging around in the filth of this world. They are like chickens scratching in a dirty barnyard. Did you ever have a mounting-up experience? This something that comes within you, by waiting, so that you feel yourself lifted above a materialistic environment! You can hardly refrain from shouting; in fact, it is not uncommon for this mounting-up experience to break forth from the heart with shouts of praise, with tears of gladness and expressions of joy! You feel like walking in the air, so light and carefree. It is an awareness inside, deep in the well-springs of the soul.

God desires that His children know His Word and believe what He says. He wants us to be fortified against fainting. The Lord lets us know the course of this present age and the end. If we have been born again, it was a supernatural birth. Therefore, God longs for us to live in companionship with a supernatural life. He would not have put in the Bible what He did not expect us to live by.

A man, reared in the Alps, published a book that also describes the nature and characteristics of an eagle, the king of all birds. He says that certain kinds live to be 100 years or older, but when they are about 60, they, like many folks, begin to mope and sit around on the crags, seemingly uninterested in the affairs of life. When the storms beat upon them, they show no desire to mount above the clouds as before. Insensible to rain and snow, there is no interest in what the younger eagles are doing.

But it is characteristic of them to wake up later. Suddenly the old bird begins to beat his wings with terrific force against the cliffs, and then at intervals hammer his beak fiercely and break off great chunks of overgrown, hard cartilage. Then he will sit back and rub his old tail feathers out against the rocks. This practice is continued for days and weeks until the stones are covered with blood from their wings, tails and beaks. When the feathers are all knocked out, new ones come. The beak is worn short like a young eagle's, and becoming sharp, it also takes on new life. Fresh plumage grows out fluffy and after awhile the old bird appears like a youngster. He has literally "renewed his youth," and is good for another half century or more!

Now when storms approach, the wind blows and lightning flashes, they put their eyes again to the skies, and with a scream, leap toward the heavens, soar above the clouds, and enjoy the beautiful sunlight while the tempests are raging beneath. The eagle renews his youth by physical exercise.

Why would God's children let a fowl, a bird of earth, follow His will more closely than they, who claim to have partaken of eternal life? If an eagle can be rejuvenated, let us, by the grace of God, endeavor to do likewise through spiritual and physical exercise. How about beating off some of our tail feathers and callousness and live anew! God has a fresh, youthful experience for His children every day of the year. This is His way for eagle saints!

I remember an old man I met many years ago. He was given up by the doctors because of serious sickness. Dilapidated and humpbacked, he started to fast as well as pray, crying to God for help and direction. "Go to Nigeria, Africa to preach the gospel," was the command. Some call that country the graveyard of the white man because of the hot climate and grave illnesses in some regions. He spent five years there in the ministry and then returned to the U. S., preaching in churches, telling people how God healed and was now greatly using him. The man looked better than he had for a long time. Filled with energy and vision, he was soon back working in Africa. Truly, our Heavenly Father gives us strength as we fulfill the commission He gives us.

If the only purpose in life would be to eat three meals and grind away on a humdrum job until the worms eat you six feet below the ground, life wouldn't mean much and barely worth living. But, thanks be to God, we are called for a higher purpose than that. May we focus our eyes again on the important matters in life and believe that all the necessary things will be added unto us as we first of all seek the kingdom of God and His righteousness (Matt. 6:33).

Wherever you read in the Holy Scriptures about an eagle, it is usually in connection with a miracle, for this is God's miracle fowl. There is no other bird like an eagle. It stands out distinct from all others.

Nowhere in the Bible does God liken His children to any other bird, such as a crow, hawk or vulture. These may be mentioned in Scripture, but never in connection with redeemed saints. However, in many places of the Bible, the peculiar, separated people of God, in both Testaments, are compared to eagles.

In the first place, I want you to notice the eagle in its normal life lives off fresh meat. The nature is to stay away from decayed carrion. They enjoy slaying their own food and thrive on fresh lamb or other clean animals.

Remember, Jesus said in John 6:53, ". . . Verily, verily, I say unto you, Except ye eat the flesh of the Son of man, and drink His blood, ye have no life in you." We become saints as we learn how to eat of His flesh and drink of His blood. He said in the discourse about His second coming, Matthew 24:28, "For wheresoever the carcass is, there will the eagles be gathered together." Of course, Jesus was referring to Himself as the slain Lamb, and was pointing to the fact that His eagle saints would be gathered.

God's children everywhere in the Bible are a separated people. Talk to nominal professing church members about the Lord Jesus Christ being slain, that we may eat His flesh and drink His blood in order to possess eternal life, and it sounds ridiculous to them, for they cannot understand that our source of life is in Him, and apart from partaking of Him there is no eternal life for any earthly being.

Jesus gave us the sacred ordinance of the Lord's Supper in order that we should keep in mind His slain body and shed blood for our eternal redemption. 1 Corinthians 11:26, "For as often as ye eat this bread, and drink this cup, ye do shew the Lord's death till He come." The way the Lord produces His eagle saints is by making them partakers of His own life.

The Word of God describes eagles as miracle birds. He said to the children of Israel after they had crossed the Red Sea, ". . . I bare you on eagles' wings, and brought you unto Myself" (Exodus 19:4). His people had been slaves in Egypt for hundreds of years. They served under hard taskmasters, and labored with tired bodies, bleeding backs and hungry stomachs.

They had cried to God, and God saw their sufferings, heard their cries, and sent Moses to deliver them, but the great Law Giver did not find it easy. The whole record is in the Book of Exodus. A time came for deliverance. Lambs were slain and blood was shed. That was not all. The blood was applied on the door posts.

"And the blood shall be to you for a token upon the houses where ye are: and when I see the blood, I will pass over you, and the plague shall not be upon you to destroy you, when I smite the land of Egypt" (Ex. 12:13).

The lambs were well roasted in the homes of Goshen; the people were commanded to eat, having their staffs in their hands. Front doors had been securely shut. Probably there were many blind, lame, aged and infirm among them, but as they ate the lamb, SHUT IN under the blood, blind eyes were opened, crutches fell from under the arms of cripples, and aged people straightened up. What divine miracles were wrought that night by the Hand of God!

The moment came to depart, and the march began, which was to take them through the Red Sea. We have on record God's own testimony, where He says when they left Egypt, ". . . there was not one feeble person among their tribes" (Psalm 105:37).

It is calculated there were at least four million Israelites concerning whom God says, "I bare you on eagles' wings" (Exodus 19:4). This certainly was a great miracle, and I repeat, the Bible usually mentions eagles in connection with some miracle. Truly, when one becomes an eagle saint, he knows it is done through the miraculous work of God Himself.

Now, shall we turn to Isaiah 40:31, "But they that wait upon the Lord shall renew their strength; they shall mount up with wings as eagles; they shall run, and not be weary; and they shall walk, and not faint." Here we find the prophet declaring that "they that wait upon the Lord shall renew their strength," that is, they shall enjoy perpetual youth in the Lord. To the natural man, this is impossible, but all things are possible to them that wait upon God.

It is always through prayer and communion with the Lord that we experience constant spiritual renewal; never through self-effort. God does not want His children always to be grumbling and complaining–a headache today, backache tomorrow, sore throat at night, tired and worn out the next day. Christians should live victoriously in their daily lives.

If those who are called by His Name all over the world would spend as much time in waiting upon the Lord as they do thumbing the pages of newspapers and magazines, listening to the radio, watching TV, engaging in worldly and semiworldly matters, they would understand what this Scripture means.

By waiting in quiet communion with God, your strength is renewed, and not only so, but you shall mount up with wings as eagles.

I pity the Christian whose experience lacks the sweet, tender motivation of the Holy Spirit. In this mounting up, the things of earth lose their attraction and your soul and spirit, through waiting upon the Lord, come into glorious fellowship and communion with God. The Word says, "They shall run, and not be weary."

Some of us know what this mounting-up experience means; probably many of you do not. To live wholly in the Spirit's fellowship means to commune with the Lord constantly. Men in other occupations, without this sanctified fellowship, must have rest and vacations often. But the one who "waits upon the Lord" and lives in the mounting-up experience, knows what it is to run on errands in his Master's service for years without a vacation. The world wonders how he does it.

"They shall walk, and not faint." Most people are fainting. You know David said, "I had fainted, unless I had believed to see the goodness of the Lord in the land of the living" (Psalm 27:13). Jesus gives us a recipe against fainting in Hebrews 12:3, "For consider Him that endured such contradiction of sinners against Himself, lest ye be wearied and faint in your minds."

We read again in Psalm 103:5, "Who satisfieth thy mouth with good things; so that thy youth is renewed like the eagle's." Did you ever think, friends, Who gave you your appetite and palate for pleasant taste? Here His Word tells us He "satisfieth thy mouth with good things." Do we thank Him for them?

Here is the purpose in this, "So that thy youth is renewed like the eagle's." Whoever thinks of God renewing youth? Most people, when they reach 60, talk about what they have done, begin to live in the past and submit themselves to the habits of old age. But this is not the Bible way for an eagle saint.

A dear old saint, in his 91st year, was as cheerful and played with the children as much as a youth. He said when he was 60 his sons and daughters begged him to retire, stating he was getting to be an old man. For a while he believed them.

But when in a dying condition, Psalm 103:5 came to him. He started to wait upon the Lord, and began to request that his mouth be satisfied with pleasant things, and his appetite improved. This passage gave him inspiration. The last time I saw him, he was as spry as a man of 30, always praising the Lord, and quoting Scripture for the encouragement of others.

We come now to notice how God produces an eagle saint. This is given to us in Deuteronomy 32:11-12, "As an eagle stirreth up her nest, fluttereth over her young, spreadeth abroad her wings, taketh them, beareth them on her wings: So the Lord alone did lead him, and there was no strange god with him." This has to do primarily with God's dealings with Jacob, as it was the divine purpose to make him and his family a peculiar treasure unto Himself. So God says, "As an eagle stirreth up her nest."

First, we notice the construction of the eagle's nest. She builds it among the crags and cliffs of the highest peaks on the mountain range. A place is selected for protection from all enemies. She first carries sticks, as large as your wrist or more, then smaller ones. These are laid crosswise, and coming nearer to the center of the nest, small twigs and limbs are used. To complete the task, she kills a sheep, lamb or goat, and with the fur makes a very soft, homelike place for her young.

When the young eagle is hatched, its first food is blood. Job 39:30, "Her young ones also suck up blood: and where the slain are, there is she." Young saints are likewise produced by the blood of Jesus Christ. The newly born eagles thrive on this and the tenderest meat that can be found. The mother cares for them lovingly as they grow and develop.

But while they sit in the nest and enjoy the comforts of a soft home, being fed and protected from storms and beasts of prey, they do not yet realize what they are.

Soon the mother bird begins stirring up the nest. Picking their comfortable home to pieces, she takes that soft wool or goat hair, carries it off, and drops it from her feet into the canyon below. Then she takes away the small sticks, and with a bump, the young bird finds itself sitting uncomfortably on the rough limbs. The mother is stirring up the nest in order to wean the young birds from that home.

So the Lord has a way of dealing with each of us! If your earthly nest is being stirred; if your money or trusted friends are gone; if you feel absolutely helpless and dependent upon God alone, cheer up, for you are being weaned from the things of the world. God's ways are seldom ours. He wants eagle saints. *We would never become saints at all if we did as we pleased.*

Remember, Brother and Sister, God has a way of weaning you from this perishing world if you will wholly follow Him. The Scriptures say that the mother bird fluttereth over her young, and again that she spreadeth abroad her wings. This is done to excite the young birds to a knowledge that their mother is more superior than any other fowl of the air. She sits down by them in the nest, spreadeth out her wings like huge curtains, and of course the two young ones crawl on her back as she intended.

The next Scripture is, she taketh them. Where does she take them? The moment she finds they are on her wings, with one mighty spring she leaps out into space! The little ones try to hold on for dear life! They put their tiny claws into the feathers and go screaming through the air. The mother soars up toward the rays of the sun–out beyond the vision of man.

Then she shakes them violently and flutters them off. They go tumbling down through space, screaming and crying because of the cruelty of their mother, wondering why they were ever born, knowing that only disaster awaits them on the rocks below.

But after they have thus fallen into space, the Scripture says she bears them on her wings. In other words, she darts under them, catches them on her wings, and when they are securely clinched to her, she again bears them into the clouds where she once more shakes them from her back. They come tumbling through space.

This experience is repeated again and again. By degrees they learn to beat their wings, exercise their muscles, and after a few practices, realize that they too are eagles. *After that, there is no longer any desire to return to the old nest.*

By these difficulties and tremendous experiences, their mother has shown them their abilities as eagles, and the next Scripture we read is, "So the Lord alone did lead him, and there was no strange god with him" (Deuteronomy 32:12).

God wants you and me as His children to learn a lesson from the eagle. He permits homes to be broken up, businesses to fail, loved ones to be removed, all for the purpose of weaning us from the present world and giving us eternal life.

He makes us know that during the storms and billows of His judgments which shake kingdoms and nations to their utter destruction, a people can mount up in Him through divine Grace. Living in the consciousness of His eternal presence with joyful hearts, right in the midst of any storm, difficulty or opposition that may blow against us in this present world, is His will.

God has made eagles that can soar above the clouds, sit on top of the wind, and relax during the most desperate storm.

When I read that, I said, Lord, help me! If God can make an eagle sit on top of the wind and thus ride a storm, *then why not make His saints to be able, by faith, to throw themselves out of joint with the trends of this evil hour and sit on top of the storms that come: home-storms, church storms–storms that blow cruelly across our Christian work, across the nation and the world–and thus triumph over the storms of life!*

Whatever the trouble is, may God help us to be able by prayer and faith in Him and His Word to move above temporary matters and ride every crisis that comes to us as His eagle saints.

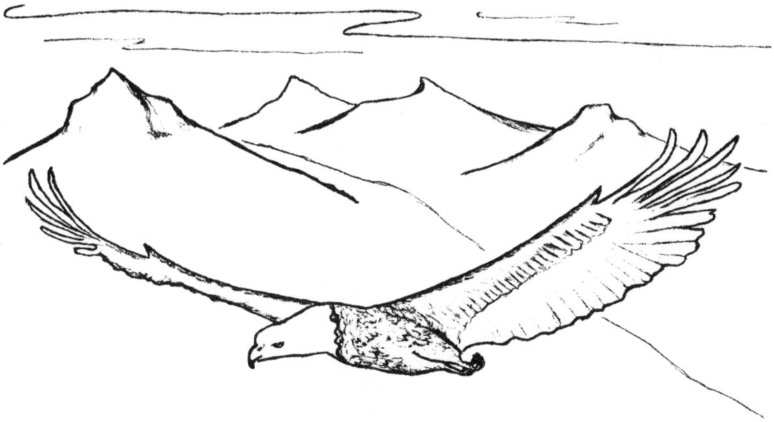

Back home after another extensive international speaking tour. 55,000 miles of global air travel through 44 countries in two years! Posing for a newspaper interview, Hans unravels a portion of his 130 plane tickets covering this trip. (Statesman photo)

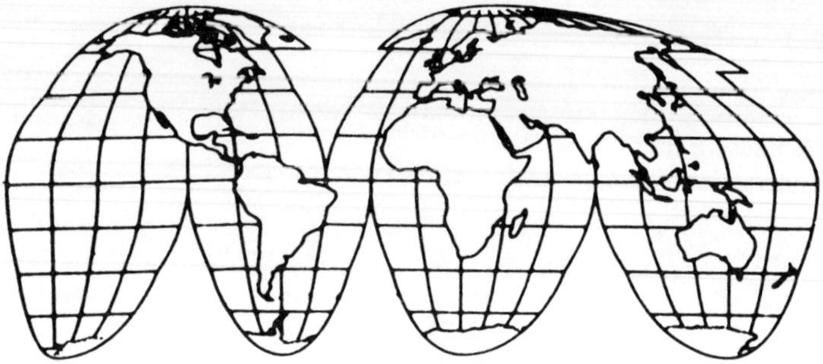

18

Circling the Globe

FORCED SHUT-DOWN OF THE JET OVER THE MIDDLE OF THE PACIFIC OCEAN

The large Pan American jetliner left Honolulu, Hawaii on time. A beautiful emerald island disappeared below giant wings as the plane went on course. Tahiti, way down in the South Pacific, was our destination. Now my boyhood dreams were going to find fulfillment as I was about to roam the South Sea Isles with a beautiful commission.

On board was much commotion. It drew a sharp contrast to the deep and silent waters below us. Beside me was seated a middle-aged multi-millionaire from Seattle, Washington. He kept the stewardess running after cigarettes and liquor. Wholly occupied by this jollification, he took the opportunity to crack plenty of questionable jokes. Evidently this short, slim entrepreneur felt that he was having a ball.

I couldn't see any sense in his foolishness and began to witness to him in short order. An abrupt wave of his hand and a sarcastic remark stopped me in my tracks. At this point I remembered how the Master had said, "Give not that which is holy unto the dogs, neither cast ye your pearls before swine, lest they trample them under their feet, and turn again and rend you" (Matt. 7:6). So I shut up and held my peace. Soon something happened which changed that.

We had been flying about 45 minutes. Suddenly the pilot broke the news, giving an all-important announcement on the public address system. "Ladies and gentlemen: We are having problems with one of our jet engines. We will have to cut off the motor and dump our gas supply into the ocean. Please don't panic and remain in your seats quietly—we will try to make it back to Honolulu, Hawaii."

What an opportunity to take up where I left off, to continue witnessing, I thought.

An icy silence spread as all the to-do abruptly ceased. In fact, it became so hushed that a person could have heard a needle drop to the floor. The man to my left was now getting very high-strung inside. I was watching him out of the corner of my eye, curious to see how he was coming along. It was impossible for him to hide the nervousness. Breathing heavily, he fumbled with his hands.

Meanwhile, the giant airliner had initiated a 180-degree turn. Silvery-white streaks appeared below the wings as the fuel was dumped into the ocean. The crew endeavored to make it back to our point of departure.

Uneasiness among the passengers, and especially within my neighbor, was increasing visibly. The atmosphere in the cabin was so tense that a spark could have easily set the whole thing off! Yet there was a peace upon me which passeth all understanding (Phil. 4:7). I now knew what the Bible meant when it says, "There is no fear in love; but *perfect love casteth out fear:* because fear hath torment. He that feareth is not made perfect in love" (1 John 4:18). Why worry? My times were in His hand (Psalm 31:15). Nothing could happen unless it were in His will. Truly, ". . . all things work together for good to them that love God, to them who are the called according to His purpose" (Rom. 8:28). It was not very long before I could recognize vividly the reality of that verse.

God was preparing the vessel beside me. Presently neither one of us spoke a word. Incidents were heavily on my side. The Almighty had taken the ship under His control and everybody involved felt dependent upon a Higher Power.

This time, I was not going to make the first move. The gentleman on my side had shut me up once before. Now it was his turn to start the conversation. There was no need for me to break the ice. Only a few minutes after the pilot had made the announcement, my fellow passenger burst out, "Eh!—didn't you tell me something about a man called Christ awhile ago?"

"Yes, I sure did," I answered happily.

"Can you tell me more about Him?" a meek voice to my left inquired.

"I certainly can. In fact, I would be delighted to do so." And then, for the entire 45 minutes of our return flight, I preached Christ and Him crucified unto my seatmate. Only our arrival at the Honolulu International Airport ended the exhortation.

"Thank you, thank you very much! I will never forget what you did for me this day. God willing, I shall stand behind such a ministry one of these days," an enthused survivor declared. With this, he handed me a $10 bill and went on his way.

MY CHILDHOOD DREAMS COME TRUE

Soon another flight winged me 2,700 miles southeast from Honolulu to Papeete, Tahiti. I arrived there late at night. Not wanting to spend the money for a hotel for what little was left of the night, I slept in a garden next to a hotel. My little travel bag was the pillow so no one could steal it and my coat served as a blanket over me.

Tahiti is famous for a perfect climate and beauty. Surrounded by coral beaches and reefs, the interior is mountainous and rugged with waterfalls and rushing streams. Palm trees and fertile gardens adorn the belt which lies between the foothills and the shore.

Waving palms, sandy beaches, and tropical flowers—my childhood dreams come true! Beauty, perfect climate, coral reefs and lagoons make the 400 square miles of Tahiti a Pacific paradise.

Many years ago, Omai, a native Tahitian, was brought to London. His gentle speech and manners and the simplicity of his actions convinced British society that the *natural* man was then the *civilized!* It and Jean Jacques Rousseau's teaching of the value of the *children of nature,* which fitted these South Sea people, promoted the romantic movement.

Not far to the north was the small, lovely island of Bora Bora. I couldn't pass that one up. My dreams of childhood days had to be thoroughly materialized now. I had travelled far enough! A few days later, I arrived there in a small plane. An old, approximately 40-mile-long, road circles the island. With a rented bicycle, I rode the entire stretch. At times natives emerged from the adjoining jungle loaded down with tropical fruits. Happily they shared their bounty with me. Most spoke a few words of English. They had picked them up from the Americans who, of course, were there during the Second World War.

I returned to the small village late in the day. While I strolled around on an evening hike, I heard some beautiful music. One could tell that whoever sang, did so with his whole heart. It was a sound one seldom hears, and then usually among inhabitants of some yet uncivilized, rather primitive region. I traced the joyful tunes and soon wound up sitting in the back rows of an old-fashioned church filled with happy singers. With tears streaming down my cheek, I gave audience to the heart-melting sonances to the end. These few moments I will treasure for the rest of my life.

All too soon I was back in Tahiti to make connections for the Fiji Islands.

PAPEETE, TAHITI TO NANDI, FIJI ISLANDS

The time had come to leave what has been called the *"Paradise of the Pacific."* Guess who was sitting beside me on board the airliner? I never thought I would meet him again. But there he was, insisting to sit at my side. It was my friend, the multimillionaire from the State of Washington! This time I had a wonderful opportunity to witness to him from the beginning. He lent me a listening ear.

Again, this trip was not without excitement. When coming in *on final* at Nandi, the pilot almost dumped the plane. We both, also being pilots, jumped to our feet, wondering what was the matter with the captain. Had he taken too many drinks in the presence of a charming island dancer in Papeete? It was not a windy day. We could not figure otherwise.

While I have been reminiscing of bygone days on South Pacific islands, winter is slowly approaching our mountain estate in southern Oregon.

Writing about my life is a joyful, yet exhausting task because of the tremendous material I have to cover. One thing brings me to the next, and the more I write, the more I remember. For this very reason, I will relegate the bulk of my life story to another forthcoming book. Mail your request and address to the publisher of this volume (please find publisher's address on title page) and you will receive an announcement as soon as my next publication becomes available.

But now let me take you right back into some more highlights of my world tours!

TAA TRANS-AUSTRALIA AIRLINES

16 Elizabeth Street, Sydney, Australia

TELEPHONE: 2 0326
P. O. BOX 4230, SYDNEY
TELEGRAMS: "TRANSAIR," SYDNEY

TJ:ar

28th January, 1965.

TO WHOM IT MAY CONCERN

The bearer of this letter, Mr. Hans Schneider is proceeding through New Guinea en route to Indonesia as part of his round world trip.

His stay is, of necessity, short but he is naturally interested of seeing as much as possible whilst in the area.

Any assistance you will be able to tender will be sincerely appreciated.

Yours faithfully,

Anthony H. Jewiss.

Australia was one of the many places I visited in the South Pacific. Letters like this helped to pave the way through the difficult territory of Papua and New Guinea.

A SPY FROM THE SKY!

While on a flight into Sukarnopura, in West Irian, Indonesia, I was the only passenger on the plane. Stringent restrictions had been passed on border flights prohibiting passengers to fly in, and I had just come from Wewak in New Guinea; however, through much prayer, I was able to circumvent those regulations. When arriving in Sukarnopura I was greeted by the staff of Missionary Aviation Fellowship, which was allowed to stay on by the Indonesian government to help them reach the jungle territories. They had been part of the crew which was in the search mission for Rockefeller's son who had gotten lost in that area. Since they knew it was nearly impossible to fly into that territory at that time, I had quite a time convincing them that I was not a spy!

"How did you ever make it in here?" they kept asking me.

Again and again I told them it was prayer to God that did it. They just couldn't believe it until I had to pray so that they would. Finally, after a long time of persuasion, they invited me to their facilities. I spent several days there and we had some wonderful fellowship in Christ.

A few weeks later, I met a representative of a church denomination in Djakarta, Indonesia. He likewise was puzzled when he heard my story. "I will give you that much money if you tell me your secret of how you made it in," he said, and offered me a certain amount of money. "We have been desperately trying to get our missionaries through there in order to save a lot of money, but we are unable to succeed." My story was the same. "It was prayer which did it."

UNEXPECTED INVITATION TO THE CONTROLS

One experience I remember was a flight I made on an Indonesian airliner to Biak. The captain was told that another pilot rode in the plane and asked me to come to the cockpit. After entering, I became engaged in a very interesting conversation. Soon the chief aviator got up from his seat and asked me to sit there. Not understanding, the suggestion was made that I fly the airliner to its destination. It was quite a challenge, as I had never flown a multi-engine plane! He helped me along with some instructions. When it was time for a landing, the pilot took over again.

An architectural masterpiece in central Java, the magnificent Borobudur *(above)*, is one of the world's greatest Buddhist sanctuaries. Built during the A. D. 700's, it is one of the eight wonders of the world.

Famous Angkor Wat, constructed more than a thousand years ago when the Hindu-Buddhist civilization flourished. Hidden by jungle growth, the ruins were rediscovered only within the last century. I marveled as I strolled through these incredible edifices which represent one of the world's richest finds for students of art history and archaeology.

On my world tours, I reached multitudes, addressing many indoor and outdoor mass meetings. It is heartwarming to see the hunger for the message of Salvation in many of these foreign lands. Notice how intently the people listen at the church in Madras, India *(above).* The pastor, a living manifestation of Christ, never made any derogatory remarks about others. At my departure, he gave me his address card which had two Bible verses on it: "Speak evil of no man" and "Follow peace with all men." He was certainly a true symbol of his message. I treasure his card unto this day.

In India, I chose to travel the Indian way by crisscrossing this subcontinent in *3rd-class trains* for two months, often surrounded by lepers and people with tuberculosis.

IMPRISONED IN BAGHDAD!

It is not very difficult to find yourself imprisoned while travelling the world, especially in certain countries. After exploring the site where the Tower of Babel had been built in the country of Iraq, I visited Baghdad, the capital. A strange thing happened there.

While walking through the streets of the city, sightseeing, I came to a tall building with one armed soldier standing in front. In keeping with my custom of climbing some high point for a nice overlook, I entered this building, took an elevator to the top floor and then walked the rest of the way to the roof. Up there I met another young fellow, who wanted to take pictures of me. I declined. After enjoying a sweeping view of the city, I walked down one flight to get the elevator. The other young man followed. While we waited for the elevator, two persons met us. They immediately started to interrogate the young fellow, tearing the sunglasses from his face and slapping it violently. Immediately after this, we were put into a small jeep and driven to a prison camp.

For some time I had been distributing Bible tracts while travelling in Iraq—a thing strictly taboo in a Moslem country. Now these Arabians apparently were catching up with me and seeking revenge.

I was held in the inner court and requests to get in touch with the German Embassy were declined. As I later found out, there was no German Embassy in Iraq at that time because they had been asked to leave on account of weapons shipments to Israel. Finally I contacted the Commercial Department at the French Embassy, also representing my country. The German head of that department came immediately and demanded an interview with the chief of the security police located at that compound. No chairs were offered to any of us, which infuriated the foreign representative, and he told the head of the constabulary, "It is completely against the keeping of recent agreements with the Federal Republic of Germany that tourism to the country of Iraq be encouraged." The security police commander indicated that they must hold me for a period of time to check me out. He promised the German representative that I would be given a decent place to stay.

Previous to this, I had been brought to the city judge, also without results.

After the Embassy official left, I was led down a narrow hallway with the other young fellow and brought to a small cell containing about two dozen prisoners. I shall never forget the way they looked at me as they realized a foreigner was about to join them. I thought that I was dreaming in the face of that stark reality. In English I said, "No, I won't go in here because I was promised a different place."

At that point a soldier stepped up to me, pulled his gun off his shoulder and poked it into my side while the gates of that cell were opened. I knew that I took my life into my own hands when repeating my request; I also was aware that practically no one understood any English.

At that very decisive moment a civilian officer walked toward me, motioning with his hand to follow him. He brought me to his office and took down more details from my passport. Then I was led to a different room where lengthy questionnaire forms were filled out and pictures taken. After this, my personal belongings, such as my watch and wallet, were returned, and I was expedited to the open street without any word of explanation!

Immediately upon my release I realized, of course, that the impossible had happened. A miracle had taken place. Walking down the city streets of Baghdad, I glanced at my watch. My eyes widened in amazement when I saw it to be seven minutes before midnight. "*Seven*—the number of God and still the same day!" Instantly I remembered how I had cried unto the Lord in the afternoon while in prison, "Please, Heavenly Father, grant that I will be released *today!*" After praying approximately half an hour regarding this matter, a wonderful joy came upon me. I took that as a sign of answered prayer. In childlike faith, I pleaded with God expecting an answer just as an infant trusts that its father will pick it up after it falls down and cries for help.

During the remainder of that day, however, things looked very bleak. I had forgotten the prayer. There seemed to be no hope. Now, at this glorious moment, I lifted my hands to the heavens and had a revival meeting all alone out there in the semidark city streets of far-away Baghdad, Iraq.

The next morning I heard a knock on the door of the church I was staying in. The German representative of the French Embassy had come to pick up my baggage for safekeeping at the consulate as I had requested. He almost fell out of his shoes when he caught sight of me, thinking he saw a ghost. "There is no chance to get out of that prison like that! What happened?" he stuttered.

"God answered my prayer. What you could not accomplish, He did," I answered joyfully, and handed him one of my Bible tracts.

While I was being kept waiting at that prison compound, I fully realized the fatal danger of that near incarceration, as I had known of people who were imprisoned in some of the Near Eastern countries and never saw daylight again. One German automobile tourist had been put into some small country jail in that area. He was eventually discovered there, more by chance than anything else. He had been held many months, even though in poor health. He doubtless would have died soon if they had not been able to trace him. One of the reasons so many of the tourists imprisoned in the Arabian countries have not been released is that the corrupt prison officials do not want to restore the personal belongings they have taken from the tourists.

19

The Family Joins Me

What a blessing to travel with your family. For the spiritual benefit and partly for training in survival matters, I have taken mine on two extensive trips which have lasted 100 days each. Most of them also accompanied me on another very challenging flight with our small plane, criss-crossing first through western Canada with its beautiful British Columbia and Yukon Territory.

HOSPITALITY UNLIMITED

I will never forget what friendly treatment was extended to us by a German family when we were rained in at Mackenzie, Canada for many days and could not fly on. We were getting cold and wet with our little baby in a small, lightweight tent which eventually was not able to withstand the torrential rains. This fellow pilot and wife invited us and again we felt right at home, also enjoying their delicious European cuisine.

Once we landed in Dawson, Yukon Territory. The only available transportation was a police car that picked us up from the airport, approximately five miles from town, and brought us to a camping place. All the hotels were full and rather expensive. We erected our pup tent, but it was rather cold for our little three-month-old son.

A French-German couple, parked alongside with their ingeniously equipped Volkswagen bus with shower, automatic throttle control and all kinds of other self-installed sophisticated gadgets, befriended us. They invited us for nice, warm meals in their camping car, took care of our little baby in the warmer bus and brought us back to the airport the next day,

Encamped in bad weather at Mackenzie, British Columbia *(above)*. Mapping our way from Dawson *(below)* to Whitehorse in Yukon Territory, Canada. Notice the primitive fueling facilities in the upper right corner. To my left is Otto Sachers who brought us back to the airport after coming to our rescue with his VW camper during a cold stay in the Klondike. Here, where one of the world's greatest gold rushes took place after news of hefty strikes spread around the world, we likewise did some "panning." In the foreground is my oldest son, Roy.

watching our plane take off. We heard from them through the years. These people certainly are living a rich and interesting life, travelling almost continuously. Whenever the money runs out, they will stay in countries of particular interest, taking on some type of job until enough funds have been saved to continue their journey. This couple's life is as varied as any life could be. There are new and practical experiences every day and they have no trouble maintaining themselves because of their many skills.

MAJESTIC ALASKA

As we continued our flight throughout Alaska we marveled at the fantastic scenery such as giant mountains, glaciers, fjords as well as the interesting wildlife in Mt. McKinley National Park. The entries in my log book remind us that Windy Pass was very calm as we flew in marginal weather from there to Anchorage. Around the Hurricane area we had to navigate at an altitude of 500 feet and could hardly see anything for miles. Later, a partial clearing permitted a view of monarchic Mt. McKinley behind us. A beautiful sunset was reflected in the many lakes and glaciers in the distance. Lighted Anchorage lay ahead. What a sight!

It was quite an experience to fly in this northern country and to sample some of the wonderful fishing at Petersburg when catching herring galore, which we marinated according to an old-fashioned German recipe—a delicacy hard to do without.

BEHAVIORAL PATTERNS IN SPARSE AND DENSE POPULATION AREAS CONTRASTED

The warm-hearted hospitality of especially the Alaskan people made us feel right at home wherever we landed. There, in the last frontier it is still possible to leave your home unlocked, especially if you dwell out in the wild, open country. If a wayfarer gets lost in the territory, it is understood that he can make himself at home in a cabin as long as he leaves it as clean as he found it. If you travel in sparsely settled places, you will find friendly folks who are glad to meet another person. Conversations tend to be interesting. However, when coming to densely populated areas, everyone wants his privacy and is tired of other people.

In very interesting tests, rats were put under the same conditions man is living under in big cities. They have proven that the rodents became very ferocious, attacking and eating each other. They would literally become insane—does this sound familiar?

I don't think that the concentration of money and wealth by joining house to house, and laying field to field, till there be no place (Isa. 5:8) is very pleasing to God. The Bible says "Woe unto them." It is further interesting that the first city builders we read about in the Scripture were Nimrod and the Canaanites, all of them descendants of *Ham*. Nimrod was the

Where glaciers meet an Alaskan bay, a mild sun casts a mellow gleam on the icy waters below us. A dramatic flight without a chance for an emergency landing.

founder of the Assyrian Empire and several Babylonian cities. It included Babel and the wicked and exceeding great city of Nineveh with more than 120,000 people (Gen. 10:8-12, Jonah 1:2, 3:3, 4:11, Nah. 3:7, Zeph. 2:13-15). The immoral places of Sodom and Gomorrah were among those which were inhabited by the Canaanites.

Here we see clearly who constructed those big, wicked metropolises. After much research as to their origin, I am even more convinced that God did not intend for man to live principally in large cities. They are usually places of vice, crime and corruption. What do you see as you walk through them? The handiwork of man. Houses, streets, cars, merchandise galore, and the latest fashion attract your attention. The many bars, vile movie houses and bookstores with filthy novels and pulp make it even worse. Very applicably do we read in Isaiah 2:8, "Their land also is full of idols; they worship the work of their own hands, that which their own fingers have made."

But as we go out into the open country, the mountains, the plains, the wilderness, we are in God's creation. Our thoughts are directed toward Him and we feel His presence much more so. Lot chose to be vexed from day to day with the filthy conversation of the wicked and saw their unlawful deeds by dwelling among them in the cities and pitching his tent toward Sodom (Gen. 13:12, 2 Peter 2:7, 8). Abraham, however, stayed away from population centers and preferred to dwell in the plain of Mamre (Gen. 13:18 and chapter 18). It was there that the Lord kept him informed about the future (Gen. 18:17). He didn't need any television or newspaper to tell him what happened in the past but, more importantly, he was briefed on things to come. It was also in the plains and away from the cities where Abraham commanded his children and his household after him, so they were going to keep the way of the LORD, to do justice and judgment (Gen. 18:19). Compare this with Lot's family life and you know the difference.

We could certainly feel the contrast in the mentality of the people living in these sparsely populated areas. We were enjoying it thoroughly.

STRONG WARNINGS RESULT IN JITTERY PASSENGERS

Then on our return trip from Juneau to Petersburg, Alaska, we encountered very bad weather and flew at times 66 feet over the sea. After a lovely visit with some nice friends, we decided to fly the coast all the way to the conterminous USA. We made a short stopover in Annette, Alaska after an 80-minute trip in order to fuel up the plane and get the latest weather reports. A long journey awaited us.

Here flight service issued strong warnings against travelling this way VFR with a small, single-engine aircraft. "Just the other day we heard an SOS from a pilot cruising along the coast nearby. Extremely bad weather made it impossible to rush to his help immediately. It can change here very quickly for the worse. All we found of him, days later, was an empty gas container floating in the ocean. We never traced him nor his plane. Along this stretch we usually have only one day of good weather per year—that is, sufficiently good for your type of aircraft. We are losing planes here all the time. It's one of the worst routes!"

That was quite a consolation. In spite of the warning, we went ahead as planned. The coastline was rugged. The shore drops straight off as mountains meet the sea, and there is no place for an emergency landing. To make it yet more exciting, the engine developed roughness south of Prince Rupert, Canada. "What if the motor quits at this time?" I comforted my wife. Otherwise, it was a nice day. No clouds, and beautiful weather most of the way. But from the middle of Vancouver Island it started to get hazy. So-called "blessings" of civilization that far north! Then finally, after a six-hour flight, we reached Snohomish County Paine

Our present plane, a Cardinal, parked beside a lonely desert strip in eastern Oregon. My son, Roy, who later became a licensed pilot also, poses in front of the Cessna 177 as he holds on to the propeller. A sample of the magnificent scenery *(below)* frequently spread underneath lofty *fire eagle.*

Field near Seattle, Washington. A month of challenging experiences in Canada and Alaska lay behind us.

WHALES, DESERTS, MOUNTAINS AND ROCKETS

I shall always recall the fantastic sights we had while flying over the Pacific Ocean adjoining Alaska, seeing a school of giant whales leaping and causing fountains of water to appear by their blowing actions. It looked just like we were over a flotilla of giant submarines. What a sight to behold!

There have been other occasions which I will relate for the enjoyment of the readers. We had an interesting experience on a 100-day trip with our Volkswagen camper. While visiting Death Valley, we arrived at a time when bad weather conditions had hit that particular area. It was getting toward evening as we were driving through the valley and the horizon had a very impressive appearance. Finally darkness came and we hit a place where flash floods had torn through the highway and moved a vast amount of gravel and sand. We took our shovel and other equipment and, by the light of the Volkswagen headlights and the moon, just dressed in bathing suits because of great heat even at night, built up enough of the road so we could continue our journey to the very beautiful Painter's Point. There we spread our sleeping bags and spent a portion of the evening looking into the lovely sky. When morning approached, we had a fantastic view down into Death Valley. Everything was so quiet and peaceful —not a sound all around. We were the only human beings there.

About two days after sampling the lowest point of the United States, we went on a hike to the highest peak in the conterminous United States. All of us, including the children, made that 26-mile trip in a day, climbing 6,128 feet from Whitney Portal (at 8,367 feet) to the top of Mt. Whitney (at 14,495 feet). Our little girl was the talk of the day as she was only five years old and able to complete that journey with us.

The next 100-day tour with the family we made with our plane. Unforgettable was the day when we flew straight toward Cape Canaveral while Apollo 11 was launched—the first manned lunar landing mission. What a sight to see the blaze and then the rocket slowly lifting up from its launching pad on a path toward the moon.

20

How to Travel on Pennies a Day and Enjoy It

A lot of American people are spending fortunes roaming overseas. I could fill a volume with hints on cheap travel alone, but it will suffice within the framework of this book just to mention a few points which should be of interest.[1]

When journeying internationally, try to stay away from hotels in general. I talked to persons who felt that they had seen the world, telling me at which Ritz, Hilton or Biltmore they had stayed. These persons might just as well have remained in the United States because hotels are about the same in every nation and they will take a lot of your money.

When travelling, you should definitely try to stay with the local folks. Only then will you get a true understanding of the country, receive genuine accounts instead of tourist stories and be appreciated more, because as a rule people like you if they see that you take an interest in them. One of the reasons Americans as a whole are not well liked abroad is that they

---

[1]For more information on this subject, consult my book, *Timely and Profitable Help for Troubled Americans,* available from the same publisher. See order form in back of book.

draw back into their own communities and do not make efforts to learn the foreign language or understand the natives; in other words, they travel and behave just as if they were in their own homeland.

I have observed over and over that people became very friendly toward me, when they found out I wanted to mingle, stay in their homes, talk and spend time with them. They usually gave an account of the true history of their nations, took me around and introduced their friends. In Taiwan, for instance, I came to meet the direct descendant of Confucius in such a manner and a very interesting king of a mountain tribe. There have been many other acquaintances, such as Djakorda (Tjokorda) Agung, a former king of Bali. A very intelligent man, he was also a friend of former President Kennedy, who visited him. He fascinated me with a chilling account of how God protected him at the base of the exploding 10,000-foot Gunung Agung (Peak of Bali) volcano. I will remember him for a long time.

A number of clubs or associations, such as Servas in Japan, will introduce you into homes where you can stay. To befriend the natives of certain countries and to get a true understanding of their customs and way of life is a very-much-needed prerequisite for a foreigner who plans to settle and make a living there. Another inexpensive place to stay is the International Youth Hostels, which have a very low fee, such as one dollar per room, and also some supply you with inexpensive food. You can have an international membership as they are located worldwide.

While searching around in various nations, it is more advisable to travel by train, bus or even as a hitchhiker (depending upon the place) than to hop from point to point by plane, in which case you do not see much of the intermediate area nor do you get the desired contacts with the people.

When travelling from one country to another internationally by aircraft, there are ways of buying tickets which will save a lot of money. For instance, you can book a trip from one city such as Sydney, Australia, to another such as San Francisco, California, and then by taking advantage of the mileage allotment for that particular leg of the journey, you can include many other stops without additional charge. Even though they would increase the travel distance, the mileage allotment is usually much larger than the direct distance between the two points. If yet more stops enroute are wanted, a person could fare much better by certain increases such as five, ten, fifteen or twenty percent of the original amount and keeping with the above method. This in most cases will be much less expensive than booking the normal way.

Don't expect your travel agent to brief you on this procedure. He lives off the percentage he makes from what you pay. At times he might not even know about this.

On one journey (see Chapter 18) which took me through 44 countries around the world and lasted two years, I paid approximately $200 (in addition to the airplane tickets), which is about 27 cents a day. This amount included train and bus fare, food and occasional lodging when accommodations with natives were not feasible. I think that this figure will speak for itself. There certainly are many ways by which a person can cut down on travelling outlays.

Certain airlines, unaffiliated with the IATA, operate as outsiders. They are not bound to the international tariff and can fly you for less. The same goes for ocean voyages. A few shipping companies are not restricted by international shipping tariffs and usually transport you for a smaller charge. Others let you travel free if you work on board ship as cook, waiter, paymaster or in a similar capacity. Places such as Australia, Canada and the Union of South Africa will either pay your trip or give you certain benefits if you immigrate. However, there are contract requirements in some cases, such as a stay of two years in Australia if that government provides for the trip.

It is more interesting to go by freighter rather than on a passenger ship, because on the latter you are one among perhaps a thousand people with no individual privileges. On a freighter you find life just like in a big family as everyone generally dines with the officers and receives a better impression of the true atmosphere aboard. Freighters are usually cheaper and often have about a dozen cabins available. In many cases they will stop in several ports along the route (depending where you travel) and there will normally be a few days at each port of call, giving you an opportunity to leave the ship and look around.

When outfitting yourself with shoes for an extended journey, be sure to purchase them at a time when you have been on your feet a good portion of the day and break them in before you leave, as nothing is more uncomfortable than to have ill-fitting shoes on a long trip. I once purchased a pair of shoes for a dollar at a Salvation Army store with thin rubber soles which lasted for seven months of a long journey, even though I hiked many miles daily. Just as in the case of the Israelites of old, I believe God watched over my clothes and shoes so they would not wear out as quickly.

If your itinerary includes Switzerland, ask about "Best Buys" in foreign currency while you are there. Also, you will find in-bond shops in Jamaica, Bermuda and aboard ships. While purchasing goods in foreign countries, stick with the products which each specializes in, such as watches in Switzerland; dresses in Italy; Venetian glass, leather goods, wall hangings, perfumes and rugs in Spain; glassware, textiles, crystals and marvelous stainless steel articles in Denmark and Sweden; mechanical items, for example, radios, phonographs, cameras, etc. in Germany; and textiles, decorative tinware, festive skirts, pre-Colombian scuplture and gold jewelry in Mexico and South America. If a lack of funds is a problem, you could sell those articles (or a portion) while still travelling wherever you find an interest, or you can bring them all home for sale later.

TRAVEL LIGHT

I might also mention that it is a great advantage to travel lightly. Many people are burdening themselves by too many unnecessary gadgets especially in America, the land of plenty. My entire baggage, on a previously mentioned two-year, 44-country trip, consisted of a small, lightweight suitcase weighing a total of seven pounds (with contents).

For those of you who may likewise be called into some type of travelling work such as the evangelistic ministry, I present at this time a suggested list of essential items:

1. **Valuables**: Wallet (including driver's license), traveller's checks, two passports* (for faster securing of visas, especially abroad when travelling extensively), extra passport photos (for visas), vaccination certificate, medical certificate,** certificate of conduct,** letters of introduction,** letters of conduct,** and travel guide books.

2. **Clothing**: A jacket or coat that does not readily admit air for keeping in warmth or shedding rain, gloves, neckerchief, two pairs of shoes (one extra pair), hat (can be used for protection from sun and rain), wash-and-wear clothing (should include a suit, casual pants, white short-sleeve shirt, colored long- and short-sleeve shirts), bow tie, belt, sweater, socks, two pairs of underwear, two handkerchiefs, pajamas (they are good because they can also be used for additional clothing under your ordinary apparel when you reach cooler areas) and bathing suit.

3. **Toiletries**: Toothbrush, toothpaste, dental floss, shaver, mirror, manicure set (including tweezers), comb, soap, wash cloth, hand lotion (has many uses), bandaids.

4. **Miscellaneous**: Watch, keys, leather pouch (worn suspended from neck in which to carry money), flashlight, sunglasses, ball point pens, pocket knife, leather string (comes in lengths which can be used for shoelaces, repairing suitcase handles, etc.), needle and thread, magnifying glass (as fire starter in emergency), compass, plastic water bottle, can opener, spoon, rubber bands and safety pins.

Packing accordingly, I was able to accommodate the suitcase underneath the seat of the plane, avoiding theft, tampering, and unnecessary damage due to rough handling. Even before the other passengers were

---

*Since most visas expire within a certain time period (usually within one to three months), you will not be able to obtain all of them before leaving on an extensive journey, which will take you longer than that period of time. You might be gone half a year or more. Therefore, you will find it a great convenience and saving of time and money to have at least two passports with you. This way you can obtain two visas at a time by submitting each passport to a different consulate. Some will not issue a visa immediately and it would be rather frustrating for you to be forced to stay for an extended period of time in the foreign city just so you can obtain perhaps half a dozen visas in two to three weeks, more or less.

**Only needed in some countries.

standing in long lines, waiting for customs clearance, I was already quickly taken care of with my few things and on the way. Usually I walked, thus avoiding the outrageous taxi rates tailored for American tourists. While other travellers had to endure lengthy, tiring checking procedures due to all their stuff, I in most cases did not even have to open my suitcase as the customs officials realized that I would not try to hide certain items in such a small container. Obviously its little space was needed to accommodate only the most necessary personal items, leaving no room for gadgets which required a customs clearance.

Life can be very simple if a person only is willing to curtail his requirements to the things absolutely necessary. He will find as an additional bonus that life will become much more joyful in the course of it. If additional items are required, they can always be bought inexpensively en route. Most travellers find that they take too many nonessentials along.

On several hikes up Mt. Whitney I pursued the same tactic by carrying practically nothing with me, for I knew that I could maintain myself without food for some time as long as I had water. In fact, the more you take with you, the more you require. In other words, if you take a lot of equipment, you need tools and items for its maintenance. Your body demands more sustenance because more energy is expended carrying the additional weight; you will travel longer, making less mileage with a greater load, again requiring more food.

In the western countries we are so used to being surrounded by all kinds of needless gadgets that we have difficulty in grasping how little actually is necessary. When I see how people even on camping trips take everything with them but "the kitchen sink," I feel sorry for them. They are not happy being *again* burdened down by all that junk. They might as well have stayed home! You would think they go camping to have a change from the daily rut and be free of time-consuming and nerve-racking materials such as radios, television, motor bikes, etc.

I have met many such unfortunate tourists abroad who forever complain when things are less comfortable and different from those at home. They are not good representatives of their country, nor even a good asset to themselves. They would be better off to travel "without themselves" (how this is done can be found in Chapter 7, entitled IMPORTANT POINTS FOR PERSONAL APPLICATION, Section two of my book *Timely and Profitable Help for Troubled Americans*[2])—that is, without their "nondesirable selves!"

We travel abroad in order to become familiar with different ways of life, cultures, foods, languages, architecture, and meet other challenges. You'd better stay here and save both your time and money if you want to find the same "homelike" things abroad. You might just desire to travel the world on the screen with armchair comfort, and if you "let your fingers

[2] See information under footnote No. 1 of this chapter.

do the walking" over the places on the map, you can say: "I've been here, I've been there—man, I've been everywhere!" Now let's go back to Mt. Whitney.

During one early climb up that mountain when I began before daybreak, I was taught a few valuable lessons. As I started out, just armed with high-topped sneakers and a few light clothes, I hurried along joyfully, singing with the birds as they started their melodious orchestra at the approach of sunrise. Well on my way I began meeting people who had encamped for the night. They were burdened down with cameras, pails, shovels, axes and extensive food supplies. They were sitting on the side of the trail breathing heavily, wanting to talk with me as they were seeking another excuse to rest. I told them they were making a mistake, for if they wanted to endure hardness as a good soldier, they should not entangle themselves so much with the affairs of this life (2 Tim. 2:3-4).

As I continued my hike, I could not help but notice that as I climbed higher, the trail became steeper, narrower and covered with a scattering of small rocks. We find that as our national as well as international problems become greater, it will have a snowballing effect in that the increasing difficulties will come thicker and faster.

ENDURANCE BRINGS REWARDS—BREATH OF FREEDOM

I had a good supply of well-trained muscles to work with to keep climbing over the rocks and mastering the steep, narrow trail. In the case of our national destiny, we know that good mental as well as physical muscles are needed to withstand the storm. The higher I climbed, the better perspective I received of things as a whole; in other words, the confusing and entangling mess we find ourselves involved in during everyday life moves into the distance as we climb out of it into more important issues. As the saying goes, "Take first things first."

Also, as I climbed higher, the noisy things of the daily routine receded into the distance. It became more quiet and when I finally arrived on the mountain top, a magnificent and comprehensive scenery opened up. I gazed toward the Pacific on the west, I saw the snow-covered Sierra Nevadas to the north and south and I looked toward Death Valley in the east. At that time it became clear to me that the reason so many people are in such a mess is because they are burdened down with too many unnecessary things of humdrum living and never make it up to the point from which they would have the perspective they need—the complete panoramic view.

Only as I arrived on the mountain top did this scene open up. Before then I had merely a partial outlook, for I kept scanning the side of the mountains and just a few vistas emerged from time to time. But on the highest place there were no further obstructions in my line of sight and I had a complete understanding of the way the countryside appeared. People still at the foot of the mountain could argue with each other about how the scenery seems from up there the rest of their lives, and they might have many different opinions; not until they arrive at the summit will they see clearly, and then all arguing becomes unnecessary.

Christians everywhere need to meet on this pinnacle of heaven's glory and they will see eye to eye. All that confusion and quibbling among them will then cease.

I wrote into the little register placed on top of that peak, *"If the creation is so great, how much greater is the Creator and to know Him is the supreme thing in our lives."*

In the confused mess we find ourselves in today with the perverted economics, politics and everything else putting their spider webs around the individual, we need this distinct, overall understanding more than ever. This is why I want to underline the necessity for the individual to get some factual material and study it in an endeavor to gain a clear-cut perception of the main issues at stake and of the underlying tendencies and motivations which brought about our present dilemma. The Bible certainly is the greatest eye opener.

TAKING ADVANTAGE OF LIFE'S EXCITEMENTS

Early in life I was influenced in my outlook, among other things, through some of the experiences we had as a family. Twice my father lost nearly all he owned during and after the First and Second World Wars. He saw many of his efforts, hopes and dreams end in smoke. While roaming the globe, I was always impressed to notice that rich people in wealthy areas, such as New York City, seemed rather unhappy. When I lived there, I counted it a rare experience to meet a joyful, smiling person on the street; yet much of the wealth of this earth is concentrated in that metropolis alone. On the other hand, as I visited poorer areas, such as Spain or even the small island Bora Bora in the South Pacific, I saw many glad, cheerful individuals.

This amply proves that genuine happiness cannot be found in the pursuit of material items. The more we have, the more burdened down we are; and even a person with great financial assets will spend a large part of his time trying to protect and watch over them. It may be partially because of the lessons I have learned that my personal goal has not been the accumulation of great treasures, but instead I have spent much of my time in matters which were of interest and enjoyment to me. I would not for any amount of money want to miss the many wonderful experiences I have gathered on my extensive economical travels. They will last as long as life and memory.

Gadgets can be stolen or lost and a person is left with nothing, as we discovered during two world wars in Germany. But the adventures a person has gathered which have broadened his horizon, will stay with him. I consider this a very good investment indeed. Under Communism, unable to travel, and living with just the barest necessities, there were times when we could divorce ourselves from the monotonous, everyday life by winging back into our past to some of the precious highlights we had stored in the years gone by. Those memories helped us to carry on through dark, dismal days.

PART V

FLYING

THROUGH THE AGES

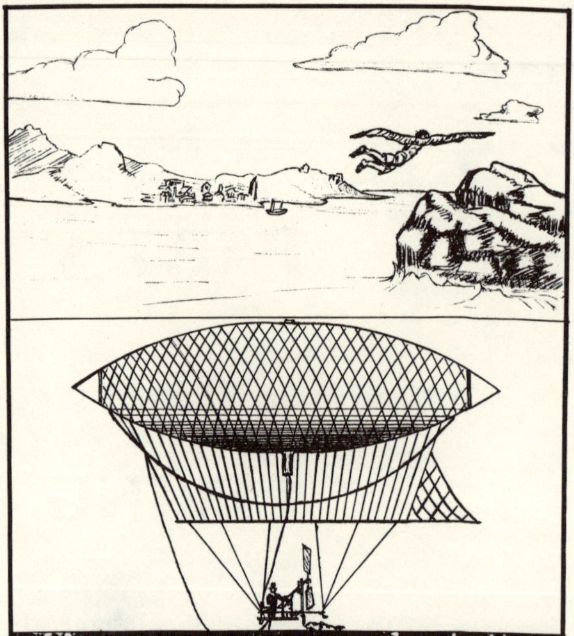

"Some men see things as they are
and say why, others dream things that
never were and say, why not?"

—Aeschylus

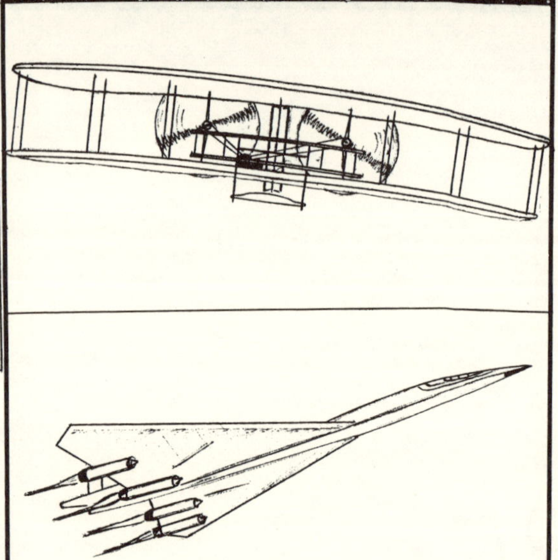

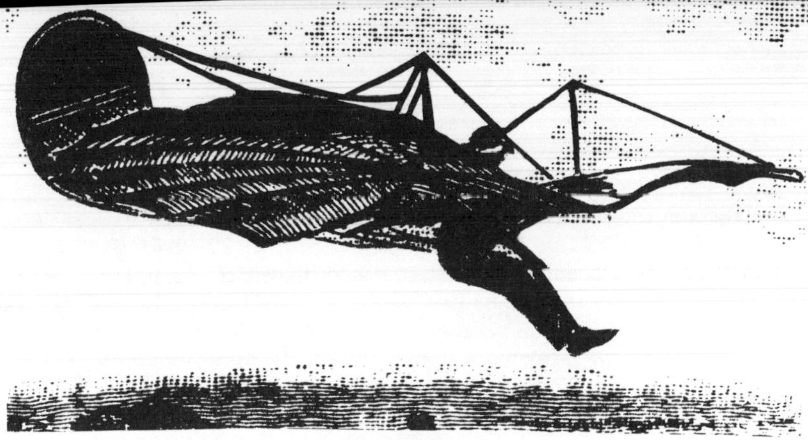

21

History of Flight

Man's age-old quest has been adventurously to conquer the expanse above him—to be able easily and lightly to drift or float around in the air, free as a bird and at random—to be eminently suspended high up in the sky beholding a great wide world below from this vantage point. Beyond ordinary limits of human experience, he could excel and enjoy the extraordinary and idealistic state of transcendency.

Down through the ages man has felt this crave. He watched light objects float through the air and birds fly, and by flapping his arms, he likewise tried to take to the sky or glide after jumping from cliffs. For thousands of years, all his endeavors ended in futility and man decided it was a privilege only the gods could enjoy.

Asshur, chief god of the Assyrians, was pictured with wings. Hermes, messenger of the Greek gods, had winged heels, helmet, and wand. Valkyries (those who choose the fallen), warlike goddess-maidens of Norse mythology, rode through the air on winged horses. Hovering over battlefields, these 12 handmaidens of the chief god Odin (Wotan) chose the heroes who were to die in battle and afterward led them to Valhalla (Hall of the Slain). Brunhild (Brünnhilde), the maiden Sigurd (Siegfried) awakened from a magic sleep, was a Valkyrie, and Richard Wagner built his opera "Die Walküre" around this theme. Though man was not able to fly himself, we see his longing for it expressed by endowing the gods and their messengers with this ability. Even the early Christians pictured angels with wings.

Early in life, I thrilled to the story of Daedalus (the cunning worker) who, according to Greek myths, made two pairs of large wings out of feathers and wax. Then he and his son Icarus, who later fell into the sea when the sun melted the wax on his wings, flew away with these fastened on their shoulders. After they managed to escape in this way from imprisonment in Crete, Daedalus was able to fly all the way to Sicily.

Fairly early in time, man also learned to send heavier-than-air objects such as stones, spears, boomerangs (whose cross section was similar to the shape now used in airplane wings), and finally kites, heavenward. The famed Greek statue, "Winged Victory," symbolized man's yearning. Many old legends tell us about this desire. It includes stories about flying carpets and horses. The ancient Greek writer Lucian wrote tales about trips to the moon. The French writer Jules Verne, the English poet Alfred, Lord Tennyson, and the American author John Trowbridge all wrote about aviation in the 19th Century. Jules Verne, still loved and read by young and old alike all over the world, wrote some of the most accurately anticipating and amazing science fiction in the 1800's. Taking the adventurous reader all around, above, and below the world by submarines, balloons, and rockets in breathless fashion, he never resorted to hideous style in a pervertedly gruesome search for excitement, but wrote in a rather wholesome manner. Even the first man who orbited the earth was greatly influenced by his writings.

In 215 B. C., at Sicily, Archimedes, a Greek, discovered the principle of floating. About 2,000 years later, this was instrumental in the making of balloons and other lighter-than-air craft. And, no matter how unbelievable it may sound, in 100 B. C. Hero discovered in Alexandria the principle of jet propulsion. Again, this was used about 2,000 years later in the construction of jet planes. Then, from the 1300's on, efforts were made to solve the problems of flying scientifically. The English scientist, Roger Bacon, was one of these pioneers.

In the 1400's, the ambidextrous genius and one of the greatest experimental scientists of his age, Leonardo da Vinci, came up with drawings of wings for man, parachutes, propellers, a helicopter, and flying machine with wings. His knowledge of aviation went far beyond his time. Having displayed brilliance in nearly all the arts and sciences, he left us almost 7,000 pages about the various fields from his notebooks. Still today, inventors find there a wealth of knowledge to fire their inquisitive spirits. Most of his notes were written backwards with his left hand, which he then read with a mirror. The International Business Machines Corporation built many models from his drawings.

In 1783 finally came the first lighter-than-air ascent in a captive hot-air balloon designed by the French Montgolfier brothers and flown to an altitude of 80 feet by François Pilâtre de Rozier as the first to fly. Man had just conquered the third dimension and a fever for further advance in this realm obtruded upon him.

Next came the first controlled engine-powered lighter-than-air flight by Henri Giffard in a steam-driven airship at five miles per hour over Paris.

Then between 1891 and 1896 Otto Lilienthal of Germany proved in thousands of glider flights that heavier-than-air machines were more than a dream. Soon after this followed the first engine-powered heavier-than-air flight by the Wright brothers at Kitty Hawk, North Carolina. Somewhat later yet, a leading aviation historian spoke of the ornithopter and the helicopter as "those last two but fading dreams." Six years later, Germany came out with the first maneuverable helicopter built by Heinrich Focke in 1937.

Then followed many high-altitude, speed, and long-range flight contests in an effort to see what planes could do. Numerous adventure stories have been written about daring airmen as aviation records started to be broken almost every week. They brought fame and fortune to many, but a lot of others found death in those years. Even the first man to fly, Pilâtre de Rozier, was killed two years later when endeavoring to cross from France to England in a balloon.

In 1919 people began to transverse the Atlantic in planes and airships. By 1926 they flew in like manner over the North Pole. Another highlight was the first nonstop trans-Atlantic solo flight by Charles Lindbergh with his Spirit of St. Louis in 1927. During 33 hours and 30 minutes, he flew 3,610 miles from New York to Paris. It tremendously boosted the cause of aviation and made people willing to invest more in that field than ever before. Then followed the first round-the-world flight by United States Army biplanes in 1924; in 175 days they flew 26,345 miles.

We would miss reminiscences of extraordinary glamor and fascination if we were not to comment briefly on the airship program of various countries during more than half a century in the 1900's. These giants of the sky were once familiar sights. After having been used as bombers over cities in the First World War, they served as passenger carriers in intercontinental traffic. Small airships, called "blimps," protected ships and attacked submarines with various weapons and depth charges during World War II and they were so effective that not a single one of 90,000 escorted United States surface vessels was lost to submarine attack.

One of the most colorful epochs of airships began when Count Ferdinand von Zeppelin, a retired German army officer, started their construction. Being an excellent engineer, he did such a tremendous job that they are often called by his name. His nation soon became a leader in that field. He launched the first in 1900 and founded the Zeppelin Airship Building Company in 1908 and from 1910 to 1914 the German Airship Transportation Company, the world's first airline, carried 35,000 passengers without a single death. Twenty-six airships were built by him before the First World War started, and another German outfit made twenty-two of them between 1910 and 1919. Beginning in 1915, that nation made about 50 bombing raids (the first planned air attack against a civilian population in history) over England with them, and used these ships for observation, scouting and supply work.

In 1924 the Germans had built the LZ-126 in spite of Allied restrictions on German airship activities until 1925. This had to be turned over to the United States and, having been renamed Los Angeles, became the most successful rigid airship of America. It weighed 46 tons, was 656 feet long, and could additionally carry the amount of its own weight in cargo. Twenty passengers were accommodated in the cabin, which was larger than a Pullman car, and that proud monarch of the sky was famous as the "queen of the air."

In 1928 Germany built the only airship to orbit the globe and named it Graf Zeppelin. This well-known Brobdingnagian, 800 feet long, 100 feet in diameter, and able to fly more than 70 miles per hour, held 50 passengers and their baggage. In its fantastically luxurious cabin with exquisite dining room and other comforts—which reminds a person of the luxury liners Queen Elizabeth and Queen Mary—people travelled between Germany and South America in regular service from 1933 to 1937.

This colossus of the sky was only surpassed by the 7,063,000-cubic-foot Hindenburg in 1936. It measured 803 feet in length and 135 feet in width, and was the largest Zeppelin ever built. After 54 flights, with 36 of them across the Atlantic, this proud queen of the airships went up in flames while approaching Lakehurst, New Jersey on May 6, 1937. Said to be caused by arson, this spectacular disaster killed 36 persons and put an end to regular passenger service by airships. A very colorful era had unfortunately come to a close, and there has been some talk in recent years about resuming such a program.

The United States Navy built two giant rigid airships, Akron and Macon, in 1931 and 1933. Being 785 feet long, they each could carry five fighter planes inside their hulls, which could be launched and received while the airships were in flight. When both of them met tragic ends in 1933 and 1935, respectively, it ceased United States manufacture of rigid airships. Finally, in 1961, the United States Navy also ended its lighter-than-air aircraft program by retiring the last operating blimps.

In the meantime, aviation has had an enormous impact on the world. Aircraft do not have to detour or slow down because of surface obstructions, such as bodies of water or mountains. They can go more direct and faster than other means of transportation. By flying the shortest distances or "great circle" routes, the world has shrunk and international relations have grown in a tremendous proportion.

At the same time, man enjoys beholding the world from above. This thrill gives flying enthusiasts, in particular, great sensations.

Unfortunately, though, man has not always looked at it in this ideal way. Much of the knowledge in this area has been used for the destruction of untold people and for the infliction of horrendous suffering and pain. One only needs to remember the devastating fire storms caused in many a great city, as for instance Dresden, Germany—centers of culture and learning—during the last World War, including the mass destruction of Japanese

LZ 127 Fahrtbetrieb: Nach der Landung

LZ 127 Einrichtung: Fahrgastraum

For many years, rigid airships, built by Zeppelin and other Germans, led the world. In 1928, the *Graf Zeppelin (above)* was completed. This giant airship was 800 feet long, 100 feet in diameter and could fly over 70 miles an hour. Its luxurious cabin *(below)* could carry 50 passengers and their baggage. The *Graf Zeppelin* was the only airship to fly completely around the world.

people in the atomic bombing of Hiroshima and Nagasaki. The Wright brothers, inventors of the airplane, were already greatly disturbed when they saw their invention being turned into an instrument of war.

One can only imagine what would have happened if the Second World War had lasted a little longer. As early as 1939 and 1940, Germany and Italy had the first jet-propelled airplanes. Then, by 1942, the German Junkers Jumo-004 jet engine was installed in the Messerschmitt Me-262 and it made the first successful jet-propelled fighter. In 1944, German fighter squadrons began using them, but they had too few jets at that time to affect the outcome of the war, and their supplies dwindled because of the heavy Allied bombings of German industrial centers and supply lines. If one visualizes that a jet plane travelling at 1,500 miles per hour hits the rain drops with a force of 70,000 pounds per square inch, it will become clear what progress was being made in the field of aviation.

Germany also took the lead during World War II in the use of jet propulsion for guided projectiles. As early as 1937, the Germans built a large missile-research center in Peenemünde. Soon they first used successfully ground-to-ground guided missiles in combat. Toward the end of the war, in 1944, the Vergeltungswaffe Eins (Vengeance Weapon One, buzz-bomb or V-1) was being introduced. Powered by a pulsejet engine and carrying one ton of explosives, it could go 360 miles per hour over a distance of 150 miles. The rocket was 25 feet four inches long.

This terrible weapon very soon was greatly overshadowed on September 8, 1944, by the much fiercer V-2 guided missile produced under the direction of Count Wernher von Braun who, after the war, came to the United States as technical adviser for the army. Looking like a giant wingless artillery shell with four arrowlike fins at its tail, it was 46 feet long. Containing 30,000 parts and an electronic brain, it was guided by an automatic pilot and dove into its target at the proper time by shutting off the rocket engine. This terrifying trajectile travelled up to more than 3,600 miles per hour to a height of 60 miles and over a range of 200 miles. It was launched straight up like a rocket and, being much faster than the speed of sound, could not be heard coming.

Today, man has gone far beyond that—to the moon, and is even on his way to Mars. What will all this scientific know-how bring in the future? Will it be utilized for his good, or is it leading us into a holocaust of unbelievable and terrible magnitude? The sad fact is that rulers use much of this progress for war efforts, and kill out of a drive to exterminate mostly young men in their prime of life and creativity. Whole cultures fall as a result.

Therefore, we must assume that people will continue to fight with each other. It is well said, "From whence come wars and fightings among you? come they not hence, even of your lusts that war in your members? Ye lust, and have not: ye kill, and desire to have, and cannot obtain: ye fight and war, yet ye have not, because ye ask not" (James 4:1-2).

Air progress!? – Where will it lead?

One way to see the denizens of this world temporarily unite would be if the beings of some faraway planet would initiate warfare against us worldlings. Then, suddenly all men probably will agree in the common warfare to drive off these intruders from outer space. For the first time in history, all inhabitants on earth would be in unison, even though short-lived. Could it be that the "Flying Saucer" phenomenon is correlated to this? Is it possible that this strange power is intervening into the affairs of mankind, for their good, in this case? Today the field of science fiction about space flight continues to inspire people everywhere. It is wide open and, besides dealing with imaginary space ventures, much territory is yet to be explored by inventive minds.

KLAUS WRITES AFTER 20 YEARS

Asian Art

Klaus G. Rügge GmbH

Dear Hans Jürgen: Hamburg, 1/23/78

Through a call from your mother, I learned that you are working on a book about our journey together. . . . I am eagerly awaiting your report. Often I have remembered this joint trip and, I believe, it was . . . the most adventuresome after all, which one has ever undertaken. Maybe I will be able to visit you sometime in America. I have just visited my daughter, who lives near San Francisco as an exchange student, and probably I will be there again in May.

As always in a rush, since the business has grown considerably (trade in antiques and art handicrafts), I remain for today with friendly greetings

Your

Klaus

Dear Hans Jürgen: Hamburg, 2/15/78

I have greatly enjoyed your letters and I regret very much that the letter of October 12, 1977 has not arrived.

. . . An article appeared at that time in a German flying magazine, but I don't think I still have the manuscript. . . .

The nicest surprise for me was always the introduction–how I visited you that time in Belgium–and expected in my boundless naivety a Lufthansa airplane. When I then saw this better plywood model, I must say I got slight shudders. I particularly still remember our first flight to Paris, which we undertook in fog and entirely lost our orientation–and then were happy, as we located the Seine; but I always advised you to go a little higher, since it is known that the Eiffel Tower is over 300 meters.

Strangely, each leg of this journey is still before my eyes as if I had experienced it yesterday, maybe since it was the first adventure which one encountered. Today it would probably be impossible to repeat such a thing.

I will most certainly come to America–only I must go to China and Korea, etc., first. After that–most likely in May–I will try to spend more time in America. You may be certain that I will visit you.

Maybe we can take a few days' time and try to recapture the "adventure."

The title, "Flying to Be Free," I find to be excellent, because I believe it was for us an "escape into freedom" from the pressure of emptiness, learning and conforming . . .

The building up of my businesses has required much of my attention in the past years; first there were the photo businesses. . . . have liquidated them; but, at the same time, I have built up my businesses in the antique trade. These have done very well and I am now at the point, however, that I would like to sell them, in order finally to enjoy life a little for once. . . .

With hearty greetings,

Klaus

EPILOGUE

A FINAL WORD TO THE READER

Individuality of life and expression is the cornerstone of any great culture. Those who seek to take these freedoms from us must, therefore, be considered the archenemies of advance, as well as mankind and life itself.
–HANS J. SCHNEIDER

There certainly are many ways to live rich and interesting lives, and the days which lay behind us greatly enhanced our outlook and scope. They engraved dramatically colorful highlights into our memories that would stay with us as long as we live.

Generally, earthly fortunes, such as money, silver, gold, and other possessions, frequently will vanish by the wayside while you are still around. During the two world wars, Klaus's and my folks twice forfeited nearly everything they had. Many people lost their life's earnings in the 1929 stock market crash or by theft, sickness, accidents, or other catastrophes. It reminds us of Matthew 6:19-21: "Lay not up for yourselves treasures upon earth, where moth and rust doth corrupt, and where thieves break through and steal: But lay up for yourselves treasures in heaven, where neither moth nor rust doth corrupt, and where thieves do not break through nor steal: For where your treasure is, there will your heart be also." No thief or economic fiasco will take from you what you treasure in your remembrance unless you become a lunatic. In that case, your wealth will be of no use to you either.

Even until today, about two decades after our fantastic flying venture, many, if not most, of the escapades we braved, linger in our memories with a clarity and brightness as if they occurred yesterday. Also, the many dramatic encounters I had since then, intensely colored my life. This, of course, applies particularly to very strong experiences a person makes. Leaving deep traces in your mind, they will be instrumental for your later life and influence your being. This book illustrates how such forces changed my entire course.

Therefore, it is important that you are choosy about the environment you subject yourself to. It will make or break you. It will help you hitch your wagon to a higher star or drag you down to hell and torment, wrecking you. There is only one short life and that will soon be past. It is important what you do with this little time span entrusted to you. The world is full of beauty and clean, worthwhile, exciting challenges.

Are you dissatisfied with your daily, monotonous routine, being trapped in an unpleasant city setting or job you are fed up with? Do you long for fulfillment of your heart's desire? Would you like a more interesting, rewarding career rather than eking out a dull, miserable existence, wondering what life is all about?

Then why not discover how you can escape that rat race, even improving your orbit beyond measure, as you separate yourself from the drab humdrumness of the masses by following God and living a creative life, spearheading something new and meritorious and enriching mankind at the same time? Despite the many difficulties and increasing turmoil facing you, life can be an adventurous, beautiful endeavor if you give heed to what truly satisfies and then will suit you most.

If the author, who once was famished, impoverished, sick unto death and enslaved under totalitarianisms—a life infinitely worse than yours probably is now—could be lifted onto a thrilling and worthwhile plateau, so certainly can you!

If your journey with us has resulted in a similar experience to mine; that is, if you have found Christ, the Saviour, then I am very happy to have had you on board. Welcome to the great family of God!

But, if you have not arrived at LIFE'S ULTIMATE after perusing the pages of this book, then I hope and pray that your day will come soon. It was likewise nice to have you with us!

THE END...

and hopefully the beginning
of a new *LIFT* in your life.

APPENDIX

ACKNOWLEDGMENTS

My profound appreciation goes to Polly M. Updegraff, R. S. Wathne, Vice-President of World Wide Publishing Corporation, and Wanna Walker, for their kind editorial help, composition suggestions and advice.

I am also grateful to the *World Book Encyclopedia* for the various information I gleaned from its pages. I relied particularly heavily upon it for the FLYING THROUGH THE AGES part.

My two sons, Roy and Tom, also assisted me in many tasks connected with this book.

At last, but not least, I am deeply thankful to my wife Inger for bearing with me while my attention was diverted to writing the manuscript and getting the book published during a period of about two years.

With all my heart, I also remember the many veteran pilots whose training afforded me the necessary know-how to make these flying ventures possible and successful.

GLOSSARY OF FLYING TERMS

Airfoil:	An aircraft control part with a flat or curved surface made to be moved through the air so as to keep the craft up or control its movements, such as a wing, rudder, propeller blade, etc.
Angle of attack:	The angle between the wing of the airplane and the actual flight path.
Angle of bank:	The degree (20°, 30°, etc.) of turn in relation to level flight. Steeper turns make the airplane stall at a higher airspeed than normal and increase the load factor.
Angle of stall:	The angle of attack at which an airplane will stall.
Bank:	To slope laterally on a turn, with the inside wing low and the outside wing high so as to prevent slipping sideways.
Base leg:	A flight path at right angles to the landing runway off its approach end and extending from downwind leg to the intersection of the extended runway center line.
Burble point:	The particular angle of attack at which the air begins to burble on top of the wings, decreasing lift. This is an indication that a stall has occurred.
Cowling:	Detachable metal covering for engine.
Downwind leg:	A flight path (usually *with* the wind) parallel to the landing runway in the direction opposite to landing.
Elevator:	A movable airfoil like a horizontal rudder, usually hinged to the tail, for use in making the craft go up or down.
Final:	A flight path in the direction of landing along the extended runway center line from the base leg to the runway.
Go-around:	When the pilot aborts the landing, reapplies power, retracts flaps and landing gear if extended, and climbs again.
Service ceiling:	Maximum altitude at which a plane can fly.
Stall speed:	The velocity at which the amount of forward speed necessary to maintain altitude and maneuverability is lost.
Touch and go:	A landing followed immediately by a takeoff (without making a full stop).
Traffic pattern:	The standard procedure to be flown by departing and inbound aircraft.
Wing over:	A lateral turning movement of an airplane.

GLOSSARY OF MISCELLANEOUS TERMS

Cancan:	A gay, wild, disorderly dance, originating in France and characterized by much high kicking and leaping.
Cassandra:	A person who prophesies misfortune, but is not believed.
Charleston:	A lively ballroom dance popular in the 1920's, noted especially for side kicks from the knee. The knees are twisted in and out and the heels are swung sharply outward on each step.
Chorea:	A nervous disorder, especially of children, marked by uncontrollable movements of the arms, legs and face. Also called St. Vitus's Dance.
Conga:	A ballroom dance that had its origins on the western coast of Africa and in the West Indies. The dancers move along in a winding line, giving a kick to the heavy drum beat on every fourth count.
Corybantic:	Wild and frenzied, from Corybant (1) one of the attendants of the ancient Asiatic goddess Cybele following her over the mountains by torchlight with wild music and dancing, (2) one of the priests of Cybele who conducted her worship with similar frenzied rites.
Fandango:	A lively Spanish dance in rhythm varying from slow to quick 3/4 time.
Flamenco:	A vigorous, rhythmic dance style of the Andalusian gypsies. People often form a circle around the dancers and sing, clap, stamp and shout in rhythm with the music.
Funambulist:	A tightrope walker or dancer.
Highland Fling:	A fast-paced dance of the Scottish Highlands.
Hootchy-kootchy:	A seductive dance consisting primarily of bodily contortions by a female performer, featured especially at carnival side shows.
Jitterbug:	A fast, acrobatic, frenzied dance performed to jazz music.
Lindy:	A kind of jitterbug especially popular in the 1930's and 1940's, also called the Lindy Hop. It was named after Charles A. Lindbergh because of the fame attached to his flying exploits.
"Old Nick":	Another term for the devil.
St. Vitus's Dance:	Same as Chorea above.

Saraband:	A graceful, stately, slow Spanish dance in triple time, developed from an earlier lively dance.
Tarantella:	A rapid, whirling southern Italian dance in 6/8 time; so called because it was popularly thought to be a remedy for tarantism (a nervous disease, characterized by hysteria and a mania for dancing, supposedly caused by the bite of the tarantula).

SYNOPSIS

(This outline is included for the benefit and convenience of librarians and reviewers.)

Flying to Be Free is the factual, humorous account of a daring aviation endeavor undertaken by the author and a photographer friend around Europe into Africa with a grossly inadequate, underpowered plane. Frequent brushes with death highlight their escapades.

CHAPTER 1: Tells when, where and why the trip was conceived. Introduces hilarious Klaus, the other daredevil, and the flimsy 65-horsepower Aeronca Chief.

CHAPTER 2: Ignoring the warnings of experts, they venture into hazardous territory covered only by antiquated aeronautical charts. The first leg of the journey ends with an emergency landing at a French military field after a panic-stricken, fog-trapped flight 180 feet over Paris in search of an airport.

CHAPTER 3: The team touches down at a rough "banana" field. The owner of an airplane factory becomes their host. A demonstration of Spanish hospitality overwhelms two exhausted fliers, but a death-defying struggle follows as they battle the fierce elements along a forbidding coast around dreaded Cape Finisterre.

CHAPTER 4: Coming to a busy international airport, their advent delays incoming airliners. Amorous Klaus meets a beautiful American girl in Lisbon, but "threw up" the romance. The plane is damaged while being cared for by hangar personnel but they fly on, hoping for the best. Arrival at fabulous Seville, Spain, a pearl among metropolises.

CHAPTER 5: From Seville to Gibraltar–but at the last possible moment the landing had to be aborted; red rockets and signal flares forced a change of plan. With practically empty tanks, Hans and Klaus head toward Africa over the shark-infested Strait. The absence of any radio equipment aboard compounds their plight; unable to file an international flight plan, they risk fighter interception. In the air once again, the plane dives toward a watery grave at those far-off shores when the overtired pilot falls asleep at the controls in a hot cockpit filled with gasoline fumes.

CHAPTER 6: Airborne from Africa only after a late, high-risk takeoff, the adventurers race the sun and the relentless gas gauge to reach an elusive airport. Following a 45-minute fruitless search, emergency landing procedures are initiated. A lively military parade launches their arrival in Andalusia. At the colorful, world-renowned Feria in Seville, Hans meets a captivating señorita, but his overtures are complicated by language barriers and an injured foot.

CHAPTER 7: A loaded day continues perilously at a short, rough airfield, succeeded by the terrorizing awareness of rapidly falling oil pressure and soaring oil temperature. In marginal visibility, flying part of the distance without a map, they lose their way. Again nearly out of gas and close to dark, a forced landing at a strategic, off-limits U. S. Air Force Base becomes necessary. The comical intrusion is received with hostility and the flying vagabonds are ushered away under the clash of machine guns. The tide turns the next morning when the two airmen leave the base under the escort of jet fighters in formation, after having been besieged by photographers and journalists.

CHAPTER 8: Hans relaxes too soon and almost crashes the plane as he is returning to their starting point. Klaus, at 100 pounds, has lost one-third of his former weight. Lantern-jawed and hatchet-faced, he is a cadaverous sight and ample evidence of their nerve-racking escapade; the homecoming of the little bird and her pilot.

CHAPTER 9: The flying venture's marvelous result on the author's life, his profound philosophy and earlier background that conditioned him. Further challenging considerations.

CHAPTER 10: A final good-bye to the mighty challenger of the continents and past adventures.

CHAPTERS 11–13: Touching experiences in Hans's new life and his deeper calling.

CHAPTERS 14–19: Interesting episodes during national and international tours, interspersed with thought-provoking assessments of life and spiritual insights.

CHAPTER 20: The author who has visited almost 100 countries reveals some of his secrets on "How to Travel on Pennies a Day and Enjoy It." He explains different ways to see the world *with a limited budget.* Hans also touches on how travelling can truly enrich personal values.

CHAPTER 21: A comprehensive history of flying. Man's dream becomes reality; it first brings fulfillment, but later developments cause much grief through terrifying wars.

REVIEWS & COMMENTS REGARDING HANS J. SCHNEIDER'S

Timely and Profitable Help for Troubled Americans

• In your book TIMELY AND PROFITABLE HELP FOR TROUBLED AMERICANS you told it like it is.—H. L. C., Goodlettsville, TN.

• If it is 50% as good as you say, it will be worth reading.—C. M. V., Detroit, MI.

• It is the best book I have read on the subject.—Dr. Marjorie Fry, Editor, Castle Rock, CO.

• I marvel at your experiences and your comprehensive understanding of National and International developments in their relationship to Bible prophecy.—E. L. M., Editor, Harrisonburg, VA.

• Your book is most appropriate for these days. Runaway inflation and civil disorder are just around the curve. Your chapter on unconventional Methods in the Absence of Medical Facilities will be most valuable in the coming days. I have seen the positive results of mud packs for swelling, splinters etc. TIMELY AND PROFITABLE HELP FOR TROUBLED AMERICANS is a good prescription for those of us who no longer expect any help from the failing institutions of this world and recognize that we must work out our own salvation—physical, mental and spiritual. Best Regards.—John R. Andrew, M.D., Ellijay, GA.

• Started your wonderful book yesterday and could not give it up until daylight failed. What a mission you have to perform to get this message to the poor fearful people. Isn't it great how your book came to help me to look up and it inspires such hope. It is truly an inspirational gift—thank you.—Mrs. M. H., Necedah, WI.

• Don't start reading the book until you have time to finish it. Once started you will not want to quit. —K. L. N., Entrepreneur, Talent, OR.

Masters of Legalized Confusion and Their Puppets

• I have seen you on TV 21, Phoenix and was shocked to hear what you had to say, but I must say, it is what is going on here in the U.S.A. Would you please send me MASTERS . . . ?—E. C., Mesa, AZ.

• I have read it several times, and marvel each time. . . . Religious writings have held great disappointment for me . . . But when I began to read MASTERS OF LEGALIZED CONFUSION, I could not take my eyes from it, and said to myself, "What manner of MAN wrote this booklet?" And, more did I wonder . . . WHO IS HE, WHERE DID HE COME FROM, WHY HAVE I NOT HEARD OF HIM? I have at least 85 hard-bound "Theological" books, not to mention the softcovers and booklets, and there is not so much truth in the pages of all these books together. . . . I can never tell you the joy it gave me, and I hope another 40,000, and still another 40,000 will be printed.—P. M., Researcher, Joseph, OR.

• I am going to translate MASTERS . . . into French for the people here. —Rev. V. B. L., Port-au-Prince, Haiti.

• I got pulled, pushed or lifted back into the presence of Jesus Christ by reading this wonderful little book. I carefully searched the scriptures it referred me to. When I read it, do you want to know how I felt? I felt like an old prospector who for years had starved out on the backside of the desert digging for something precious and finally struck it rich. Now I want to demonstrate what I have found. —E. B., Eugene, OR.

• Just received your book by Hans J. Schneider and thank you a Million for it. It's a Knockout, for I can only sanction its contents 100%, that's for sure.—Evangelist E. B., Fountain, CO.

• Mail me 10 more COD.—M. D., Choudrant, LA.

A contemporary Thoreau, Schneider is an advocate of the rural life. – Chico *Enterprise-Record*, Chico, California.

Sympathy and concern for an American populace headed toward what he feels is another period of "hard times" prompted Hans J. Schneider to write *Timely and Profitable Help for Troubled Americans*. – Medford *Mail Tribune*, Medford, Oregon.

TIMELY AND PROFITABLE HELP FOR TROUBLED AMERICANS

Are you dissatisfied with your daily, monotonous routine, being trapped in an unpleasant city environment or job? Do you long for a more interesting, rewarding career rather than eking out a dull, miserable existence wondering what life is all about? Do you feel uneasy about the economic conditions or worried what might happen if you suddenly couldn't work? —THIS IS THE BOOK FOR YOU!!!

If the author, who was once famished, impoverished, sick unto death and enslaved under totalitarianisms—a life infinitely worse than yours probably is now—could be lifted into a thrilling and worthwhile plateau, so certainly can you!

This book is a gold mine of pertinent information, such as: How to cut expenses; how to add to your income; proper investments of funds; exciting occupations and what to beware of; how to get more out of life; choosing the lifestyle that appeals to you most and finding the right place to live; how to ensure your children a meaningful, thorough education, solving the generation gap and juvenile delinquency problem at the same time; and how to find freedom. Your eyes will be opened by his accounts of how people acted under extremely adverse conditions and by the piercing analysis of our shaky, already-failing economy which clearly shows you what may well be ahead for America and why and in what manner you and your family should prepare. Finally, look behind the scenes and discover what powers are manipulating our country and the world and how you may properly protect yourself from their schemes.

This manual is comprehensive, which enables you quickly to gain a broad and practical understanding of many vital fields which concern you RIGHT NOW! Therefore, treat yourself to the thrilling experience of a lifetime by reading this book (one of the best investments you will ever make) and, more important than that, APPLYING these life-challenging suggestions.

ABOUT THE AUTHOR

HANS J. SCHNEIDER, author, lecturer, economist, pilot, world traveller and son of a former multimillionaire-industrialist, has predicted our present crisis in speeches around the world since 1961. Born in Breslau, Germany in 1935, he endured physical suffering and privation under Hitler's and Stalin's dictatorships. While his country struggled through a complete economic and political crash coupled with monetary chaos, a long, serious illness almost took his life. Conditions were so bad that the family searched the forests for food to survive.

In 1950 he settled in West Germany and studied extensively. Shipbroker, textile, import-export work in various nations and attendance at foreign trade seminars were complemented by focussing his attention, in recent years, toward the developing international economic and political upheaval, its reasons and how to avoid the catastrophic effects on a personal basis through sound investment strategies and other measures. This, combined with his unique background, gives him a distinctly original and realistic approach in this matter.

While piloting small planes on dangerous aviation ventures in different parts of the world, he faced many encounters with death. He later journeyed under survival conditions on pennies a day through nearly 100 countries, including all over America where he now lives with his wife and five children.

As a man of many lifestyles—referred to by his friends as having lived seven lives—he has received a lot of practical, field-tested knowledge. Multi-lingual, he speed reads through much material of different nations. It all combines to enrich his books.

MASTERS OF LEGALIZED CONFUSION AND THEIR PUPPETS

An eye-opening, controversial exposé about the spiritual confusion so prevalent today! A far cry from narrow, denominational reading, it includes: Impostors and their dupes; last-day signs; confrontation with the living God; fundamentalism; houses of spiritual prostitution; searchlight on spiritual magicians and their tricks; and wholesale "march of death" in man's civilization and its system of brainwashing.

Read this astonishing, frank work by one who grew up under godless Communist occupation when facilities for formal schooling were unavailable and religious worship was taboo, who later intensively studied philosophy and religions of mankind (including Buddhism and Yoga), finally finding spiritual reality when faced with the imminence of death many times during a bone-chilling flying venture around Europe and into Africa.

Hans J. Schneider, who has travelled and lectured as an evangelist in almost 100 countries, witnesses also in radio, television and newspaper interviews and via his writings. MASTERS OF LEGALIZED CONFUSION AND THEIR PUPPETS has been translated, read and studied worldwide and many letters of appreciation have been received. The first edition of an amazing 40,000 copies is almost gone.

To receive genuine help, ORDER THESE CHALLENGING BOOKS, exposing truth without compromise, for yourself and your friends today! (Order form on reverse side)